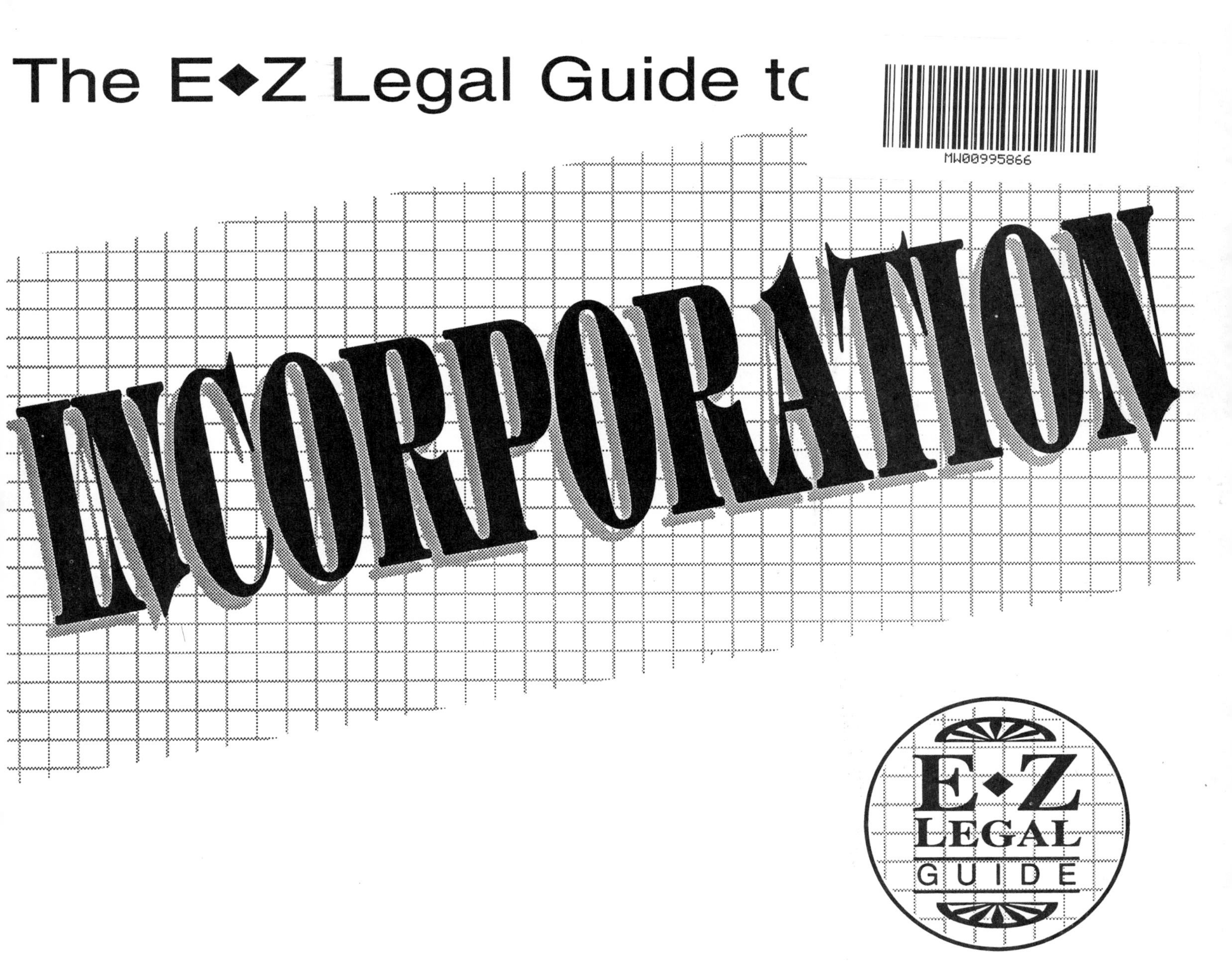

E◆Z Legal Books
Deerfield Beach, Florida

Printed in the United States of America

E•Z LEGAL FORMS®

384 South Military Trail Deerfield Beach, FL 33442
Tel. 954-480-8933 Fax 954-480-8906

Distributed by E-Z Legal Forms, Inc.

2 3 4 5 6 7 8 9 10 CPC

This book is sold with the understanding that neither the author nor the publisher is engaged in rendering legal advice. If legal advice is required, the services of an attorney should be sought. Publisher and author cannot in any way guarantee that the forms in this book are being used for the purposes intended and, therefore, assume no responsibility for their proper and correct use.

Library of Congress Catalog Card Number: 94-061616

The E-Z Legal Guide to Incorporating Your Business
p. cm.

ISBN 1-56382-401-9: $14.95

Title: The E-Z Legal Guide to Incorporating Your Business.

Incorporation

Important facts

E-Z Legal products are designed to provide authoritative and accurate information in regard to the subject matter covered. However, neither this nor any other publication can take the place of an attorney on important legal matters.

Information in this guide has been carefully compiled from sources believed to be reliable, but the accuracy of the information is not guaranteed, as laws and regulations may change or be subject to differing interpretations.

Why not have your attorney review this guide? We encourage it.

Limited warranty and disclaimer

This is a self-help legal product and is intended to be used by the consumer for his or her own benefit. Use of this product to benefit a second party may be considered the unauthorized practice of law.

As with any legal matter, common sense should determine whether you need the assistance of an attorney. We urge you to consult with an attorney whenever large amounts of money are involved or on any matter when you do not understand how to properly complete a form or question its adequacy to protect you.

It is understood that by using this legal guide you are acting as your own attorney. Accordingly, the publisher, author, distributor and retailer shall have neither liability nor responsibility to any party for any loss or damage caused or alleged to be caused by use of this guide. This guide is sold with the understanding that the publisher, author, distributor and retailer are not engaged in rendering legal services. If legal services or other expert assistance are required, the services of a competent professional should be sought.

Money-back guarantee

E-Z Legal Forms offers you a limited guarantee. If E-Z Legal Forms are found to be defective, you may return your purchase to us within 30 days for a full refund of the list or purchase price, whichever is lower. In no event shall our liability – or the liability of any retailer – exceed the purchase price of the product. Use of the product constitutes acceptance of these terms.

Copyright Permission Certificate

The purchaser of this guide is hereby authorized to reproduce in any form or by any means, electronic or mechanical, including photocopying, all forms and documents contained in this guide, provided it is for nonprofit, educational or private use. Such reproduction requires no further permission from the publisher and/or payment of any permission fee.

The reproduction of any form or document in any other publication intended for sale is prohibited without the written permission of the publisher.

Publication for nonprofit use should provide proper attribution to E-Z Legal Forms.

Barry S. Chesler, President, E-Z Legal Forms

Incorporation

Table of contents

Incorporation

How to use this E-Z Legal Guide

E-Z Legal Guides can help you achieve an important legal objective conveniently, efficiently and economically. But it is nevertheless important for you to properly use this guide if you are to avoid later difficulties.

Step-by-step instructions for using this guide:

1. Carefully read all information, warnings and disclaimers concerning the legal forms in this guide. If after thorough examination you decide that you have circumstances that are not covered by the forms in this guide, or you do not feel confident about preparing your own documents, consult an attorney.

2. Before filling out a form, make several copies of the original to practice on, and for future use and updates. **All documents submitted to the court must be printed on one side only.** You should also make copies of the completed forms. Create a record-keeping system for both sets of copies.

3. Complete each blank on each legal form. Do not skip over inapplicable blanks or lines intended to be completed. If the blank is inapplicable, mark "N/A" or "None" or use a dash. This shows you have not overlooked the item.

4. Always use pen or type on legal documents. Never use pencil.

5. Avoid erasing or crossing out anything you've written on final documents.

6. It is important to remember that on legal contracts or agreements between parties all terms and conditions must be clearly stated. Provisions may not be enforceable unless in writing. All parties to the agreement should receive a copy.

7. You may find more specific instructions within this guide for completing some forms. These instructions are for your benefit and protection, so follow them closely.

8. You will find a helpful glossary of terms at the end of this guide. Refer to this glossary if you encounter unfamiliar terms.

9. Always keep legal documents in a safe place and in a location known to your spouse, family, personal representative or attorney.

CHAPTER 1

Should you incorporate your business?

Whether to incorporate or to conduct a business in some other form – a sole proprietorship or a partnership, for example – involves many considerations. If you are currently in business, you are busy running the business, which often prevents you from taking time out to carefully consider your options, assess your situation and plan. Even if you are not yet in business but planning to start a new enterprise, do not rush into business without first deciding on the best form of organization. Many factors determine the form and structure of a business enterprise.

Some of the more important considerations in determining what type of business entity is best for your situation include:

1) Liability and personal exposure
2) Costs, including filing fees and tax considerations
3) The available methods of raising capital

The four basic forms of business entity are:

1) individual or sole proprietorship
2) partnership
3) limited liability company
4) corporation.

Each offers unique advantages and disadvantages.

Sole proprietorship

The sole proprietorship is the simplest form of business organization. A sole proprietorship is a business that is owned by an individual who is solely responsible for all aspects of the business. The owner is personally responsible for all debts of the business, even in excess of the amount invested. The business and its owner are thus considered the same entity.

The advantages of a sole proprietorship include:

a. Low start-up costs, as legal and filing fees are at a minimum. However, many states and cities require a filing with the county clerk, especially if a fictitious business name is adopted. A fictitious name is any name other than the registered name, under which the company does business. A fictitious name is often referred to by the letters DBA (doing business as....)

b. Greatest freedom from regulation and paperwork.

c. Owner is in direct control, with no interference from other owners.

d. Taxes may be lower than for regular corporations.

The disadvantages of a sole proprietorship include:

a. Unlimited liability. The proprietor is responsible for the full amount of business debts no matter how incurred, which means that his personal property may be taken to cover debts of the business. This, of course, is a significant disadvantage.

b. Unstable business life, since the sole owner's death or illness would terminate the business.

c. Difficulty in raising capital and in obtaining long-term financing, because an ownership interest in the business cannot readily be sold.

Highlight

The proprietor is responsible for the full amount of business debts no matter how incurred, which means that his personal property may be taken to cover debts of the business.

Partnership

A partnership is a legal entity that is jointly owned by two or more individuals (although in some cases partners may also be corporations or other entities). As with a sole proprietorship, the owners are personally liable for all debts of the firm unless a special type of partnership, the limited partnership, is set up. Limited partnerships are complex legal structures, and one partner must retain unlimited liability for the debts of the firm. Even partnership agreements for regular partnerships can be quite complex.

The advantages of a partnership include:

a. Low start-up costs, usually with fewer filing fees and franchise taxes.

b. A broader management base than a sole proprietorship, and a more flexible management structure than a corporation.

c. Possible tax advantages, since it avoids the double taxation of corporations and because income can be taxed at personal income rates. Naturally, the personal income situations of the partners could make this a disadvantage.

d. The potential for additional sources of capital and leverage by adding limited and special partners.

Highlight

Forming a limited liability company provides management with a great deal of organizational flexibility.

e. The duration of the entity can be limited to a stated time, or can continue indefinitely by amendment.

The disadvantages of a partnership include:

a. Unlimited liability of at least one partner and possibly all partners, except in limited partnership situations. The personal assets of the general partners are available to satisfy partnership debts.

b. The life of a partnership is unstable, since changing partners by adding new ones or by death or departure of partners causes the partnership to terminate.

c. Obtaining large sums of capital is relatively difficult, as financing cannot be obtained from the public through a stock offering.

d. The acts of just one partner, even unauthorized acts in many cases, bind all partners.

e. An individual partnership interest cannot be sold or transferred easily.

f. Most tax-supported fringe benefits, such as pension and profit-sharing arrangements available to corporations, are unavailable to partnerships.

Limited liability company

A limited liability company is a business entity created by legislation. It combines the advantages of a corporation with those of a partnership. This type of company is similar to a corporation in that it offers limited personal liability to its owners. It is similar to a partnership in that it offers the partnership's tax advantages to its owners. Therefore, forming a limited liability company provides management with a great deal of organizational flexibility.

The advantages of a limited liability company include:

a. Double taxation is avoided. Since it is not a corporation, there is no corporate income tax. Income is based on the personal level, as in a partnership.

b. Personal liability is limited. All personal assets of the partners are protected from corporate creditors. Managers and officers are also protected if they participate in the operation of the company.

c. There is relatively little paperwork and recordkeeping beyond a simple operating agreement or statement of the principles of the organization.

d. You can form a limited liability company yourself. The forms are available from the secretary of state of the state in which you want to form the company. You do not need an attorney.

e. You can convert your present corporation to a limited liability company and begin receiving the benefits immediately.

f. It is relatively inexpensive to establish a limited liability company. It usually costs less than $500 to register with the state.

g. Annual registration fees are low, under $250 in most states.

The disadvantages of a limited liability company include:

a. Although most states recognize the limited liability company, there is still a lack of widespread public acceptance, because this type of company is relatively new. Limited liability companies have only been recognized by the IRS since 1988.

b. Multi-state businesses may have tax problems if they conduct business in states that recognize limited liability companies and in states that do not.

c. IRS rules governing insolvency may create problems for the owners of the limited liability company.

d. Limited liability companies do not enjoy the advantages of IRS rulings when there is a sale of worthless stock or stock sold at a loss.

e. The sale of 50 percent or more of the ownership of the limited liability company in any 12-month period ends any tax advantages the company may have had with the IRS.

f. Limited liability companies may not engage in tax-free reorganizations.

Highlight

You can form a limited liability company yourself. The forms are available from the secretary of state of the state in which you want to form the company. You do not need an attorney.

As the public, accountants and financial planners become more familiar with the limited liability company, the popularity of this form of business organization is expected to grow.

Corporation

A corporation is a business that is formed and authorized by law to act as a single entity, although it may be owned by one or more persons. It is legally endowed with rights and responsibilities and has a life of its own independent of the owners and operators. It has been defined by the United States Supreme Court as "an artificial being, invisible, intangible and existing only in contemplation of the law." To fully understand the concept of a corporation you must think of it as a distinct and independent entity and one separate from its owners.

Highlight

To fully understand the concept of a corporation you must think of it as a distinct and independent entity and one separate from its owners.

The advantages of a corporation include:

a. Limited liability. The owners are not personally liable for debts and obligations of the corporation. They can personally lose only to the extent of their investment in the corporation, with the exception that they can be personally liable for certain types of taxes, such as payroll taxes withheld from the employees' paychecks but not paid to the IRS and state tax authorities. If the business fails or loses a lawsuit, the general creditors cannot attach the owners' homes, cars and other personal property. Limited liability is the one major reason so many businesses are incorporated.

b. Capital can be raised more easily than under other forms of ownership. This does not mean, however, that a new corporation can sell shares of stock easily. The sale of stock is highly regulated by both federal and state governments, and obtaining bank loans for a fledgling business may be no easier for a new corporation than for a partnership or proprietorship.

c. Ownership in a corporation is more easily transferable; this includes transferring shares to family members as gifts or otherwise, as well as selling your interest to some other person. However, in many small corporations it is advisable to put restrictions on transfer of shares, especially if the persons owning and working in the business must be able to work closely together. This is generally accomplished by stockholder agreements. The stockholder's agreement is an agreement between a shareholder and the corporation. It may state, for example, that the shareholder may not sell his shares for a specific period of time after acquiring them or that the shareholder must, under certain conditions, sell the shares back to the corporation.

d. Since the corporation is an independent legal entity, it has a life of its own, or a continuous existence. It does not cease simply because one of the owners dies or wishes to retire.

e. A corporation has a defined, centralized management. Control rests in the board of directors, whose powers are exercised through the officers.

f. Many companies offer discounts (in areas like travel) to corporations.

g. Retirement funds, defined-contribution plans, money-purchase plans and other profit-sharing, pension and stock-option plans may be more easily set up with a corporation.

The disadvantages of a corporation include:

a. Corporations are subject to more governmental regulations than either partnerships or sole proprietorships.

b. Corporations are among the most expensive form of business to organize, although a partnership may be equally expensive.

c. There is double taxation, since both the corporate entity and the individual owners have to file tax returns. As you will see, this may be avoided with a Subchapter S Corporation.

d. Record-keeping requirements can be more extensive with a corporation.

e. Operating across state lines can be complicated because corporations need to "qualify to do business" in states where they are not incorporated. This is explained later in greater detail.

f. Ending the corporate existence, and in many cases even changing the structure of the organization, can be more complicated and costly than for partnerships and proprietorships.

The selection of the form of organization of a business should be decided with professional assistance. Nevertheless, the prevailing attitude is that a corporation is the preferred form of organization, since its advantages far outweigh its disadvantages.

This guide takes you through the incorporation process. Once you have decided that the corporation is the correct form of organization for your business, you must go through the legal steps required to create your corporation. These steps vary from state to state. They also vary in complexity. But with careful planning, most people can organize their own corporation without a lawyer, thus saving hundreds of dollars in legal fees.

Highlight

The prevailing attitude is that a corporation is the preferred form of organization, since its advantages far outweigh its disadvantages.

CHAPTER

Where to incorporate

The first step is to choose the state within which to organize your corporation. There are 50 states and the District of Columbia to choose from.

You may have heard of the advantages of incorporating in the state of Delaware, and it is true that a great percentage of the publicly held corporations in this country are incorporated there. There are reasons for this—many of which are no longer valid for public corporations, and most of which never had importance for a small corporation. As a matter of fact, many of the large Delaware corporations started out in other states; only when they grew in size to become large national corporations did they move their corporate entity to Delaware.

Delaware's Division of Incorporations suggests these advantages to incorporating in that state:

1) The franchise tax compares favorably with that of any other state.

2) Shares of stock owned by persons outside of the state are not subject to taxation.

3) Shares of stock that are part of the estate of a non-resident decedent are exempt from the state Inheritance Tax Law.

4) Delaware courts construe the Corporation Law liberally, allowing investors confidence in the security of their investment.

5) Directors have greater statutory protection from liability in Delaware.

Although the above advantages are true, it does not necessarily follow that Delaware should be the location of your corporation. There are many reasons for incorporating elsewhere. First, of course, is that most corporations will operate businesses located somewhere else in the country and are not likely ever to do business in Delaware.

If your business is, for example, going to be a retail store in New York City, it would be more advisable to set up a New York corporation. If you were to set up a Delaware corporation and operate a store in New York City, you would still have to qualify "to do business" in the state of New York, which would then require:

1) Filing an application to do business as a "foreign," or out-of-state, corporation
2) Paying franchise taxes as a foreign corporation in New York
3) Reporting and paying annual taxes in New York as well as Delaware

Highlight

Base your decision regarding where to incorporate on the important factors. The location of your physical facilities can be the most important factor.

The advantages of Delaware incorporation would have to be very great indeed to overcome the burden for most small businesses of being subject to regulation by two states. If you plan to do business outside your company's resident state, you may have to qualify as a foreign corporation in every state where you do business. Later we will discuss what constitutes "doing business" and when your business requires such qualification in various states.

Needless to say, incorporating in the state where you are located makes the greatest sense.

Favorable Delaware Corporation Law was more a reason for incorporating there in the past than it is now. It is true that at one time Delaware had the most liberal statute in the country for corporations, which allowed the management of a corporation great flexibility in the operations of the business. Nevertheless, this flexibility is most valuable for corporations that have thousands of stockholders all over the world. It is fairly meaningless to the small corporation that is not publicly owned.

Furthermore, other states have revised their own Corporation Laws so that the advantages that once were available only in Delaware are available in many states. Nevada is such a state, and has become even more popular than Delaware as a state within which to incorporate. Nevada offers lower taxes, no corporate franchise fees and more protection and privacy for corporate officers, directors and stockholders than does Delaware.

Base your decision regarding where to incorporate on the important factors. The location of your physical facilities can be the most important factor. Consider the costs of incorporating in that state, and if you incorporate in a state other than the one you're physically located in, consider what it will cost to become authorized to do business in that state.

These costs include fees to check and reserve the name you want to use for your corporation, the cost of filing incorporation papers, and whether there is a one-time organizational fee or franchise tax (this is often based upon the number of shares you will have authorized for the corporation to issue).

In addition to the initial costs, you must determine what the annual fees are in the states you are considering. For example, if there is an annual report to file with the secretary of state, what is the filing fee? Is there an annual franchise tax? Is there a state or local income tax, and how is it determined?

Highlight

Martindale-Hubbell Law Directory, found in public and law libraries, contains summaries of the laws of all 50 states. Read the incorporation statutes for the appropriate state before filing your incorporation papers.

In addition to financial considerations, the laws governing corporations in your state of choice can be another important factor. For example, some states require three incorporators and three directors. If you plan to have a corporation owned or controlled by one person, your state may require you to have more board members than you want. These requirements vary from state to state; in almost all instances, however, it is advisable for a small business corporation to organize within the state where business will actually be conducted, as it is usually easy to comply with those corporate requirements. Consideration of other states is only recommended when the business will, in fact, do business in other states.

A publication titled Martindale-Hubbell Law Directory, found in public and law libraries, contains summaries of the laws of all 50 states. The forms and information in this guide notwithstanding, you should read the incorporation statutes for the appropriate state before filing your incorporation papers.

Once you have decided what state to incorporate in, a great deal of information about how to set up that corporation free or for minimal fees can be obtained from the appropriate secretary of state. A listing of the address and telephone number of the department to contact in your state is contained in the back of this guide.

The registered agent

States generally require that their corporations maintain a registered agent in the state in order to receive communications and summonses in a lawsuit. Generally, this agent may be the office of the corporation itself. If you are physically located in the state of incorporation the corporation itself or an officer would be the registered agent.

If you incorporate in a state where you do not actually have an office, you need a local agent. There are many organizations in the business of representing corporations for a small annual fee. These are easily found in law directories.

Highlight

If you incorporate in a state where you do not actually have an office, you need a local agent.

CHAPTER 3

Selection and reservation of the corporate name

Once you are ready to set up your own corporation, you must next select a corporate name and then check to see if the state in which you are going to incorporate will allow you to use the name.

The first obstacle, other than your own originality, will be the state statutes, which prohibit use of certain words. Not all states have the same prohibitions, so you should check your particular state. However, words that typically cannot be used include: Bank, Banking, Cooperative, Engineering, Trust, National, Federal, United States, Insurance, Acceptance, Guaranty, Pharmacy, Credit Union, Medical, Architect, Indemnity, Thrift, Certified Accountant, Board of Trade, Chamber of Commerce, Lawyer, State Police, Urban Development, Urban Relocation, Underwriter, Loan, Mortgage, Savings, Endowment, and Doctor.

These words are, of course, used in the names of organizations or corporations, but only in fields in which special licensing or regulation is required. Such corporations must be organized pursuant to statutes regulating their particular fields. It is not advisable to attempt to set up such a corporation without the assistance of a lawyer.

When considering your corporate name, also check what must be included in the name. All states require that a corporate name include an indication of limited liability, so that people dealing with the organization know that if it fails, they cannot collect their debts from the owners personally. The words that indicate this are: Association, Corporation, Corp., Foundation, Incorporated, Inc., Limited, Ltd., Syndicate, Company, Co., Club, Fund, Institute, and Society.

This requirement should be checked carefully before selecting the name. New York, for example, allows only Corporation, Incorporated, Limited or their abbreviations.

Once you've decided on a name, you must investigate whether the name you want is already being used by someone else. Even similar names can cause problems, because most states will not allow a name that is the same or "deceptively similar" to a name already on record in the state. Therefore, your XYZ Corp. restaurant may be a problem, for example, if there is already an XYZ Inc. bakery in the state.

Highlight

Once you've **decided on a** name, you **must investigate** whether the **name you want** is already **being used by** someone else.

One useful thing to keep in mind is to choose a descriptive word and a proper name for your corporation. Perhaps XYZ Restaurant Corp., or XYZ Foods Corp., in the above example, would be accepted, whereas XYZ Corp. might be refused on the basis of its being "deceptively similar" to the XYZ, Inc. already in existence.

The materials you obtain from the secretary of state will help you learn how to reserve the name. Usually it is done by submitting a letter or a form with the required fee and waiting to receive clearance. In some cases you can check the availability of the name with a telephone call. Always clear the proposed corporate name before you prepare and file your corporate papers.

CHAPTER

Types of corporate stock

The stockholders of a corporation are the owners of the corporation. When a business incorporates, it issues units of stock indicating who owns what "share" of the incorporated business. These shares are paid for, in turn, with money, property, or services. Thus, if a corporation's net worth is $30,000, and there are 300 shares issued, each share would be worth $100. If there are two people who each own 150 shares of the stock, then each person (shareholder) owns half of the corporation.

The two main types of stock a corporation may issue are:

1) common stock

2) preferred stock.

Common stock

Holders of common stock are entitled to have the primary voice in selecting directors. Voting rights are attached to each share of stock, usually one vote per share. Furthermore, common stockholders are entitled to share in the profits and in final distribution of the corporate assets on dissolution.

More than one kind, or "class," of common stock may be issued. Certain conditions may be imposed upon each class, such as restrictions on voting rights. Common stock is designated in terms of what rights its owners may be entitled to: Class A-voting stock, Class B-voting stock, etc.

Preferred stock

The holders of preferred stock are usually entitled to "preference" over the holders of common stock with respect to receipt of dividends and distribution of assets upon the dissolution of the corporation. They usually do not have voting rights, however. Preferred shares are generally not issued by smaller corporations.

For our purposes in this guide, and for the purposes of most small or medium-sized corporations, only common stock is important and one class of common stock is generally sufficient. For a small or medium-sized corporation it is not necessary to authorize or issue a large number of shares of common stock; the minimum number of shares allowed under the state law will be sufficient for most purposes. Beyond this minimum, the state usually imposes a proportionately higher filing fee and tax.

Highlight

For our purposes in this guide, and for the purposes of most small or medium-sized corporations, only common stock is important and one class of common stock is generally sufficient.

No-par value stock

No-par value stock bears no stated or nominal value on the face of the stock certificate; hence, it does not purport to represent anything more than the given number of shares or ownership interest in the corporation. The actual value represented by the stock will depend, therefore, on what an investor is willing to pay for it, based on such factors as the product line or the assets of the corporation, the profitability of its business, the quality of its management, its record of past performance and dividend payouts, etc.

Par value stock

Par value stock, on the other hand, bears a stated or nominal value on the face of the stock certificate (i.e., $10), which represents the amount contributed by the shareholder(s) to buy each share of stock. Because the value of any share of stock generally fluctuates from day to day, the "par value" of stock can be misleading if used to measure the worth of a stock. Merely because a share of stock says it has a "$10 par value" does not necessarily mean the stock is actually worth that amount.

CHAPTER

Drafting a corporate purpose

In order to incorporate, it is necessary to record the purpose of your company. Great care should be taken when stating the intended purpose of the proposed corporation, since the activities of the corporation may be unduly limited unless carefully written to be as broad and inclusive as possible. When the powers granted to the corporation are not broad enough for its needs, the corporation must petition the state to amend its corporate charter (by filing a Certificate of Amendment) before it may expand its activities beyond those originally approved.

To draft appropriate purposes and activities for the corporation, follow these two steps:

1) Write down a statement setting forth the specific objectives, purposes, and activities the corporation will engage in, including all related lines of business.

2) Add the statement below to allow for future contingencies and to protect the right of the corporation to expand future activities:

The foregoing purposes and activities will be interpreted as examples only and not as limitations, and nothing therein shall be deemed as prohibiting the corporation from extending its activities to any related or otherwise permissible lawful business purposes which may become necessary, profitable or desirable for the furtherance of the corporate objectives expressed above.

The following examples illustrate how two different businesses might state their corporate purposes.

1) Construction business

Purposes: To engage in the construction, repair and remodeling of buildings and public works of all kinds, and in the improvement of real estate, and in doing any other business and contracting work incidental to or connected with such work, including demolition.

The foregoing purposes and activities will be interpreted as examples only and not as limitations, and nothing therein shall be deemed as prohibiting the corporation from extending its activities to any related or otherwise permissible lawful business purposes which may become necessary, profitable or desirable for the furtherance of the corporate objectives expressed above.

2) General merchandising business

Purposes: To manufacture, produce, purchase or otherwise acquire, sell, import, export, distribute and deal in goods, wares, merchandise and materials of any kind and description.

The foregoing purposes and activities will be interpreted as examples only and not as limitations . . . (complete as in the last paragraph of the first illustration above).

CHAPTER

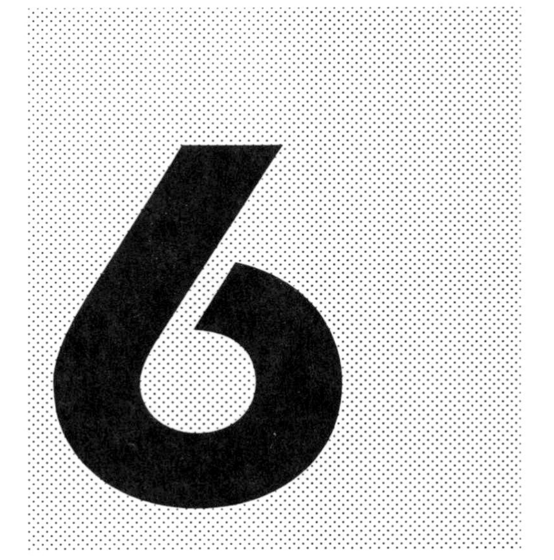

Choosing a fiscal year

You will note on form SS-4 in the back of this guide that the IRS Request for Employer Identification Number asks for your fiscal year. In some states the Certificate of Incorporation also requires the fiscal year to be given.

It is easiest to choose the calendar year as your corporation's fiscal year; you will have fewer tax forms to file that way.

However, there are tax advantages to choosing a fiscal year that is not the calendar year. A second choice would be July 1 to June 30. In that case, for your first year of incorporation you would have to file two sets of income tax forms: For the first half of the year you would file as a sole proprietor (individual return) using Schedule C and any other appropriate schedules. For the second half of the year you would file a corporate return (Form 1120, or Form 1120S, if you make the Subchapter S election), and an individual return because you are now an employee of your corporation.

Similarly, if you choose April 1 or October 1 as the beginning of your fiscal year, you will have to file the same two sets of tax returns for your first year of incorporation. If you choose April 1, you would file as a sole proprietor for the first quarter (January 1 to March 31), and you would file corporate and individual returns for the last three quarters (April 1 to December 31). If you choose October 1 you would file as a sole proprietor for the first three quarters (January 1 to September 30), and you would file corporate and individual returns for the last quarter (October 1 to December 31).

The advantage of separate years is that it allows flexibility in tax planning. For instance, you can contract the amount of salary you pay yourself as late as December 31 and have it taxed personally. If you decide on a small amount, it will reduce your personal tax accordingly, leave money in the corporation for its use, and gain additional time to find a suitable tax angle to avoid paying the resultant corporate tax – a business trip, for example, which is deductible and reduces corporate profits.

And the tax savings, corporate and personal, can be significant. You may want to choose a fiscal year by following the advice of your accountant, who can determine the fiscal year most advantageous to you.

Highlight

You may want to choose a fiscal year by following the advice of your accountant, who can determine the fiscal year most advantageous to you.

CHAPTER

The corporate board and directors

The management of a corporation consists of the corporate directors and the corporate officers.

Corporate directors

Subject to any restrictions imposed by the corporate charter or bylaws, the right and responsibility to determine policy and conduct the business of the corporation lies with the board of directors. The number of those who make up the board is usually set by the bylaws of the corporation.

Bylaws are drawn up and adopted at the first meeting of the stockholders. The directors are elected by the stockholders and are ultimately responsible to the stockholders. Stockholders have the power to remove directors, with or without cause, when the charter of incorporation or the bylaws so authorize and at any special meeting of the stockholders called for that purpose. Directors are usually elected at the annual meeting of stockholders.

It is important to remember that stockholders actually vote their shares of stock. Thus, if there are three stockholders but one owns 80 percent of the shares of stock, that stockholder will control the vote based on the amount of stock ownership.

If any restrictions imposed on the general powers of the directors are contained in the corporation's charter, third persons, such as creditors, are also bound by them, since the charter is considered a public record. Restrictions embodied only in the corporate bylaws, however, are not binding upon third persons, as bylaws are not publicly filed or recorded.

Directors must act as a body. They can bind the corporation only by actions taken at a board meeting with the necessary quorum. They cannot vote by proxy and their duties generally may not be delegated to others. A resolution not passed at a board meeting but signed by each individual director at his or her home would be invalid, unless the directors were the sole stockholders.

The directors are generally required by law to meet at least once every year, although as a practical matter this is rarely done in family or small corporations. In such meetings of the directors, the directors appoint the corporate officers (the same officers are often re-elected), ratify acts of the prior year, review important business matters and set broad policy objectives. The corporate secretary then writes up minutes as a record of the meetings.

Highlight

The directors appoint the corporate officers (the same officers are often re-elected), ratify acts of the prior year, review important business matters and set broad policy objectives.

The directors may also authorize dividends, a new contract, a new lease, a loan, or major purchases or projects. Such actions are then recorded as corporate resolutions and are formally recorded in the minutes book of the corporation.

As a practical matter, minutes of directors' and stockholders' meetings are often very helpful as an instrument of management, since they are frequently the only official record of what was done or decided upon by these bodies. When accurately and adequately kept, the minutes will sometimes help avoid misunderstandings or potential lawsuits.

Provided the board of directors acts honestly, the directors can generally bind the corporation by actions taken at board meetings and are not personally liable for any such actions. Hence, if an honest but bad or imprudent judgment should result in business losses, the directors may not be held personally liable unless the action was grossly negligent or made in bad faith.

Directors may be personally liable if they:

a. Exploit their office for personal gain at the expense of the corporation or its stockholders. The directors are usually said to have a "fiduciary" relationship with the stockholders, meaning one that presumes the utmost good faith and trust.

b. Wrongfully dispose of corporate assets or declare and pay dividends when no surplus or profit exists.

c. Authorize the issue of unissued stock to themselves for the purpose of converting themselves from minority to majority stockholders.

d. Issue, as fully paid, shares of stock not paid for.

e. Improperly lend corporate funds to stockholders when such funds remain unpaid or uncollectible.

Corporate officers

The president, vice president, treasurer and secretary (and such other officers as the particular corporation may choose to have) are appointed by the board of directors; their salaries, duties and conditions of employment are fixed by the board.

Highlight

Corporations are required **to have** a president, **treasurer** and secretary (or clerk).

The officers run and manage the corporation from day to day. However, they have only such legitimate responsibilities and authority to act on behalf of the board of directors as are conferred upon them by the board, or as are specified in the bylaws of the corporation.

Corporations are required to have a president, treasurer and secretary (or clerk). Other officers, such as chairperson, vice president, or assistant treasurer, are optional and are not usually included in the Articles of Incorporation.

CHAPTER

The Certificate or Articles of Incorporation

You are now ready to prepare and file a Certificate of Incorporation (in may states it is titled Articles of Incorporation). Many states will supply you with a blank form or with a model form that must be retyped. Note: Call the secretary of state in the state where you intend to incorporate to determine whether a specific state form is required. If no specific form is required, find out what specific information is required in the Certificate or Articles of Incorporation.

The following items of information are typically required in a Certificate of Incorporation:

1) Name and address of the corporation
2) Fiscal year
3) Purposes of the corporation
4) Total number of shares authorized for issuance (including the par value of shares, and the classes of shares if more than one class)
5) Preferences, limitations, and relative rights of each class of stock
6) Initial capital paid into the corporation
7) Number of directors constituting initial board of directors
8) Name and address of each of the initial directors
9) Name and address of the president, treasurer and secretary
10) Name and address of each incorporator

Not all of these items may be required in your state, and many will not apply or be appropriate in your case. Note: Some states, i.e. South Carolina, require that an attorney certify that your Articles of Incorporation conform to your state's statutory requirements. The only way to be certain what is required is to call your secretary of state and ask for a sample Certificate of Incorporation. See the Appendix for the appropriate telephone number in your state.

For the purposes of this guide we have limited our discussion to business corporations. Professional corporations and corporations in highly regulated industries may require more complicated corporate documents. People in those fields should seek legal counsel in setting up their businesses.

We have also not covered not-for-profit corporations, since the procedures are more complicated. In many states approvals must be sought from numerous state agencies to begin a charitable corporation, and the procedure for obtaining a tax exemption may require the aid of professionals familiar with that area of tax law. There are many groups of volunteer lawyers around the country that will organize charitable corporations for free. Check with your local bar association or local or state arts counsel for the names of such volunteers.

Highlight

Once the documents have been filed, the incorporator should hold the initial meeting of the corporation, elect the board of directors and turn the management of the corporation over to them.

Once your Certificate of Incorporation has been drafted and signed, it should be mailed or delivered to the secretary of state's office or other state office as is proper, along with the required fees. The fee is usually based on the number of pages in the certificate and is usually only a few dollars.

You will be notified by return mail that the certificate has been accepted and filed. Your evidence of filing is generally a receipt from the state. You may also request a copy of the Certificate of Incorporation with the state certificate of filing and the official incorporation date.

Once the documents have been filed, the incorporator should hold the initial meeting of the corporation, elect the board of directors and turn the management of the corporation over to them. In many states the initial board of directors must be listed in the Certificate of Incorporation. The incorporators' meeting, depending on state law, may be an actual meeting or may be evidenced by a signed statement of action.

Certain states allow the board (and the stockholders) to transact business without actually meeting if they all sign a written statement setting forth the action they have transacted. Some states allow a meeting to take place with the directors communicating by conference telephone call. In this way they can be all over the world and still legally conduct business. Check the law in your state to see if these types of meetings or consents are legal.

The initial activity of the board of directors will include such start-up activities as:

1) electing the officers

2) opening a bank account

3) adopting a corporate seal and form of a stock certificate

5) issuing stock

Highlight

The corporate seal is a simple impression seal that usually contains the name of the corporation, the year of incorporation and the state of incorporation

The corporate seal is a simple impression seal that usually contains the name of the corporation, the year of incorporation and the state of incorporation. It can be bought at most legal stationery stores at nominal cost.

Additional stock certificates can be purchased there also. You can have the stationer print the name of the corporation on the certificates or you can type it in yourself. Again, check the state law to make certain your stock certificate contains all the required information. Usually it must state the name of the corporation, the state of incorporation, the type of stock (common, preferred, etc.) the par value of the shares, any preferences that these or other shares have, the name of the holder, the signatures of officers of the corporation, and the corporate seal.

CHAPTER

Establishing your corporation

With your corporation organized, how do you operate and manage it? Listed below are a few guiding pointers:

Transfer assets to the corporation

If you have been operating a business prior to incorporation (as many people do) you can transfer the assets and debts of the business to the new corporation for an agreed sum or consideration, and receive shares of stock in exchange. You cannot, however, burden the corporation with more debts than assets. Further, you cannot sell your personal property to the corporation at inflated prices, or exchange its stock for personal property that is overvalued.

Notify your customers

A sound business practice is to notify all existing business associates, creditors and customers or clients of the change to a corporate status. This can be done by personal communication (telephone or letter) or by a small newspaper notice. Generally, all subsequent company records and transactions should be changed to reflect the new corporate status of the organization, including the printing of new letterheads, business cards, stationery and signs.

Determine state and local requirements

The parties starting a new business must consider not only the formalities for incorporation, but other possible regulations and requirements. Permits and licenses, for example, are required for such businesses as real estate brokers, barbers, hairdressers, private investigators, cosmetologists, billiard rooms, pharmacies, nursing homes, notaries, peddlers, newsstands, employment agencies, businesses serving or selling alcoholic beverages, health concerns, hospitals and educational institutions.

Many businesses are regulated by federal agencies, such as brokerage and securities businesses, air transportation, banking, and drug manufacturing companies. Before commencing any new business, consider what regulations are applicable so that your business will not be conducted in violation of these rules and regulations.

Highlight

In most startups of small businesses, the number of owners of stock is so few that neither the state nor federal governments need be involved.

In addition, any business that hires employees must consider personnel issues such as:

- whether it is subject to rules relating to withholding of taxes for local, state and federal governments
- whether it must pay Social Security tax, unemployment insurance or workmen's compensation
- whether any unions have jurisdiction and what pension or other payments must be made to them
- whether minimum wage requirements are applicable
- whether hiring minors is permissible
- any occupational safety and health regulations.

Be open to advice

There are a number of federal and local agencies besides the office of the secretary of state that can assist you in incorporating your business.

First is your state department of securities and the regional office of the Securities and Exchange Commission. These agencies regulate the sale of securities. In most startups of small businesses, the number of owners of stock is so few that neither the state nor federal governments need be involved. They usually become involved only when you are selling stock to more than 25 people or making what is known as a "public offering." However, even with fewer stockholders, there may be questions as to whether your stock sale or your proposed financing must be cleared with the authorities.

The Small Business Administration of the federal government was established by Congress in 1953 to provide prospective, new, and established members of the small business community with financial and management training and counseling. Check your Yellow Pages for their local office. Counseling sponsored by the Service Corps Of Retired Executives (SCORE) is extremely helpful, and they may offer free on-site counseling services, workshops and seminars. Also contact your local trade associations and the local chamber of commerce. They, too, can give you much advice and assistance.

Keep separate corporate records

Highlights

To avoid potential IRS problems, you must maintain separate sets of records, one for your personal affairs and one for the affairs of the corporation.

Remember that your corporation is viewed in the eyes of the law as a different "legal entity," separate and apart from the owner(s). Hence, to avoid potential IRS problems, you must maintain separate sets of records, one for your personal affairs and one for the affairs of the corporation. As a rule, however, it is not necessary to maintain an elaborate bookkeeping system. A separate bank account and bookkeeping that clearly show what you and the corporation separately earn and pay out is usually sufficient. A local bookkeeper or accountant can set up a convenient accounting and tax system for your business.

Set up your corporate bank accounts

To open a corporate bank account, you need an Employer Identification Number for your corporation. To obtain this, file application form SS-4 with the IRS. If you already have an Employer Identification Number for a Keogh Plan account or because you have had employees in an unincorporated business, you nevertheless need a new number for the corporation, as the corporation is a new person or entity. The bank will probably also require a Corporate Resolution, duly signed with the corporate seal, as an official corporate indication of authorization to open a bank account.

Verify whether you're doing business in another state

If your new corporation is strictly a local business, it is unlikely that you will need to be authorized or qualified to do business in another state. You clearly are doing business in only one place.

But what happens if you start advertising in magazines and you get orders from out of state? Are you now doing business in more than one state? Or what if you are in the sales business, have a store or sales office in only one place, but have sales representatives who drive to other states and call on potential customers? Does this mean you are now doing business elsewhere? If you start expanding and open up new stores, then you would clearly be doing business in these other locations.

Before we go further into how you decide whether you are doing business in another state, let's look at why it matters. If you are doing business in another state but have not qualified by filing the proper papers and paying the fees, the consequences can be serious. In all states, an unqualified foreign corporation is denied access to the courts of the state, which would mean you could not sue someone in that state to enforce a contract or obligation. In addition, many states impose fines when they discover a corporation doing business without being qualified; in some cases directors, officers or agents may be subject to these fines. These consequences could be serious to your business.

Highlight

If you are doing business in another state but have not qualified by filing the proper papers and paying the fees, the consequences can be serious.

The statutes of many states define what constitutes "doing business" within that state; these statutes should be consulted.

If you do have to become authorized to do business as a foreign corporation, the procedure is relatively simple. You obtain from the secretary of state the application form, complete it and file it with the proper fees.

The Model Corporation Act

The Model Corporation Act, drafted by a group of lawyers and law professors, gives a list of activities that, in and of themselves, do not constitute doing business. Since this act is the basis for the laws in many states, it is a good guide as to what you can do without having to qualify. The language reads as follows:

Without excluding other activities which may not constitute transacting business in this state, a foreign corporation shall not be considered to be transacting business in this state, for the purposes of this Act, by reason of carrying on in this state any one or more of the following activities:

a. Maintaining or defending any action or suit or any administrative or arbitration proceeding, or effecting the settlement thereof or the settlement of claims or disputes.

b. Holding meetings of its directors or shareholders or carrying on other activities concerning its internal affairs.

c. Maintaining bank accounts.

d. Maintaining offices or agencies for the transfer, exchange and registration of its securities or appointing and maintaining trustees or depositories with relation to its securities.

e. Effecting sales through independent contractors.

f. Soliciting or procuring orders, whether by mail or through employees or agents or otherwise, where such orders require acceptance without this state before becoming binding contracts.

g. Creating as borrower or lender, or acquiring indebtedness or mortgages or other security interests in real or personal property.

h. Securing or collecting debts or enforcing any rights in property securing the same.

i. Transacting any business in interstate commerce.

j. Conducting an isolated transaction completed within a period of thirty days and not in the course of a number of repeated transactions of like nature.

CHAPTER

Incorporation checklist

Steps in the incorporation process:

1) Decide whether to incorporate.
2) Decide where to incorporate.
3) Select a corporate name.
4) Select a registered agent, if necessary.
5) Draft a Certificate or Articles of Incorporation.
6) Sign the Certificate of Incorporation and file with the secretary of state, with appropriate filing fees.
7) Hold incorporator's initial meeting to elect directors and transact first business.
8) Hold organizational meeting of initial board of directors.
9) Select a corporate seal and stock certificates, issue shares, elect officers and open bank accounts.
10) Apply for Employer Identification Number.
11) Choose a fiscal year.
12) File a "doing business as" certificate, if necessary.
13) Apply for authorization to do business in other states, if necessary.
14) Obtain necessary state and local licenses and/or permits.

CHAPTER 11

The S Corporation election

An S Corporation (previously a Subchapter S Corporation, also called a Small Business Corporation,) is, for most tax purposes, treated by the IRS as if it were a partnership or sole proprietorship. This means that it is not a tax-paying entity, as a regular C Corporation is.

If you form a C Corporation, the profits of that business are taxed twice. First the corporation pays a corporate tax on the profit. Then, when the after-tax profit is distributed to you as a shareholder, you pay a hefty income tax on it as dividend income. This is the double taxation that is imposed on corporate profits.

The S Corporation, on the other hand, is viewed only as a financial channel through which its income, deductions, credits and losses are passed to its shareholders. It is these shareholders who must pay whatever tax is due. If at the end of the year your S Corporation earns a profit, it does not pay any taxes on that profit. Instead, the profit is considered your income and you pay the tax.

Can you benefit from an S Corporation?

Virtually every type of business operation can benefit by being operated as an S Corporation, with the possible exception of businesses that expect to retain rather than distribute profits. Because it is treated as a partnership, an S Corporation must report that its shareholders have earned profits even if it does not distribute these profits. But even in this situation, the fact that individual tax rates are lower than corporate rates may justify a decision in favor of the S Corporation.

How and when to use an S Corporation

Use of the S Corporation should depend upon several factors:

1) The type of business that you own

2) The profitability of your business

3) Your personal tax bracket

4) The types of assets used by your business

5) The growth prospects for your business

6) The recognition of an S Corporation by your state

Highlight

Forming an S Corporation is one of many tax strategies available to small-business owners. Like other tax-saving techniques, it is not recommended in all cases.

Which businesses benefit most?

1) Service industries with modest equipment or capital asset requirements

2) Fully developed businesses that will not require additional capital investments

3) Enterprises that will invest in real estate, equipment, or other property that will rapidly appreciate in value

4) Start-up ventures that are expected to operate at a loss for the first year or two

When to be taxed as a regular corporation

Forming an S Corporation is one of many tax strategies available to small-business owners. Like other tax-saving techniques, it is not recommended in all cases. You should decide to be taxed as a regular corporation when:

1) Your business becomes profitable and you want to build up your company earnings to expand your business.

2) You have owned a profitable service business for several years and, rather than drain the earnings from the company, you now want to accumulate them in the corporation and diversify. Regular corporate tax rates may leave more cash for reinvestment. Of course, it may be possible to pull sufficient income out of the corporation as salary to avoid double taxation.

3) You formed your S Corporation several years ago as a tax shelter. The shelter's earnings have risen and it is now about to become very profitable, throwing these profits into your high-bracket personal return. The solution is to give up S Corporation status and let the profits be taxed at corporate rates.

4) There are considerable passive losses, such as through tax credits, depreciation, or real estate investments. Even though these losses result from accounting strategies, the items should be taken out of the S Corporation and placed under the ownership of a C Corporation or held personally.

5) There are more than 35 shareholders in your S Corporation. (stock in the S Corporation that is jointly held by a husband and wife is treated as if owned by one shareholder). Since 35 is the maximum limit allowed by law, beyond this number your S Corporation will automatically revert back to C Corporation status.

Highlights

Many small corporations are electing to be S Corporations because, under the new Tax Reform Act, individuals pay lower taxes than do corporations.

The S Corporation and the limited liability company

The S Corporation is similar in many respects to the limited liability company. However, even though both types of business provide limited liability and similar tax advantages, there are five important differences. Unlike a limited liability company, an S Corporation:

1) Enjoys widespread popularity
2) May not own more than 80 percent of another corporation
3) May not have more than 35 shareholders
4) May not have more than one class of stock
5) May not have a non-resident alien, partnership, or corporation as a shareholder

To take advantage of the S provision:

1) Complete and file with the IRS a simple one-page form, IRS form 2553 (this permits tax filing as a small-business corporation).

2) Complete and file an individual tax return, IRS form 1120S, when it comes time to pay your taxes.

Form 2553 must be filed by the 15th day of the third month of the first taxable year. All S Corporations incorporated after 1982 must adopt the calendar year as their tax year, but they have some leeway as to a fiscal year within three months either side of a calendar year. These forms can be obtained at no charge by calling (or visiting) a local IRS Service Office. Forms 2553 and 1120S are also contained in this manual.

Many small corporations are electing to be S Corporations because, under the new Tax Reform Act, individuals pay lower taxes than do corporations. Therefore, the business profits are more advantageously taxed at the lower individual rates. Nevertheless, the decision to become an S Corporation should be made after consulting with your attorney or accountant.

CHAPTER 12

Maintaining corporate records

Once organized, the corporation must maintain a continuous record of all authorized actions approved by its stockholders or directors.

A complete and detailed record of stockholders' and directors' meetings, or minutes, as they are called, is important for many reasons:

1) Parties dealing with the corporation may want evidence that the corporate action was approved.

2) Officers and employees within the corporation are entitled to protection if their acts were approved.

3) Accurate minutes are frequently necessary to preserve certain tax benefits or to avoid tax liabilities and penalties.

4) Minutes are often necessary to prove that the corporation is operated as a separate entity independent of its principals.

The forms in this guide will help you maintain a well-documented written record of stockholders' and directors' actions, in a format that meets legal standards. By using these forms you can create a complete corporate biography, detailing the important events during the life of the corporation.

Generally, you need only complete the resolution form that conforms to the corporate action voted. Occasionally, however, you may need to modify the form to suit your particular needs. Always be certain the resolution accurately states the corporate action approved. In some cases, particularly on more important transactions, you may find it necessary to have an attorney decide what the resolution should contain. While these prepared forms can greatly simplify your recordkeeping requirements, they are not a substitute for your good judgment in deciding how you should document the actions of your corporation.

CHAPTER 13

Records of stockholder actions

Stockholders can usually vote in person or by proxy, on the broadest issues relating to the corporation. These typically include changes of corporate name, address, purpose, the amount or type of shares, and other matters involving the corporate structure. Stockholders' action may also be needed on major legal or financial issues, such as whether to mortgage, encumber, pledge or lease all or substantially all of the corporate assets or to file bankruptcy, merge or consolidate. There are, of course, many other actions that can be taken by stockholders. The primary function of the stockholders, however, is to elect the board of directors, through whose governance the corporation is actually managed.

Stockholders can act officially only as a group. This means that a formal meeting is needed before they can legally bind the corporation. There are some exceptions where the stockholders can consent in writing to a particular action without having to hold a meeting. These instances, however, are rare.

Certain rules and procedures have to be followed for stockholders to properly conduct an official stockholder meeting:

1) Every stockholder has to be properly notified about the time and place of the meeting, who is calling the meeting, and any matters that will be considered at the meeting.

It is common in small corporations for the stockholders to do without a formal notice, especially when the bylaws set the time and place of the regular annual meeting of stockholders. This can be done by having all the stockholders sign a waiver of notice at the meeting. Unscheduled or special meetings of stockholders may require notice, although a signed waiver of notice can also be used at these meetings. For an unscheduled meeting to be legally convened, it is essential that the records show that proper notice was given, or that the stockholders signed a waiver of notice.

Your Articles of Incorporation or bylaws will specify where and when a stockholder meeting can legally be held; the book of minutes should show the time and place of each meeting. In this way, you can prove that the meeting complied with the legal requirements.

2) No business can be transacted at a stockholders' meeting unless a quorum is present. Therefore, it is essential that the book of minutes reflect that a quorum of stockholders attended the meeting.

Highlight

If there is no rule on a quorum, then whatever number of stockholders shows up for the meeting will constitute a quorum.

The Articles of Incorporation or the bylaws will usually state the size of the quorum, either in terms of the number of stockholders or the number of shares that must be represented at the meeting. For example, a bylaw that "two-thirds of all stockholders shall constitute a quorum" applies to the number of stockholders, and not to the amount of the stock they own. On the other hand, a bylaw that states "a majority of the outstanding stock shall constitute a quorum" means that a certain number of shares of stock must be represented, regardless of whether the stock is owned by one person or by thousands of people. If there is no rule on a quorum, then whatever number of stockholders shows up for the meeting will constitute a quorum.

3) Stockholder meetings must have a chairperson to preside over the meeting. They must also have a secretary to record what happens. The bylaws will ordinarily designate these officials by specifying that the president serve as chairperson and the secretary act as secretary; however, substitutes are usually allowable.

4) The first item of business at every stockholder meeting should be to approve the minutes of the previous meeting. Once the minutes are approved, they legally document what occurred at the meeting. Minutes are the most nearly conclusive proof of what the corporation is authorized to do. That is why it is important to show that the minutes have been approved as accurate, or that necessary changes have been made.

5) Parliamentary procedure governs the conduct of meetings. It is not generally necessary to identify the person making the motion or seconding a motion, nor is it essential to record the exact tally of votes, as long as the action approved is clear.

CHAPTER 14

Records of director actions

Most of the rules and procedures that apply to stockholder meetings apply equally to meetings of the board of directors with these exceptions:

1) Directors will meet far more often than stockholders; in large corporations they may meet monthly. The directors can also hold special meetings for interim board action; in more active corporations they will routinely meet more often.

2) As with stockholders, the board can function only through a duly called meeting where a quorum of directors (as defined in the bylaws) is present. Directors who may be in conflict with the interests of the corporation may not be counted toward the quorum, nor be entitled to vote.

3) The board must be particularly careful to document not only its actions but why the action was taken. Because the board has responsibility to stockholders and potential liability to other constituencies, it may be called upon to show why its action was prudent, particularly in areas of dividends, loans to officers, major contracts, compensation, and policy-making. It is especially critical for the minutes to include or refer to reports, arguments, opinions and other documents to support the reasonableness of the board's actions.

Many additional forms that allow the corporate board of directors to act on a wide variety of matters are available in the *E-Z Legal Corporate Secretary*, available as a book or software.

All records, resolutions and minutes should be kept within the corporate minute book for no fewer than six years, although retaining the records longer is recommended, considering the numerous types of claims that are possible and the varying statutes of limitations.

Properly used, the forms in this guide will provide you with a simple, easy-to-use and legally sound records system for your corporation.

CHAPTER

Dissolving your corporation

There are many ways to dissolve a corporation, depending upon state law.

A corporation may be dissolved by:

1) ***Expiration*** of the period specified in the corporate charter (Certificate of Incorporation) if any expiration date is stated.

2) ***A surrender of the charter***. When the shareholders of a corporation, by majority vote, surrender the corporate charter to the state and it is formally accepted, the corporation is dissolved.

3) ***Filing a Certificate of Dissolution*** with the secretary of state in the state of incorporation.

4) ***Consolidation.*** When corporation A unites with corporation, B to form a third but entirely separate corporation C, corporations A and B cease to exist and are said to have been dissolved "by consolidation." The new corporation C assumes all the assets, property rights, privileges and liabilities of former corporations A and B.

5) ***Merger***. When corporation A merges into corporation B, only corporation A is dissolved "by merger." Corporation B survives. The surviving corporation absorbs all the assets, property rights, privileges, and often the liabilities of the absorbed corporation, but continues its own separate corporate existence thereafter.

6) ***The occurrence of a condition***. A corporation may be dissolved when a condition clearly specified in the corporate charter occurs, such as the death of a principal. This provision is rare, however, as corporations have a perpetual life independent of their principals.

7) ***Legislative repeal***. Under the inherent rights reserved by most states to "alter, amend, or repeal" the charter granted to a corporation, a legislature may, for some reason, find it necessary to revoke a corporate charter, thereby terminating the corporate existence. This is more commonly exercised with non-profit corporations.

8) ***Action by the attorney general.*** The state (and only the state) can sue to terminate the existence of a corporation. And if satisfied that the state has proven its case (e.g. when the court finds a corporation has not filed required taxes or documents or that it has abused or neglected to use its powers), the court may revoke the corporate charter.

9) ***Directors' or shareholders' petition.*** The board of directors (or a majority thereof) may be empowered by statute to petition for the dissolution of a corporation upon the occurrence of certain events, e.g. when the assets of the corporation are not sufficient to discharge its liabilities. The stockholders of a majority of all outstanding shares entitled to vote on the issue may also be empowered by statute to make such petition to the court on similar grounds.

Highlight

The dissolution of a corporation carries with it important tax and liability questions.

10) ***Shareholders' petition under deadlock statutes.*** A typical so-called "deadlock statute" commonly provides: "Unless otherwise provided in the Certificate of Incorporation, the holders of one-half of all outstanding shares of a corporation entitled to vote in an election of directors may present a petition for dissolution on one or more of the following grounds:

(a) That the directors are so divided respecting the management of the corporation's affairs that the votes required for action by the board cannot be obtained.

(b) That the shareholders are so divided that the votes required for the election of directors cannot be obtained.

(c) That there is internal dissension and two or more factions of shareholders are so divided that dissolution would be beneficial to the shareholders."

The dissolution of a corporation carries with it important tax and liability questions. Therefore dissolution should be undertaken only after consulting with an attorney and accountant.

Glossary of useful terms

A-F

Assets - Anything owned with monetary value. This includes both real and personal property.

Authorized shares - The number of shares a corporation is authorized to sell.

Bylaws - Rules adopted by the corporation itself for the regulation of a corporation's own actions; a subordinate law adopted by a corporation, association, or other body for its self-government or to regulate the rights and duties of its officers and members.

C corporation - A regular corporation that is not an S corporation

Calendar year - The accounting year beginning on January 1 and ending on December 31.

Certificate or Articles of Incorporation-The document that creates a corporation according to the laws of the state. This must be filed and approved by the state.

Consolidation - When two corporations combine, creating a third.

Deceptively similar - A name so similar to another name that the two become confused in the public eye.

Dividend income - Dividends that must be declared as regular income for income tax purposes

Fiscal year - Any 12-month period used by a business as its fiscal accounting period. Such accounting period may, for example, run from July 1 of one year through June 30 of the next year.

Foreign corporation - A corporation formed in one state or country but conducting some or all of its business in another state or country.

I-P

Incorporate - To form a corporation or to organize and be granted status as a corporation by following procedures prescribed by law.

Incorporator - The person who signs the Articles of Incorporation upon petitioning the state for a corporate charter.

Insolvency - Bankruptcy

Issued shares - The number of shares actually sold by the corporation.

Merger - The absorption of one corporation by another.

Minority stockholder - One who owns or controls less than 50 percent of the stock in a corporation.

Minutes - Written records of formal proceedings of stockholders' and directors' meetings.

Non-par value stock - Shares of stock without specified value.

Not-for-profit corporation - A corporation organized for some charitable, civil, social or other purpose that does not entail the generation of profit or the distribution of its income to members, principals, shareholders, officers or others affiliated with it. Such corporations are accorded special treatment under the law for some purposes, including taxation.

Parliamentary procedure - Rules such as "Roberts Rules of Order," which govern stockholders' meetings, directors' meetings, etc.

Par value stock - Shares of stock with a specified value.

Proxy - Authorization by a stockholder allowing another to vote his shares of stock.

Publicly owned corporation - One whose stock is owned by more than 25 stockholders and is regulated by the Securities and Exchange Commission.

Q-S

Quorum - A majority of the stockholders or directors necessary for vote-counting and decision-making at a meeting. While a quorum is usually a majority of either the total membership or the members present, a quorum may consist of a greater number than a simple majority if desired and stated in the bylaws.

Regular corporation - Also known as a C Corporation

Service business - A business that sells service or advice instead of a tangible product

Shareholder - See Stockholder.

Start-up venture - A new business having no track record

State statutes - Laws created by a state legislature

Statutory agent - A lawyer, corporation or individual who has assumed the responsibility of being the legal representative for the corporation for purposes of accepting legal service in a certain state.

S Corporation (Subchapter S Corporation)- A small business corporation which elects to be taxed as a partnership or proprietorship for federal income tax purposes. Individual shareholders enjoy the benefits under state law of limited corporate liability, but avoid corporate federal taxes.

Stock certificate - Written instrument evidencing a share in the ownership of a corporation.

Stockholder - A holder of one or more shares of the stock of a corporation. A stockholder may be called a "shareholder."

Subsidiary - A corporation owned by another corporation.

DEPARTMENTS OF CORPORATION

BY STATE

Every state provides its own specific Certificate (or Articles) of Incorporation. Refer to the following pages to find the appropriate address and phone number for the state in which you will incorporate.

DEPARTMENTS OF CORPORATION

ALABAMA
Secretary of State
State Capital-Corporations Divisions
P.O. Box 5616
Montgomery, AL 36103-5616
(205)242-5324

ALASKA
State of Alaska
Department of Commerce and
Economic Development
Corporation
Juneau, AK 99811
(907)465-2530

ARIZONA
Arizona Corporation Commission
Incorporating Division
1300 W. Washington
Phoenix, AZ 85007
(602)542-3026

ARKANSAS
Secretary of State
State Capital-Corporations Divisions
Little Rock, AR 72201-1094
(501)682-1010

CALIFORNIA
Secretary of State
1230 J Street
Sacramento, CA 95814
(916)445-0620

COLORADO
Secretary of State
1575 Sherman Street, 2nd Floor
Denver, CO 80203
(303)894-2251

CONNECTICUT
Office of the Secretary of State
State of Connecticut-Corporations Division
30 Trinity Street
Hartford, CT 06106
(203)566-8570

DELAWARE
State of Delaware
Department of State, Division of Incorporation
townsend Building
P.O. Box 898
Dover, DE 19903
(302)739-3073

DISTRICT OF COLUMBIA
Dept. of Consumer Regulatory Affairs
614 "H" Street N.W., Room 407
Washington, DC 20001
(202)727-7278

FLORIDA
Division of Incorporation
P.O. Box 6327
Tallahassee, FL 32314
(904)488-9000

GEORGIA
Secretary of State
Corporations Department
2 Martin Luther King Drive
Suite 315, West Tower
Atlanta, GA 30334
(404)656-2817

HAWAII
Director of the Dept. of Regulatory Agencies
State Capital
Honolulu, HA 96813
(808)586-2727

IDAHO
Secretary of State
State House, Room 203
Boise, ID 83720
(208)334-2300

ILLINOIS
Secretary of State
Springfield, IL 62756
(217)782-7880

INDIANA
Secretary of State
302 W. Washington St., Room E018
Indianapolis, IN 46204
(317)232-6576

IOWA
Secretary of State
State Capitol
Des Moines, IA 50319
(515)281-5204

KANSAS
State of Kansas
Department of Incorporation
1500 S.W. Arrowhead Drive
Topeka, KS 66604-4027
(913)296-4564

KENTUCKY
Secretary of State
P.O. Box 718
Frankfort, KY 40602-0718
(502)564-2848

LOUISIANA
Secretary of State
P.O. Box 94125
Baton Rouge, LA 70804-9125
(504)925-4704

MAINE
Secretary of State
Department of Incorporation
State House, Station 101
(207)289-4195

MARYLAND
State Dept. of Assessments and Taxation
301 W. Preston St., Room 809
Baltimore, MD 21201
(410)225-1350

MASSACHUSETTS
Secretary of State
Corporations Division
1 Ashburton Place, 17th Floor
Boston, MA 02108
(6617)727-9640

MICHIGAN
State of Michigan
Department of Commerce
Corporation Division
P.O. Box 30054
Lansing, MI 48909
(517)334-6302

MINNESOTA
Secretary of State
180 State Office Building
St. Paul, MN 55155
(612)296-2803

MISSISSIPPI
Secretary of State
Office of Incorporation
P.O. Box 136
Jackson, MS 39205
(601)359-1633

MISSOURI
Secretary of State
Jefferson City, MO 65101
(314)751-4153

MONTANA
Secretary of State
Capitol Bldg., Room 225
Helena, MT 59620
(406)444-2034

NEBRASKA
Secretary of State-Corporate Division
Suite 1301, Capitol Bldg.
Lincoln, NE 68509
(402)471-4079

NEVADA
Secretary of State-Capital Complex
Carson City, NV 89710
(702)687-5203

NEW HAMPSHIRE
Department of Revenue Administration
Return Processing Division
P.O. Box 637
Concord, NH 03301
(603)271-3246

NEW JERSEY
State of New Jersey
Department of State
P.O. Box 1330
Trenton, NJ 08625
(609)530-6400

NEW MEXICO
State Corporation Commission
Franchise Tax Department
P.O. Drawer 1269
Santa Fe, NM 87504-1269
(505)827-4504

NEW YORK
Please see the coupon in this guide

NORTH CAROLINA
Secretary of State
Raleigh, NC 27603
(919)733-4201

NORTH DAKOTA
Secretary of State
Bismark, ND 58505
(701)224-4284

OHIO
Secretary of State
30 East Broad Street, 14th Floor
Columbus, OH 43266-0418
(614)466-3910

OKLAHOMA
Secretary of State
101 State Capitol
Oklahoma City, OK 73105
(405)521-3911

OREGON
Department of Commerce
Corporation Division
158 12th street N.E.
Salem, OR 97310
(503)378-4166

PENNSYLVANIA
Commonwealth of Pennsylvania
Corporations Office
Department of State
301 N. Office Bldg.
Harrisburg, PA 17120
(717)787-1057

PUERTO RICO
Commonwealth of Puerto Rico
Department of State
P.O. Box 3271
San Juan, Puerto Rico 00902-3271
(809)722-2121

RHODE ISLAND
1900 Kawanaha Blvd. E
State House
100 N. Main Street
Providence, RI 02903
(401)277-3040

SOUTH CAROLINA
P.O. Box 11350
Columbia, SC 29211
(803)734-2158

SOUTH DAKOTA
Secretary of State-Attn. Corporations
500 E. Capitol
Pierre, SD 57501
(605)773-4845

TENNESSEE
Department of State
Division of Services, Suite 1800
James K. Polk Building
Nashville, TN 37243-0306
(615)741-2286

TEXAS
Secretary of State
Austin, TX 78711
(512)463-5555

UTAH
Department of Commerce
Heber M.Wells Building
160 E. 300 South, 2nd Floor
Salt Lake City, UT 84111
(801)530-4849

VERMONT
Secretary of State-Corporations Division
109 State Street
Montpelier, VT 05609-1104
(802)828-2386

VIRGINIA
Commonwealth of Virginia
State Corporation Commission
P.O. Box 1197
Richmond, VA 23209
(804)371-753-7115

WASHINGTON
Secretary of State
Olympia, WA 98504
(206)753-7115

WEST VIRGINIA
Secretary of State-Corporations Division
Bldg. 1, Room 139 West
1900 Kawanaha Blvd. E.
Charleston, WV 25305
(304)558-8000

WISCONSIN
Secretary of State
P.O. Box 7846
Madison, WI 53707
(608)266-3590

WYOMING
Secretary of State-Corporations Division
State Capitol Bldg.
Cheyenne, WY 82002
(307)777-7311

Incorporation

The forms in this guide

Businesses incorporating in New York can get a *Certificate of Incorporation* form that complies with New York statutes by filling out this coupon.

Send to: **E•Z LEGAL® FORMS,**
384 S. Military Trail,
Deerfield Beach, FL 33442

CERTIFICATE OF INCORPORATION FOR NEW YORK

Please send me one blank *Certificate of Incorporation* for businesses incorporating in the state of New York. I understand that this is a basic form and may require customizing depending on my needs and the type of business being incorporated.

Send to: ______________________________
name

____
address

____

Bylaws

of

____

adopted________________________

BYLAWS
OF

____

ARTICLE I
OFFICES

The principal office of the Corporation in the State of shall be located in , County of . The Corporation may have such other offices, either within or without the State of , as the Board of Directors may designate or as the business of the Corporation may require from time to time.

ARTICLE II
SHAREHOLDERS

SECTION 1. Annual Meeting. The annual meeting of the shareholders shall be held on the day in the month of in each year, beginning with the year 19 , at the hour of o'clock .m., for the purpose of electing Directors and for the transaction of such other business as may come before the meeting. If the day fixed for the annual meeting shall be a legal holiday in the State of , such meeting shall be held on the next succeeding business day. If the election of Directors shall not be held on the day designated herein for any annual meeting of the shareholders, or at any adjournment thereof, the Board of Directors shall cause the election to be held at a special meeting of the shareholders as soon thereafter as conveniently may be.

SECTION 2. Special Meetings. Special meetings of the shareholders, for any purpose or purposes, unless otherwise prescribed by statute, may be called by the President or by the Board of Directors, and shall be called by the President at the request of the holders of not less than percent (%) of all the outstanding shares of the Corporation entitled to vote at the meeting.

SECTION 3. Place of Meeting. The Board of Directors may designate any place, either within or without the State of , unless otherwise prescribed by statute, as the place of meeting for any annual meeting or for any special meeting. A waiver of notice signed by all shareholders entitled to vote at a meeting may designate any place, either within or without the State of , unless otherwise prescribed by statute, as the place for the holding of such meeting. If no designation is made, the place of meeting shall be the principal office of the Corporation.

SECTION 4. Notice of Meeting. Written notice stating the place, day and hour of the meeting and, in case of a special meeting, the purpose or purposes for which the meeting is called, shall unless otherwise prescribed by statute, be delivered not less than ( ) nor more than ( ) days before the date of the meeting, to each shareholder of record entitled to vote at such meeting. If mailed, such notice shall be deemed to be delivered when deposited in the United States Mail, addressed to the shareholder at his address as it appears on the stock transfer books of the Corporation, with postage thereon prepaid.

SECTION 5. Closing of Transfer Books or Fixing of Record. For the purpose of determining shareholders entitled to notice of or to vote at any meeting of shareholders or any adjournment thereof, or shareholders entitled to receive payment of any dividend, or in order to make a determination of shareholders for any other proper purpose, the Board of Directors of the Corporation may provide that the stock transfer books shall be closed for a stated period, but not to exceed in any case fifty (50) days. If the stock transfer books shall be closed for the purpose of determining shareholders entitled to notice of or to vote at a meeting of share-holders, such books shall be closed for at least ( ) days immediately preceding such meeting. In lieu of closing the stock transfer books, the Board of Directors may fix in advance a date as the record date for any such determination of shareholders, such date in any case to be not more than ( ) days and, in case of a meeting of shareholders, not less than ( ) days, prior to the date on which the particular action requiring such determination of shareholders is to be taken. If the stock transfer books are not closed and no record date is fixed for the determination of shareholders entitled to notice of or to vote at a meeting of shareholders, or shareholders entitled to receive payment of a dividend, the date on which notice of the meeting is mailed or the date on which the resolution of the Board of Directors declaring such dividend is adopted, as the case may be, shall be the record date for such determination of shareholders. When a determination of shareholders entitled to vote at any meeting of shareholders has been made as provided in this section, such determination shall apply to any adjournment thereof.

SECTION 6. Voting Lists. The officer or agent having charge of the stock transfer books for shares of the corporation shall make a complete list of the shareholders entitled to vote at each meeting of shareholders or any adjournment thereof, arranged in alphabetical order, with the address of and the number of shares held by each. Such list shall be produced and kept open at the time and place of the meeting and shall be subject to the inspection of any shareholder during the whole time of the meeting for the purposes thereof.

SECTION 7. Quorum. A majority of the outstanding shares of the Corporation entitled to vote, represented in person or by proxy, shall constitute a quorum at a meeting of shareholders. If less than a majority of the outstanding shares are represented at a meeting, a majority of the shares so represented may adjourn the meeting from time to time without further notice. At such adjourned meeting at which a quorum shall be present or represented, any business may be transacted which might have been transacted at the meeting as originally noticed. The shareholders present at a duly organized meeting may continue to transact business until adjournment, notwithstanding the withdrawal of enough shareholders to leave less than a quorum.

SECTION 8. Proxies. At all meetings of shareholders, a shareholder may vote in person or by proxy executed in writing by the shareholder or by his duly authorized attorney-in-fact. Such proxy shall be filed with the secretary of the Corporation before or at the time of the meeting. A meeting of the Board of Directors may be had by means of a telephone conference or similar communications equipment by which all persons participating in the meeting can hear each other, and participation in a meeting under such circumstances shall constitute presence at the meeting.

SECTION 9. Voting of Shares. Each outstanding share entitled to vote shall be entitled to one vote upon each matter submitted to a vote at a meeting of shareholders.

SECTION 10. Voting of Shares by Certain Holders. Shares standing in the name of another corporation may be voted by such officer, agent or proxy as the Bylaws of such corporation may precribeor, in the absence of such provision, as the Board of Directors of such corporation may determine.

Shares held by an administrator, executor, guardian or conservator may be voted by him, either in person or by proxy, without a transfer of such shares into his name. Shares standing in the name of a trustee may be voted by him, either in person or by proxy, but no trustee shall be entitled to vote shares held by him without a transfer of such shares into his name.

Shares standing in the name of a receiver may be voted by such receiver, and shares held by or under the control of a receiver may be voted by such receiver without the transfer thereof into his name, if authority so to do be contained in an appropriate order of the court by which such receiver was appointed.

A shareholder whose shares are pledged shall be entitled to vote such shares until the shares have been transferred into the name of the pledgee, and thereafter the pledgee shall be entitled to vote the shares so transferred.

Shares of its own stock belonging to the Corporation shall not be voted, directly or indirectly, at any meeting, and shall not be counted in determining the total number of outstanding shares at any given time.

SECTION 11. Informal Action by Shareholders. Unless otherwise provided by law, any action required to be taken at a meeting of the shareholders, or any other action which may be taken at a meeting of the shareholders, may be taken without a meeting if a consent in writing, setting forth the action so taken, shall be signed by all of the shareholders entitled to vote with respect to the subject matter thereof.

ARTICLE III
BOARD OF DIRECTORS

SECTION 1. General Powers. The business and affairs of the Corporation shall be managed by its Board of Directors.

SECTION 2. Number, Tenure and Qualifications. The number of directors of the Corporation shall be fixed by the Board of Directors, but in no event shall be less than
(   ). Each director shall hold office until the next annual meeting of shareholders and until his successor shall have been elected and qualified.

SECTION 3. Regular Meetings. A regular meeting of the Board of Directors shall be held without other notice than this Bylaw immediately after, and at the same place as, the annual meeting of shareholders. The Board of Directors may provide, by resolution, the time and place for the holding of additional regular meetings without notice other than such resolution.

SECTION 4. Special Meetings. Special meetings of the Board of Directors may be called by or at the request of the President or any two directors. The person or persons authorized to call special meetings of the Board of Directors may fix the place for holding any special meeting of the Board of Directors called by them.

SECTION 5. Notice. Notice of any special meeting shall be given at least one (1) day previous thereto by written notice delivered personally or mailed to each director at his business address, or by telegram. If mailed, such notice shall be deemed to be delivered when deposited in the United States Mail so addressed, with postage thereon prepaid. If notice be given by telegram, such notice shall be deemed to be delivered when the telegram is delivered to the telegraph company. Any directors may waive notice of any meeting. The attendance of a director at a meeting shall constitute a waiver of notice of such meeting, except where a director attends a meeting for the express purpose of objecting to the transaction of any business because the meeting is not lawfully called or convened.

SECTION 6. Quorum. A majority of the number of directors fixed by Section 2 of this Article III shall constitute a quorum for the transaction of business at any meeting of the Board of Directors, but if less than such majority is present at a meeting, a majority of the directors present may adjourn the meeting from time to time without further notice.

SECTION 7. Manner of Acting. The act of the majority of the directors present at a meeting at which a quorum is present shall be the act of the Board of Directors.

SECTION 8. Action Without a Meeting. Any action that may be taken by the Board of Directors at a meeting may be taken without a meeting if a consent in writing, setting forth the action so to be taken, shall be signed before such action by all of the directors.

SECTION 9. Vacancies. Any vacancy occurring in the Board of Directors may be filled by the affirmative vote of a majority of the remaining directors though less than a quorum of the Board of Directors, unless otherwise provided by law. A director elected to fill a vacancy shall be elected for the unexpired term of his predecessor in office. Any directorship to be filled by reason of an increase in the number of directors may be filled by election by the Board of Directors for a term of office continuing only until the next election of directors by the shareholders.

SECTION 10. Compensation. By resolution of the Board of Directors, each director may be paid his expenses, if any, of attendance at each meeting of the Board of Directors, and may be paid a stated salary as director or a fixed sum for attendance at each meeting of the Board of Directors or both. No such payment shall preclude any director from serving the Corporation in any other capacity and receiving compensation therefor.

SECTION 11. Presumption of Assent. A director of the Corporation who is present at a meeting of the Board of Directors at which action on any corporate matter is taken shall be presumed to have assented to the action taken unless his dissent shall be entered in the minutes of the meeting or unless he shall file his written dissent to such action with the person acting as the Secretary of the meeting before the adjournment thereof, or shall forward such dissent by registered mail to the Secretary of the Corporation immediately after the adjournment of the meeting. Such right to dissent shall not apply to a director who voted in favor of such action.

ARTICLE IV
OFFICERS

SECTION 1. Number. The officers of the Corporation shall be a President, one or more Vice Presidents, a Secretary and a Treasurer, each of whom shall be elected by the Board of Directors. Such other officers and assistant officers as may be deemed necessary may be elected or appointed by the Board of Directors, including a Chairman of the Board. In its discretion, the Board of Directors may leave unfilled for any such period as it may determine any office except those of President and Secretary. Any two or more offices may be held by the same person, except for the offices of President and Secretary which may not be held by the same person. Officers may be directors or shareholders of the Corporation.

SECTION 2. Election and Term of Office. The officers of the Corporation to be elected by the Board of Directors shall be elected annually by the Board of Directors at the first meeting of the Board of Directors held after each annual meeting of the shareholders. If the election of officers shall not be held at such meeting, such election shall be held as soon thereafter as conveniently may be. Each officer shall hold office until his successor shall have been duly elected and shall have qualified, or until his death, or until he shall resign or shall have been removed in the manner hereinafter provided.

SECTION 3. Removal. Any officer or agent may be removed by the Board of Directors whenever, in its judgement, the best interests of the Corporation will be served thereby, but such removal shall be without prejudice to the contract rights, if any, of the person so removed. Election or appointment of an officer or agent shall not of itself create contract rights, and such appointment shall be terminable at will.

SECTION 4. Vacancies. A vacancy in any office because of death, resignation, removal, disqualification or otherwise, may be filled by the Board of Directors for the unexpired portion of the term.

SECTION 5. President. The President shall be the principal executive officer of the Corporation and, subject to the control of the Board of Directors, shall in general supervise and control all of the business and affairs of the Corporation. He shall, when present, preside at all meetings of the shareholders and of the Board of Directors, unless there is a Chairman of the Board, in which case the Chairman shall preside. He may sign, with the Secretary or any other proper officer of the Corporation thereunto authorized by the Board of Directors, certificates for shares of the Corporation, any deeds, mortgages, bonds, contracts, or other instruments which the Board of Directors has authorized to be executed, except in cases where the signing and execution thereof shall be expressly delegated by the Board of Directors or by these Bylaws to some other officer or agent of the Corporation, or shall be required by law to be otherwise signed or executed; and in general shall perform all duties incident to the office of President and such other duties as may be prescribed by the Board of Directors from time to time.

SECTION 6. Vice President. In the absence of the President or in event of his death, inability or refusal to act, the Vice President shall perform the duties of the President, and when so acting, shall have all the powers of and be subject to all the restrictions upon the President. The Vice President shall perform such other duties as from time to time may be assigned to him by the President or by the Board of Directors. If there is more than one Vice President, each Vice President shall succeed to the duties of the President in order of rank as determined by the Board of Directors. If no such rank has been determined, then each Vice President shall succeed to the duties of the President in order of date of election, the earliest date having the first rank.

SECTION 7. Secretary. The Secretary shall: (a) keep the minutes of the proceedings of the shareholders and of the Board of Directors in one or more minute books provided for that purpose; (b) see that all notices are duly given in accordance with the provisions of these Bylaws or as required by law; (c) be custodian of the corporate records and of the seal of the Corporation and see that the seal of the Corporation is affixed to all documents, the execution of which on behalf of the Corporation under its seal is duly authorized; (d) keep a register of the post office address of each shareholder which shall be furnished to the Secretary by such shareholder; (e) sign with the President certificates for shares of the Corporation, the issuance of which shall have been authorized by resolution of the Board of Directors; (f) have general charge of the stock transfer books of the Corporation; and (g) in general perform all duties incident to the office of the Secretary and such other duties as from time to time may be assigned to him by the President or by the Board of Directors.

SECTION 8. Treasurer. The Treasurer shall: (a) have charge and custody of and be responsible for all funds and securities of the Corporation; (b) receive and give receipts for moneys due and payable to the Corporation from any source what-soever, and deposit all such moneys in the name of the Corporation in such banks, trust companies or other depositories as shall be selected in accordance with the provisions of Article VI of these Bylaws; and (c) in general perform all of the duties incident to the office of Treasurer and such other duties as from time to time may be assigned to him by the President or by the Board of Directors. If required by the Board of Directors, the Treasurer shall give a bond for the faithful discharge of his duties in such sum and with such sureties as the Board of Directors shall determine.

SECTION 9. Salaries. The salaries of the officers shall be fixed from time to time by the Board of Directors, and no officer shall be prevented from receiving such salary by reason of the fact that he is also a director of the Corporation.

ARTICLE V
INDEMNITY

The Corporation shall indemnify its directors, officers and employees as follows:

(a) Every director, officer, or employee of the Corporation shall be indemnified by the Corporation against all expenses and liabilities, including counsel fees, reasonably incurred by or imposed upon him in connection with any proceeding to which he may be made a party, or in which he may become involved, by reason of his being or having been a director, officer, employee or agent of the Corporation or is or was serving at the request of the Corporation as a director, officer, employee or agent of the corporation, partnership, joint venture, trust or enterprise, or any settlement thereof, whether or not he is a director, officer, employee or agent at the time such expenses are incurred, except in such cases wherein the director, officer, or employee is adjudged guilty of willful misfeasance or malfeasance in the performance of his duties; provided that in the event of a settlement the indemnification herein shall apply only when the Board of Directors approves such settlement and reimbursement as being for the best interests of the Corporation.

(b) The Corporation shall provide to any person who is or was a director, officer, employee, or agent of the Corporation or is or was serving at the request of the Corporation as a director, officer, employee or agent of the corporation, partnership, joint venture, trust or enterprise, the indemnity against expenses of suit, litigation or other proceedings which is specifically permissible under applicable law.

(c) The Board of Directors may, in its discretion, direct the purchase of liability insurance by way of implementing the provisions of this Article V.

ARTICLE VI
CONTRACTS, LOANS, CHECKS AND DEPOSITS

SECTION 1. Contracts. The Board of Directors may authorize any officer or officers, agent or agents, to enter into any contract or execute and deliver any instrument in the name of and on behalf of the Corporation, and such authority may be general or confined to specific instances.

SECTION 2. Loans. No loans shall be contracted on behalf of the Corporation and no evidences of indebtedness shall be issued in its name unless authorized by a resolution of the Board of Directors. Such authority may be general or confined to specific instances.

SECTION 3. Checks, Drafts, etc. All checks, drafts or other orders for the payment of money, notes or other evidences of indebtedness issued in the name of the Corporation, shall be signed by such officer or officers, agent or agents of the Corporation and in such manner as shall from time to time be determined by resolution of the Board of Directors.

SECTION 4. Deposits. All funds of the Corporation not otherwise employed shall be deposited from time to time to the credit of the Corporation in such banks, trust companies or other depositories as the Board of Directors may select.

ARTICLE VII
CERTIFICATES FOR SHARES AND THEIR TRANSFER

SECTION 1. Certificates for Shares. Certificates representing shares of the Corporation shall be in such form as shall be determined by the Board of Directors. Such certificates shall be signed by the President and by the Secretary or by such other officers authorized by law and by the Board of Directors so to do, and sealed with the corporate seal. All certificates for shares shall be consecutively numbered or otherwise identified. The name and address of the person to whom the shares represented thereby are issued, with the number of shares and date of issue, shall be entered on the stock transfer books of the Corporation. All certificates surrendered to the Corporation for transfer shall be cancelled and no new certificate shall be issued until the former certificate for a like number of shares shall have been surrendered and cancelled, except that in case of a lost, destroyed or mutilated certificate, a new one may be issued therefor upon such terms and indemnity to the Corporation as the Board of Directors may prescribe.

SECTION 2. Transfer of Shares. Transfer of shares of the Corporation shall be made only on the stock transfer books of the Corporation by the holder of record thereof or by his legal representative, who shall furnish proper evidence of authority to transfer, or by his attorney thereunto authorized by power of attorney duly executed and filed with the Secretary of the Corporation, and on surrender for cancellation of the certificate for such shares. The person in whose name shares stand on the books of the Corporation shall be deemed by the Corporation to be the owner thereof for all purposes. Provided, however, that upon any action undertaken by the shareholders to elect S Corporation status pursuant to Section 1362 of the Internal Revenue Code and upon any shareholders agreement thereto restricting the transfer of said shares so as to disqualify said S Corporation status, said restriction on transfer shall be made a part of the bylaws so long as said agreement is in force and effect.

ARTICLE VIII
FISCAL YEAR

The fiscal year of the Corporation shall begin on the day of and end on the day of of each year.

ARTICLE IX
DIVIDENDS

The Board of Directors may from time to time declare, and the Corporation may pay, dividends on its outstanding shares in the manner and upon the terms and conditions provided by law and its Articles of Incorporation.

ARTICLE X
CORPORATE SEAL

The Board of Directors shall provide a corporate seal which shall be circular in form and shall have inscribed thereon the name of the Corporation and the state of incorporation and the words, "Corporate Seal".

ARTICLE XI
WAIVER OF NOTICE

Unless otherwise provided by law, whenever any notice is required to be given to any shareholder or director of the Corporation under the provisions of these Bylaws or under the provisions of the Articles of Incorporation or under the provisions of the applicable Business Corporation Act, a waiver thereof in writing, signed by the person or persons entitled to such notice, whether before or after the time stated therein, shall be deemed equivalent to the giving of such notice.

ARTICLE XII
AMENDMENTS

These Bylaws may be altered, amended or repealed and new Bylaws may be adopted by the Board of Directors at any regular or special meeting of the Board of Directors.

The above Bylaws are certified to have been adopted by the Board of Directors of the Corporation on the   day of   , 19

____
Secretary

WAIVER OF NOTICE OF MEETING OF INCORPORATORS AND DIRECTORS OF

____

We the undersigned do hereby constitute all the incorporators and directors of the above-named corporation and do hereby waive notice as to time and place of the first meeting of incorporators and directors of the aforesaid corporation.

Furthermore, we hereby consent and agree that said meeting shall be held at o'clock .m. on , 19 at the following place:

____

We do hereby affix our names to show our waiver of notice of said meeting.

______________________ ______________________

______________________ ______________________

______________________ ______________________

______________________ ______________________

______________________ ______________________

Dated:

NOTICE OF ORGANIZATION MEETING
OF INCORPORATORS AND DIRECTORS

TO: ______________________________

____

____

PLEASE BE ADVISED THAT:

We, the undersigned, do hereby constitute a majority of the directors named in the Articles of Incorporation of ________________________, a corporation;

Pursuant to state law, we are hereby calling an organization meeting of the Board of Directors and incorporators named in the Articles of Incorporation of the above named corporation; for the purpose of adopting bylaws, electing officers, and transacting such other business as may come before the meeting; and

Said organization meeting shall be held at ____________________________

____ on
19 , at o'clock .m.

______________________________ ______________________________

______________________________ ______________________________

______________________________ ______________________________

______________________________ ______________________________

RECEIPT OF NOTICE

______________________________ ______________________________
Addressee-Director Date Received

MINUTES OF ORGANIZATION MEETING OF BOARD OF DIRECTORS OF

____

The organizational meeting of the Board of Directors of
was held at
on , 19 , at :00 .m. Present were:

______________________ ______________________

______________________ ______________________

______________________ ______________________

being persons designated as the Directors in the Articles of Incorporation.

Absent from the meeting were:

______________________ ______________________

______________________ ______________________

______________________ ______________________

acted as temporary Chairman of the meeting and
acted as temporary Secretary.

The Chairman announced that the meeting had been duly called by the Incorporators of the Corporation.

The Chairman reported that the Articles of Incorporation of the Corporation had been duly filed with the State of on , 19 . The Certificate of Incorporation and a copy of said Articles of Incorporation were ordered to be inserted in the Minutes as a part of the records of the meeting.

A proposed form of Bylaws for the regulation and the management of the affairs of the Corporation was then presented at the meeting. The Bylaws were read and considered and, upon motion duly made and seconded, it was:

RESOLVED, that the form of Bylaws of the Corporation, as presented to this meeting, a copy of which is directed to be inserted in the Minute Book of the Corporation be, and the same are hereby approved and adopted as the Bylaws of the Corporation.

The following persons were nominated officers of the Corporation to serve until their respective successors are chosen and qualify:

PRESIDENT:
VICE PRESIDENT:
SECRETARY:
TREASURER:

The Chairman announced that the aforenamed persons had been elected to the office set opposite their respective names.

The President thereupon took the chair and the Secretary immediately assumed the discharge of the duties of that office.

The President then stated that there were a number of organizational matters to be considered at the meeting and a number of resolutions to be adopted by the Board of Directors.

The form of stock certificates was then exhibited at the meeting. Thereupon, a motion duly made and seconded, it was:

RESOLVED, that the form of stock certificates presented at this meeting be, and the same is hereby adopted and approved as the stock certificate of the Corporation, a specimen copy of the stock certificate to be inserted with these Minutes.

FURTHER RESOLVED, that the officers are hereby authorized to pay or reimburse the payment of all fees and expenses incident to and necessary for the organization of this Corporation.

The Board of Directors then considered the opening of a corporate bank account to serve as a depository for the funds of the Corporation. Following discussion, on motion duly made and seconded, it was:

RESOLVED, that the Treasurer be authorized, empowered and directed to open an account with and to deposit all funds of the Corporation, all drafts, checks and notes of the Corporation, payable on said account to be made in the corporate name signed by

FURTHER RESOLVED, that officers are hereby authorized to execute such resolutions (including formal Bank Resolutions), documents and other instruments as may be necessary or advisable in opening or continuing said bank account. A copy of the applicable printed form of Bank Resolution hereby adopted to supplement these Minutes is ordered appended to the Minutes of this meeting.

It is announced that the following persons have offered to transfer the property listed below in exchange for the following shares of the stock of the Corporation:

Name	Payment Consideration, or Property	Number of Shares

Upon motion duly made and seconded, it was:

RESOLVED, that acceptance of the offer of the above-named stock subscribers is in the best interest of the Corporation and necessary for carrying out the corporate business, and in the judgement of the Board of Directors, the assets proposed to be transferred to the Corporation are reasonably worth the amount of consideration deemed therefor, and the same hereby is accepted, and that upon receipt of the consideration indicated above, the President and the Secretary are authorized to issue certificates of fully-paid, non-assessable capital stock of this Corporation in the amounts indicated to the above-named persons.

In order to provide for the payment of expenses of incorporation and organization of the Corporation, on motion duly made, seconded and unanimously carried, the following resolution was adopted:

RESOLVED, that the President and the Secretary and/or Treasurer of this Corporation be and they are hereby authorized and directed to pay the expenses of this Corporation, including attorney's fees for incorporation, and to reimburse the persons who have made disbursements thereof.

After consideration of the pertinent issues with regard to the tax year and accounting basis, on motion duly made, and seconded and unanimously carried, the following resolution was adopted:

RESOLVED, that the first fiscal year of the Corporation shall commence on
, and end on

FURTHER RESOLVED, that the President be and is hereby authorized and directed to enter into employment contracts with certain employees, such contract shall be for the term and the rate stated in the attached Employment Agreements.

FURTHER RESOLVED, that it shall be the policy of the Corporation to reimburse each employee or to pay directly on his behalf all expenses incidental to his attendance at conventions and seminars as may be approved by the President. Reimbursement shall include full reimbursement for commercial and private transportation expenses, plus other necessary and ordinary out-of-pocket expenses incidental to the said travel, including meals and lodging.

A general discussion was then held concerning the immediate commencement of business operations as a Corporation and it was determined that business operations of the Corporation would commence as of It was agreed that no fixed date would be set for holding meetings of the Board of Directors except the regular meetings to be held immediately after the annual meetings of shareholders as provided in the Bylaws of the Corporation but that meetings of the Directors would be periodically called by the President and Secretary or others as provided by the Bylaws. Upon motion duly made, seconded and unanimously carried, it was:

RESOLVED, that the officers of the Corporation are hereby authorized to do any and all things necessary to conduct the business of the Corporation as set forth in the Articles of Incorporation and Bylaws of the Corporation.

Upon motion duly made, seconded, and unanimously carried the following resolution was adopted:

RESOLVED, that, if required, that
be, and hereby is, appointed Resident Agent in the State of

The office of the Resident Agent will be located at

The Chairman then presented to the meeting the question of electing the provisions of Section 1244 of the Internal Revenue Code. He noted that this Section permits ordinary loss treatment when either the holder of Section 1244 stock sells or exchanges such stock at a loss or when such stock becomes worthless. After a discussion, the following preamble was stated and the following resolution was unanimously:

RESOLVED, THAT:

WHEREAS, this Corporation qualifies as a small business corporation as defined in Section 1244, but

WHEREAS, the Board of Directors are concerned over future tax law changes modifying Section 1244 as presently enacted (subsequent to the Revenue Act of 1978) and thus desire to safeguard this Corporation's 1244 election by complying with prior law as well as present law, and

WHEREAS, pursuant to the requirements of Section 1244 and the Regulations issued thereunder, the following plan has been submitted to the Corporation by the Board of Directors of the Corporation:

(a) The plan as hereafter set forth shall, upon its adoption by the Board of Directors of the Corporation immediately become effective.

(b) No more than shares of common stock are authorized to be issued under this plan, such stock to have a par value of $ per share.

(c) Stock authorized under this plan shall be issued only in exchange for money, or property susceptible to monetary valuation other than capital stock, securities or services rendered or to be rendered. The aggregate dollar amount to be received for such stock shall not exceed $1,000,000, and the sum of each aggregate dollar amount and the equity capital of the Corporation (determined on the date of adoption of the plan) shall not exceed $1,000,000.

(d) Any stock options granted during the life of this plan which apply to the stock issuable hereunder shall apply solely to such stock and to no other and must be exercised within the period in which the plan is effective.

(e) Such other action as may be necessary shall be taken by the Corporation to qualify the stock to be offered and issued under this plan as "Section 1244 Stock," as such term is defined in the Internal Revenue Code and the regulations issued thereunder.

NOW, THEREFORE, the foregoing plan to issue Section 1244 Stock is adopted by the Corporation and the appropriate officers of the Corporation are authorized and directed to take all actions deemed by them necessary to carry out the intent and purpose of the recited plan.

There being no further business requiring Board action or consideration;

On motion duly made, seconded and carried, the meeting was adjourned.

Dated:

____

Secretary of the Meeting

WAIVER OF NOTICE,
FIRST MEETING OF SHAREHOLDERS

We the undersigned, being the shareholders of the
, agree that the first meeting of shareholders be on the date and at the time and place stated below in order to elect officers and transact such other business as may lawfully come before the meeting. We hereby waive all notice of such meeting and of any adjournment thereof.

Place of Meeting:____

Date of Meeting:____

Time of Meeting:____

____

____

____

____

____

Dated:________________________ ________________________________

Shareholders

MINUTES, FIRST MEETING OF SHAREHOLDERS

The first meeting of the shareholders of
was held at
on the day of , 19 , at . m.

The meeting was duly called to order by the President. He stated the purpose of the meeting.

Next, the Secretary read the list of shareholders as they appear in the record book of the Corporation. He reported the presence of a quorum of shareholders.

Next, the Secretary read a waiver of notice of the meeting, signed by all shareholders. On a motion duly made, seconded and carried, the waiver was ordered appended to the minutes of this meeting.

Next, the President asked the Secretary to read:

(1) the minutes of the organization meeting of the Corporation; and
(2) the minutes of the first meeting of the Board of Directors.

A motion was duly made, seconded and carried unanimously that the following resolution be adopted:

WHEREAS, the minutes of the organization meeting of the Corporation and the minutes of the first meeting of the Board of Directors have been read to this meeting, and

WHEREAS, byaws were adopted and directors and officers were elected at the organization meeting, it is hereby

RESOLVED that this meeting approves and ratifies the election of the said directors and officers of this Corporation for the term of years, and approves, ratifies and adopts said by-laws as the by-laws of the corporation. It is further

RESOLVED that all acts taken and decisions made at the organization meeting and the first meeting of the Board are approved and ratified. It is further

RESOLVED that signing of these minutes constitutes full ratification by the signatories and waiver of notice of the meeting.

There being no further business, the meeting was adjourned.

Dated the day of , 19

____
Secretary

____
Director

____
Director

____
Director

____
Director

Appended hereto: Waiver of notice of meeting.

MINUTES, SHAREHOLDERS' ANNUAL MEETING

The Annual Meeting of Shareholders of ______________________________

______________________ was held at __________________________, State of

______________________, on the ________ day of ______________________, 19______, at

__________ o'clock, _____.m.

The President duly called the meeting to order and outlined its purposes.

The Secretary next stated that a notice of meeting had been properly served, introducing an affidavit to this effect which was ordered placed on file. (OR: The Secretary stated that a waiver of notice of the meeting had been properly signed by the shareholders and it was placed on file.)

The President proposed the immediate election of a Chairman. A motion to that effect was duly made and carried.

It being determined that a quorum was present either in person or by proxy, a voice vote of shareholders was taken. ______________________________ was elected Chairman of the meeting.

A motion was duly made and carried that the Secretary read the minutes of the preceding meeting of shareholders. Upon completion of the reading, a motion was duly made and carried that the minutes be approved as read. (OR: A motion was duly made and carried that a reading of the preceding meeting of shareholders be waived.)

The President then presented his annual report. (Include report.)

A motion was duly made, seconded and carried that the report be received and filed.

The Secretary next presented his report. (Include report.)

A motion was duly made, seconded and carried that the report be received and filed.

The Treasurer then presented his report. (Include report.)

A motion was duly made, seconded and carried that the report be received and filed.

The Chairman said that election of directors of the Corporation for the coming year was the next order of business.

The following were nominated as directors.

_______________________________ _______________________________

_______________________________ _______________________________

_______________________________ _______________________________

The Chairman then stated that the Board has appointed ________________________ ________________________and________________________ as inspectors of election and that they would receive and tally the ballots.

Each shareholder was asked to place his vote in a ballot, stating the number of shares voted, and to sign his name.

The inspectors, after completing a tally of the vote, declared that the following votes had been cast:

Names of Nominees	Number of Votes
_______________________________	__________________________
_______________________________	__________________________
_______________________________	__________________________
_______________________________	__________________________
_______________________________	__________________________

The Chairman then announced that the following persons had been elected directors:

____

____.

A motion was duly made, seconded and carried that the inspectors file the report with the Clerk of ________________________ County (when required by law) and the the Secretary of the Corporation.

There being no further business, a motion was duly made, seconded and carried that the meeting be adjourned.

Dated the _________ day of _______________________, 19_____.

____

Secretary

NOTICE TO DIRECTORS OF REGULAR BOARD MEETING

A meeting of the Board of ___________________________ will be held at the office of the Corporation at ______________________________, City of_______________ ________________, State of _________________, on the______ day of __________________, 19_____, at ________ o'clock ____.m., for the purpose of transacting all such business as may properly come before the same.

Dated the _________day of __________________, 19_____.

____
Secretary

MINUTES OF DIRECTORS' MEETINGS

____

A regular meeting of the Board of Directors of the Corporation was held at the office of the Corporation, at , on , 19 , at o'clock .m.

There were present and participating at the meeting:

______________________	______________________
______________________	______________________
______________________	______________________
______________________	______________________

Being a quorum of the directors of the Corporation.

, President of the Corporation, acted as Chairman of the meeting, and , Secretary of the Corporation, acted as Secretary of the meeting.

The Secretary presented notice or a waiver of notice of the meeting, signed by all the directors.

The meeting, having been duly convened, was ready to proceed with its business, whereupon it was:

RESOLVED, That the salary of , as President of the Corporation, be fixed at Dollars ($) per year.

RESOLVED, Further that the salary of , as Vice President of the Corporation, be fixed at Dollars ($) per year.

RESOLVED, Further that the salary of , as Treasurer of the Corporation, be fixed at Dollars ($) per year.

RESOLVED, Further that the salary of , as Secretary of the Corporation, be fixed at

Dollars ($) per year.

RESOLVED, That in addition to their present salaries, the officers of the Corporation, comprising , ,

, and ,

holding, respectively, the offices of ,

, , and

, shall participate in all fringe benefit programs available to employees of the Corporation from time to time.

A True Record

Attest

____
Chairman

____
Secretary

ASSIGNMENT OF ASSETS

This agreement is made and entered into this day of , 19 , by and between (Stockholder) and , a Corporation hereinafter referred to as "Corporation."

WITNESSETH:

WHEREAS, on the day of , 19 , the Corporation will have been formed by Articles of Incorporation being filed with the Secretary of State of and at the time it was necessary to transfer certain assets into the Corporation in order to capitalize the Corporation; and

WHEREAS, is desirous of transferring to the Corporation certain assets shown on the attached Exhibit "A", and the Corporation is desirous of receiving said assets.

NOW, THEREFORE, for and in consideration of the mutual covenants and agreements hereinafter entered into, it is agreed as follows:

1. does hereby transfer and assign those assets listed on the attached Exhibit "A" to the Corporation.

2. In consideration for said transfer the Corporation issues to , ( ) shares of stock in the Corporation, par value $ per share.

DATED this day of , 19

____
Stockholder

Corporation

By:______________________________

MEDICAL CARE REIMBURSEMENT PLAN
OF

____

FIRST: The Corporation shall reimburse all eligible employees for expenses incurred by themselves and their dependents, and defined in Internal Revenue Code, Section 152, as amended, for medical care, as defined in Internal Revenue Code, Section 213(3), as amended, subject to the conditions and limitations as hereinafter set forth. It is the intention of the Corporation that the benefits payable to eligible employees hereunder shall be excluded from their gross income pursuant to Internal Revenue Code, Section 105, as amended.

SECOND: All corporate officers employed on a full-time basis at the date of inception of this Plan, including those who may be absent due to illness or injury on said date, are eligible employees under the Plan. A corporate officer shall be considered employed on a full-time basis if said officer customarily works at least seven months in each year and twenty hours in each week. Any person hereafter becoming an officer of the Corporation employed on a full-time basis shall be eligible under this Plan.

THIRD: (a) The Corporation shall reimburse any eligible employee (check one) ___ without limitation ___ no more than $_____________ in any fiscal year for medical care expenses, (b) Reimbursement or payment is not provided under any insurance policy(ies), whether owned by the Corporation or the employee, or under any health and accident or wage-continuation plan. In the event that there is such an insurance policy or plan in effect, providing for reimbursement in whole or in part, then to the extent of the coverage under such policy or plan, the Corporation shall be relieved of any liability hereunder.

FOURTH: Any eligible employee applying for reimbursement under this Plan shall submit to the Corporation, at least quarterly, all bills for medical care including premium notices for accident or health insurance, for verification by the Corporation prior to payment. Failure to comply herewith may, at the discretion of the Corporation, terminate such eligible employee's right to said reimbursement.

FIFTH: The Plan shall be subject to termination, at any time, by vote of the board of directors of the Corporation; provided, however, that medical care expenses incurred prior to such termination shall be reimbursed or paid in accordance with this Plan.

SIXTH: The president shall determine all questions arising from the administration and interpretation of the Plan except where reimbursement is claimed by the president. In such case, determination shall be made by the board of directors.

ADOPTED this day of , 19

By:______________________________
President

____
Secretary

____
For the Board of Directors

RESOLUTION RATIFYING THE ANNEXED MEDICAL CARE REIMBURSEMENT PLAN

Pursuant to the By-laws of
, a(n) corporation, the undersigned, representing (check one) ___ all ___ a majority of the members of the Board of Directors of said corporation, hereby enact the following resolution:

RESOLVED, that the "Medical Care Reimbursement Plan" presented to this meeting is hereby approved and adopted; that a copy of the Plan is annexed to this Resolution; and that the proper Officers of the corporation are hereby authorized to take whatever action is necessary to implement the Plan.

AND IT IS FURTHER RESOLVED, that the signing of this Resolution by the directors shall constitute full ratification thereof.

RATIFIED this day of , 19

_______________________ _______________________

_______________________ _______________________

_______________________ _______________________

_______________________ _______________________

_______________________ _______________________

RESOLUTION

RESOLVED,

.

The undersigned hereby certifies that he/she is the duly elected and qualified Secretary and the custodian of the books and records and seal of ,
a corporation duly formed pursuant to the laws of the State of ,
and that the foregoing is a true record of a resolution duly adopted at a meeting of the Board of Directors, and that said meeting was held in accordance with state law and the Bylaws of the above-named Corporation on , 19 , and that said resolution is now in full force and effect without modification or rescission.

IN WITNESS WHEREOF, I have executed my name as Secretary and have hereunto affixed the corporate seal of the above-named Corporation this day of , 19 .

A True Record.

Attest.

____

Secretary

RESOLUTION

WHEREAS,

RESOLVED,

The undersigned hereby certifies that he/she is the duly elected and qualified Secretary and the custodian of
: books and records and seal of , a corporation
ly formed pursuant to the laws of the State of , and that the fore-
ing is a true record of a resolution duly adopted at a meeting of the Board of Directors, and that said meeting
ıs held in accordance with state law and the Bylaws of the above-named Corporation on
9 , and that said resolution is now in full force and effect without modification or rescission.

IN WITNESS WHEREOF, I have executed my name as Secretary and have hereunto affixed the corporate
al of the above-named Corporation this day of , 19 .

True Record.

test.

____

Secretary

NOTICE TO SHAREHOLDERS OF ANNUAL MEETING

The Annual Meeting of Shareholders of ______________________________ ____________________ for the purpose of electing __________________Directors, and transacting such other business as may properly come before the meeting, will be held on the ____________day of____________________________, 19______, at ___________ o'clock ____.m., at the office of ____, City of _________________________ and State of __________________________.

Transfer books will remain closed from the __________________day of _________________________, 19_______, until the __________________day of _________________________, 19_______.

Dated the __________ day of ____________________________, 19_______.

____
Secretary

STOCK LEDGER AND TRANSFER LEDGER

NAME AND ADDRESS OF STOCKHOLDERS	DATE ISSUED	NAME OF SECURITY	CERTIF. NUMBER	VALUE OF SHARES	DATE TRANSFERRED	CERTIF. TRANSFERRED	SHARES TRANSFERRED	BALANCE OF SHARES

STOCKHOLDER'S PROXY

KNOWN ALL MEN BY THESE PRESENTS, that

, the undersigned, being the owner(s) of ( ) shares of Stock of , a(n) Corporation, do hereby constitute and appoint , whose address is , in the City of , State of , my (our) true and lawful Attorney-In-Fact, for and in my (our) name, place and stead, to vote upon the Stock owned by me (us), or standing in my (our) name, as my (our) PROXY at the Meeting of the Stockholders of said Corporation, to be held at , in the City of , State of on , 19 , at the hour of o'clock .m., or such other day and time as the meeting may be thereafter held by adjournment or otherwise according the number of votes now, or may then be entitled to be voted, hereby granting said Attorney-In-Fact full power and authority to act for me (us) and in my (our) name at the meeting or meetings in the transaction of such other business as may come before the meeting, as fully as I (we) could do if personally present, with full power of substitution and revocation, hereby ratifying and confirming all that my (our) said Attorney-In-Fact or substitute may do in my (our) place, name and stead.

This Proxy is to continue in full force until , 19 , but may be revoked at any time by notice thereof in writing, filed with the Secretary of the Corporation.

IN WITNESS WHEREOF, I (WE) have hereunto set my(our) hand(s) and seal this day of , 19 .

______________________________ ______________________________

State of }
County of }

On before me, ,
appeared
personally known to me (or proved to me on the basis of satisfactory evidence) to be the person(s) whose name(s) is/are subscribed to the within instrument and acknowledged to me that he/she/they executed the same in his/her/their authorized capacity(ies), and that by his/her/their signature(s) on the instrument the person(s), or the entity upon behalf of which the person(s) acted, executed the instrument.
WITNESS my hand and official seal.

Signature______________________________

(Seal)

Form **2553**

(Rev. September 1993)

Department of the Treasury
Internal Revenue Service

Election by a Small Business Corporation

(Under section 1362 of the Internal Revenue Code)

▶ For Paperwork Reduction Act Notice, see page 1 of instructions.

▶ See separate instructions.

OMB No. 1545-0146
Expires 8-31-96

Notes: 1. *This election, to be an "S corporation," can be accepted only if all the tests are met under Who May Elect on page 1 of the instructions; all signatures in Parts I and III are originals (no photocopies); and the exact name and address of the corporation and other required form information are provided.*

2. *Do not file Form 1120S, U.S. Income Tax Return for an S Corporation, until you are notified that your election is accepted.*

Part I Election Information

Please Type or Print		
	Name of corporation (see instructions)	A Employer identification number (EIN)
	Number, street, and room or suite no. (If a P.O. box, see instructions.)	B Date incorporated
	City or town, state, and ZIP code	C State of incorporation

D Election is to be effective for tax year beginning (month, day, year) . . . . ▶ / /

E Name and title of officer or legal representative who the IRS may call for more information

F Telephone number of officer or legal representative ( )

G If the corporation changed its name or address after applying for the EIN shown in A, check this box . . . . ▶ ☐

H If this election takes effect for the first tax year the corporation exists, enter month, day, and year of the earliest of the following: (1) date the corporation first had shareholders, (2) date the corporation first had assets, or (3) date the corporation began doing business . . . . ▶ / /

I Selected tax year: Annual return will be filed for tax year ending (month and day) ▶ ....

If the tax year ends on any date other than December 31, except for an automatic 52-53-week tax year ending with reference to the month of December, you must complete Part II on the back. If the date you enter is the ending date of an automatic 52-53-week tax year, write "52-53-week year" to the right of the date. See Temporary Regulations section 1.441-2T(e)(3).

J Name and address of each shareholder, shareholder's spouse having a community property interest in the corporation's stock, and each tenant in common, joint tenant, and tenant by the entirety. (A husband and wife (and their estates) are counted as one shareholder in determining the number of shareholders without regard to the manner in which the stock is owned.)	K Shareholders' Consent Statement. Under penalties of perjury, we declare that we consent to the election of the above-named corporation to be an "S corporation" under section 1362(a) and that we have examined this consent statement, including accompanying schedules and statements, and to the best of our knowledge and belief, it is true, correct, and complete. (Shareholders sign and date below.)*		L Stock owned		M Social security number or employer identification number (see instructions)	N Share-holder's tax year ends (month and day)
	Signature	Date	Number of shares	Dates acquired		

*For this election to be valid, the consent of each shareholder, shareholder's spouse having a community property interest in the corporation's stock, and each tenant in common, joint tenant, and tenant by the entirety must either appear above or be attached to this form. (See instructions for Column K if a continuation sheet or a separate consent statement is needed.)

Under penalties of perjury, I declare that I have examined this election, including accompanying schedules and statements, and to the best of my knowledge and belief, it is true, correct, and complete.

Signature of officer ▶ Title ▶ Date ▶

Part II Selection of Fiscal Tax Year (All corporations using this part must complete item O and one of items P, Q, or R.)

O Check the applicable box below to indicate whether the corporation is:

1. ☐ A new corporation adopting the tax year entered in item I, Part I.
2. ☐ An existing corporation retaining the tax year entered in item I, Part I.
3. ☐ An existing corporation changing to the tax year entered in item I, Part I.

P Complete item P if the corporation is using the expeditious approval provisions of Revenue Procedure 87-32, 1987-2 C.B. 396, to request: (1) a natural business year (as defined in section 4.01(1) of Rev. Proc. 87-32), or (2) a year that satisfies the ownership tax year test in section 4.01(2) of Rev. Proc. 87-32. Check the applicable box below to indicate the representation statement the corporation is making as required under section 4 of Rev. Proc. 87-32.

1. Natural Business Year ▶ ☐ I represent that the corporation is retaining or changing to a tax year that coincides with its natural business year as defined in section 4.01(1) of Rev. Proc. 87-32 and as verified by its satisfaction of the requirements of section 4.02(1) of Rev. Proc. 87-32. In addition, if the corporation is changing to a natural business year as defined in section 4.01(1), I further represent that such tax year results in less deferral of income to the owners than the corporation's present tax year. I also represent that the corporation is not described in section 3.01(2) of Rev. Proc. 87-32. (See instructions for additional information that must be attached.)

2. Ownership Tax Year ▶ ☐ I represent that shareholders holding more than half of the shares of the stock (as of the first day of the tax year to which the request relates) of the corporation have the same tax year or are concurrently changing to the tax year that the corporation adopts, retains, or changes to per item I, Part I. I also represent that the corporation is not described in section 3.01(2) of Rev. Proc. 87-32.

Note: *If you do not use item P and the corporation wants a fiscal tax year, complete either item Q or R below. Item Q is used to request a fiscal tax year based on a business purpose and to make a back-up section 444 election. Item R is used to make a regular section 444 election.*

Q Business Purpose—To request a fiscal tax year based on a business purpose, you must check box Q1 and pay a user fee. See instructions for details. You may also check box Q2 and/or box Q3.

1. Check here ▶ ☐ if the fiscal year entered in item I, Part I, is requested under the provisions of section 6.03 of Rev. Proc. 87-32. Attach to Form 2553 a statement showing the business purpose for the requested fiscal year. See instructions for additional information that must be attached.

2. Check here ▶ ☐ to show that the corporation intends to make a back-up section 444 election in the event the corporation's business purpose request is not approved by the IRS. (See instructions for more information.)

3. Check here ▶ ☐ to show that the corporation agrees to adopt or change to a tax year ending December 31 if necessary for the IRS to accept this election for S corporation status in the event: (1) the corporation's business purpose request is not approved and the corporation makes a back-up section 444 election, but is ultimately not qualified to make a section 444 election, or (2) the corporation's business purpose request is not approved and the corporation did not make a back-up section 444 election.

R Section 444 Election—To make a section 444 election, you must check box R1 and you may also check box R2.

1. Check here ▶ ☐ to show the corporation will make, if qualified, a section 444 election to have the fiscal tax year shown in item I, Part I. To make the election, you must complete **Form 8716,** Election To Have a Tax Year Other Than a Required Tax Year, and either attach it to Form 2553 or file it separately.

2. Check here ▶ ☐ to show that the corporation agrees to adopt or change to a tax year ending December 31 if necessary for the IRS to accept this election for S corporation status in the event the corporation is ultimately not qualified to make a section 444 election.

Part III Qualified Subchapter S Trust (QSST) Election Under Section 1361(d)(2)**

Income beneficiary's name and address	Social security number
Trust's name and address	Employer identification number

Date on which stock of the corporation was transferred to the trust (month, day, year) . . . . ▶ / /

In order for the trust named above to be a QSST and thus a qualifying shareholder of the S corporation for which this Form 2553 is filed, I hereby make the election under section 1361(d)(2). Under penalties of perjury, I certify that the trust meets the definitional requirements of section 1361(d)(3) and that all other information provided in Part III is true, correct, and complete.

Signature of income beneficiary or signature and title of legal representative or other qualified person making the election Date

**Use of Part III to make the QSST election may be made only if stock of the corporation has been transferred to the trust on or before the date on which the corporation makes its election to be an S corporation. The QSST election must be made and filed separately if stock of the corporation is transferred to the trust after the date on which the corporation makes the S election.

Department of the Treasury
Internal Revenue Service

Instructions for Form 2553

(Revised September 1993)

Election by a Small Business Corporation

Section references are to the Internal Revenue Code unless otherwise noted.

Paperwork Reduction Act Notice.—We ask for the information on this form to carry out the Internal Revenue laws of the United States. You are required to give us the information. We need it to ensure that you are complying with these laws and to allow us to figure and collect the right amount of tax.

The time needed to complete and file this form will vary depending on individual circumstances. The estimated average time is:

Recordkeeping . . . . . 6 hr., 13 min.
Learning about the law or the form . . . . . 2 hr., 59 min.
Preparing, copying, assembling, and sending the form to the IRS . . . . 3 hr., 13 min.

If you have comments concerning the accuracy of these time estimates or suggestions for making this form more simple, we would be happy to hear from you. You can write to both the **Internal Revenue Service,** Attention: Reports Clearance Officer, T:FP, Washington, DC 20224; and the **Office of Management and Budget,** Paperwork Reduction Project (1545-0146), Washington, DC 20503. **DO NOT** send the tax form to either of these offices. Instead, see **Where To File** below.

General Instructions

Purpose.—To elect to be an "S corporation," a corporation must file Form 2553. The election permits the income of the S corporation to be taxed to the shareholders of the corporation rather than to the corporation itself, except as provided in Subchapter S of the Code. For more information, get **Pub. 589,** Tax Information on S Corporations.

Who May Elect.—A corporation may elect to be an S corporation only if it meets **all** of the following tests:

1. It is a domestic corporation.

2. It has no more than 35 shareholders. A husband and wife (and their estates) are treated as one shareholder for this requirement. All other persons are treated as separate shareholders.

3. It has only individuals, estates, or certain trusts as shareholders. See the instructions for Part III regarding qualified subchapter S trusts.

4. It has no nonresident alien shareholders.

5. It has only one class of stock (disregarding differences in voting rights). Generally, a corporation is treated as having only one class of stock if all outstanding shares of the corporation's stock confer identical rights to distribution and liquidation proceeds. See Regulations section 1.1361-1(l) for more details.

6. It is not one of the following ineligible corporations:

a. A corporation that owns 80% or more of the stock of another corporation, unless the other corporation has not begun business and has no gross income;

b. A bank or thrift institution;

c. An insurance company subject to tax under the special rules of Subchapter L of the Code;

d. A corporation that has elected to be treated as a possessions corporation under section 936; or

e. A domestic international sales corporation (DISC) or former DISC.

7. It has a permitted tax year as required by section 1378 or makes a section 444 election to have a tax year other than a permitted tax year. Section 1378 defines a permitted tax year as a tax year ending December 31, or any other tax year for which the corporation establishes a business purpose to the satisfaction of the IRS. See Part II for details on requesting a fiscal tax year based on a business purpose or on making a section 444 election.

8. Each shareholder consents as explained in the instructions for Column K.

See sections 1361, 1362, and 1378 for additional information on the above tests.

Where To File.—File this election with the Internal Revenue Service Center listed below.

If the corporation's principal business, office, or agency is located in	Use the following Internal Revenue Service Center address
New Jersey, New York (New York City and counties of Nassau, Rockland, Suffolk, and Westchester)	Holtsville, NY 00501
New York (all other counties), Connecticut, Maine, Massachusetts, New Hampshire, Rhode Island, Vermont	Andover, MA 05501
Illinois, Iowa, Minnesota, Missouri, Wisconsin	Kansas City, MO 64999
Delaware, District of Columbia, Maryland, Pennsylvania, Virginia	Philadelphia, PA 19255
Florida, Georgia, South Carolina	Atlanta, GA 39901
Indiana, Kentucky, Michigan, Ohio, West Virginia	Cincinnati, OH 45999
Kansas, New Mexico, Oklahoma, Texas	Austin, TX 73301
Alaska, Arizona, California (counties of Alpine, Amador, Butte, Calaveras, Colusa, Contra Costa, Del Norte, El Dorado, Glenn, Humboldt, Lake, Lassen, Marin, Mendocino, Modoc, Napa, Nevada, Placer, Plumas, Sacramento, San Joaquin, Shasta, Sierra, Siskiyou, Solano, Sonoma, Sutter, Tehama, Trinity, Yolo, and Yuba), Colorado, Idaho, Montana, Nebraska, Nevada, North Dakota, Oregon, South Dakota, Utah, Washington, Wyoming	Ogden, UT 84201
California (all other counties), Hawaii	Fresno, CA 93888
Alabama, Arkansas, Louisiana, Mississippi, North Carolina, Tennessee	Memphis, TN 37501

When To Make the Election.—Complete and file Form 2553 (a) at any time before the 16th day of the third month of the tax year, if filed during the tax year the election is to take effect, or (b) at any time during the preceding tax year. An election made no later than 2 months and 15 days after the beginning of a tax year that is less than 2½ months long is treated as timely made for that tax year. An election made after the 15th day of the third month but before the end of the tax year is effective for the next year. For example, if a calendar tax year corporation makes the election in April 1994, it is effective for the corporation's 1995 calendar tax year. See section 1362(b) for more information.

Acceptance or Nonacceptance of Election.—The Service Center will notify the corporation if its election is accepted and when it will take effect. The corporation will also be notified if its election is not accepted. The corporation should generally receive a determination on its election within 60 days after it has filed Form 2553. If box Q1 in Part II is checked on page 2, the corporation will receive a ruling letter from the IRS in Washington, DC, that either approves or denies the selected tax year. When box Q1 is checked, it will generally take an additional 90 days for the Form 2553 to be accepted.

Do not file Form 1120S until the corporation is notified that its election has been accepted. If the corporation is now required to file Form 1120, U.S. Corporation Income Tax Return, or any other applicable tax return, continue filing it until the election takes effect.

Care should be exercised to ensure that the IRS receives the election. If the corporation is not notified of acceptance or nonacceptance of its election within 3 months of date of filing (date mailed), or within 6 months if box Q1 is checked, please take follow-up action by corresponding with the Service Center where the corporation filed the election. If the IRS questions whether Form 2553 was filed, an acceptable proof of filing is: (a) certified or registered mail receipt (timely filed); (b) Form 2553 with accepted stamp; (c) Form 2553 with stamped IRS received date; or (d) IRS letter stating that Form 2553 has been accepted.

End of Election.— Once the election is made, it stays in effect for all years until it is terminated. During the 5 years after the election is terminated under section 1362(d), the corporation (or a successor corporation) can make another election on Form 2553 only with IRS consent. See Regulations section 1.1362-5 for more details.

Specific Instructions

Part I

Part I must be completed by all corporations.

Name and Address of Corporation.—Enter the true corporate name as set forth in the corporate charter or other legal document creating it. If the corporation's mailing address is the same as someone else's, such as a shareholder's, please enter "c/o" and this person's name following the name of the corporation. Include the suite, room, or other unit number after the street address. If the Post Office does not deliver to the street address and the corporation has a P.O. box, show the box number instead of the street address. If the corporation changed its name or address after applying for its EIN, be sure to check the box in item G of Part I.

Item A. Employer Identification Number.—If the corporation has applied for an employer identification number (EIN) but has not received it, enter "applied for." If the corporation does not have an EIN, it should apply for one on **Form SS-4,** Application for Employer Identification Number, available from most IRS and Social Security Administration offices.

Item D. Effective Date of Election.—Enter the beginning effective date (month, day, year) of the tax year requested for the S corporation. Generally, this will be the beginning date of the tax year for which the ending effective date is required to be shown in item I, Part I. For a new corporation (first year the corporation exists) it will generally be the date required to be shown in item H, Part I. The tax year of a new corporation starts on the date that it has shareholders, acquires assets, or begins doing business, whichever happens first. If the effective date for item D for a newly formed corporation is later than the date in item H, the corporation should file Form 1120 or Form 1120-A, for the tax period between these dates.

Column K. Shareholders' Consent Statement.—Each shareholder who owns (or is deemed to own) stock at the time the election is made must consent to the election. If the election is made during the corporation's tax year for which it first takes effect, any person who held stock at any time during the part of that year that occurs before the election is made, must consent to the election, even though the person may have sold or transferred his or her stock before the election is made. Each shareholder consents by signing and dating in column K or signing and dating a separate consent statement described below.

An election made during the first 2½ months of the tax year is effective for the following tax year if any person who held stock in the corporation during the part of the tax year before the election was made, and who did not hold stock at the time the election was made, did not consent to the election.

If a husband and wife have a community interest in the stock or in the income from it, both must consent. Each tenant in common, joint tenant, and tenant by the entirety also must consent.

A minor's consent is made by the minor or the legal representative of the minor, or by a natural or adoptive parent of the minor if no legal representative has been appointed.

The consent of an estate is made by an executor or administrator.

If stock is owned by a trust that is a qualified shareholder, the deemed owner of the trust must consent. See section 1361(c)(2) for details regarding qualified trusts that may be shareholders and rules on determining who is the deemed owner of the trust.

Continuation sheet or separate consent statement.—If you need a continuation sheet or use a separate consent statement, attach it to Form 2553. The separate consent statement must contain the name, address, and employer identification number of the corporation and the shareholder information requested in columns J through N of Part I.

If you want, you may combine all the shareholders' consents in one statement.

Column L.—Enter the number of shares of stock each shareholder owns and the dates the stock was acquired. If the election is made during the corporation's tax year for which it first takes effect, do not list the shares of stock for those shareholders who sold or transferred all of their stock before the election was made. However, these shareholders must still consent to the election for it to be effective for the tax year.

Column M.—Enter the social security number of each shareholder who is an individual. Enter the employer identification number of each shareholder that is an estate or a qualified trust.

Column N.—Enter the month and day that each shareholder's tax year ends. If a shareholder is changing his or her tax year, enter the tax year the shareholder is changing to, and attach an explanation indicating the present tax year and the basis for the change (e.g., automatic revenue procedure or letter ruling request).

If the election is made during the corporation's tax year for which it first takes effect, you do not have to enter the tax year of any shareholder who sold or transferred all of his or her stock before the election was made.

Signature.—Form 2553 must be signed by the president, treasurer, assistant treasurer, chief accounting officer, or other corporate officer (such as tax officer) authorized to sign.

Part II

Complete Part II if you selected a tax year ending on any date other than December 31 (other than a 52-53-week tax year ending with reference to the month of December).

Box P1.—Attach a statement showing separately for each month the amount of gross receipts for the most recent 47 months as required by section 4.03(3) of Revenue Procedure 87-32, 1987-2 C.B. 396. A corporation that does not have a 47-month period of gross receipts cannot establish a natural business year under section 4.01(1).

Box Q1.—For examples of an acceptable business purpose for requesting a fiscal tax year, see Revenue Ruling 87-57, 1987-2 C.B. 117.

In addition to a statement showing the business purpose for the requested fiscal year, you must attach the other information necessary to meet the ruling request requirements of Revenue Procedure 93-1, 1993-1 I.R.B. 10 (updated annually). Also attach a statement that shows separately the amount of gross receipts from sales or services (and inventory costs, if applicable) for each of the 36 months preceding the effective date of the election to be an S corporation. If the corporation has been in existence for fewer than 36 months, submit figures for the period of existence.

If you check box Q1, you must also pay a user fee of $200 (subject to change). Do not pay the fee when filing Form 2553. The Service Center will send Form 2553 to the IRS in Washington, DC, who, in turn, will notify the corporation that the fee is due. See Revenue Procedure 93-23, 1993-19 I.R.B. 6.

Box Q2.—If the corporation makes a back-up section 444 election for which it is qualified, then the election must be exercised in the event the business purpose request is not approved. Under certain circumstances, the tax year requested under the back-up section 444 election may be different than the tax year requested under business purpose. See **Form 8716,** Election To Have a Tax Year Other Than a Required Tax Year, for details on making a back-up section 444 election.

Boxes Q2 and R2.—If the corporation is not qualified to make the section 444 election after making the item Q2 back-up section 444 election or indicating its intention to make the election in item R1, and therefore it later files a calendar year return, it should write "Section 444 Election Not Made" in the top left corner of the 1st calendar year Form 1120S it files.

Part III

Certain Qualified Subchapter S Trusts (QSSTs) may make the QSST election required by section 1361(d)(2) in Part III. Part III may be used to make the QSST election only if corporate stock has been transferred to the trust on or before the date on which the corporation makes its election to be an S corporation. However, a statement can be used in lieu of Part III to make the election.

Note: *Part III may be used only in conjunction with making the Part I election (i.e., Form 2553 cannot be filed with only Part III completed).*

The deemed owner of the QSST must also consent to the S corporation election in column K, page 1, of Form 2553. See section 1361(c)(2).

Form **1120S**

Department of the Treasury
Internal Revenue Service

U.S. Income Tax Return for an S Corporation

▶ **Do not file this form unless the corporation has timely filed Form 2553 to elect to be an S corporation.**

▶ **See separate instructions.**

OMB No. 1545-0130

1993

For calendar year 1993, or tax year beginning ...., 1993, and ending ...., 19 .....

A Date of election as an S corporation	Use IRS label. Otherwise, please print or type.	Name	C Employer identification number
		Number, street, and room or suite no. (If a P.O. box, see page 9 of the instructions.)	D Date incorporated
B Business code no. (see Specific Instructions)		City or town, state, and ZIP code	E Total assets (see Specific Instructions) $

F Check applicable boxes: (1) ☐ Initial return (2) ☐ Final return (3) ☐ Change in address (4) ☐ Amended return

G Check this box if this S corporation is subject to the consolidated audit procedures of sections 6241 through 6245 (see instructions before checking this box) . ▶ ☐

H Enter number of shareholders in the corporation at end of the tax year . . . . . . ▶

Caution: *Include **only** trade or business income and expenses on lines 1a through 21. See the instructions for more information.*

Section	Line	Description	Box	Amount
Income	1a	Gross receipts or sales ____ **b** Less returns and allowances ____ **c** Bal ▶	1c	
	2	Cost of goods sold (Schedule A, line 8)	2	
	3	Gross profit. Subtract line 2 from line 1c	3	
	4	Net gain (loss) from Form 4797, Part II, line 20 *(attach Form 4797)*	4	
	5	Other income (loss) (see instructions) *(attach schedule)*	5	
	6	**Total income (loss).** Combine lines 3 through 5 ▶	6	
Deductions (See instructions for limitations.)	7	Compensation of officers	7	
	8a	Salaries and wages ____ **b** Less employment credits ____ **c** Bal ▶	8c	
	9	Repairs and maintenance	9	
	10	Bad debts	10	
	11	Rents	11	
	12	Taxes and licenses	12	
	13	Interest	13	
	14a	Depreciation (see instructions) . . . 14a		
	b	Depreciation claimed on Schedule A and elsewhere on return . . 14b		
	c	Subtract line 14b from line 14a	14c	
	15	Depletion **(Do not deduct oil and gas depletion.)**	15	
	16	Advertising	16	
	17	Pension, profit-sharing, etc., plans	17	
	18	Employee benefit programs	18	
	19	Other deductions (see instructions) *(attach schedule)*	19	
	20	**Total deductions.** Add lines 7 through 19 ▶	20	
	21	Ordinary income (loss) from trade or business activities. Subtract line 20 from line 6	21	
Tax and Payments	22	**Tax:** **a** Excess net passive income tax *(attach schedule)* . . . 22a		
	b	Tax from Schedule D (Form 1120S) . . . 22b		
	c	Add lines 22a and 22b (see instructions for additional taxes)	22c	
	23	**Payments:** **a** 1993 estimated tax payments . . . 23a		
	b	Tax deposited with Form 7004 . . . 23b		
	c	Credit for Federal tax paid on fuels *(attach Form 4136)* . . . 23c		
	d	Add lines 23a through 23c	23d	
	24	Estimated tax penalty (see instructions). Check if Form 2220 is attached ▶ ☐	24	
	25	**Tax due.** If the total of lines 22c and 24 is larger than line 23d, enter amount owed. See instructions for depositary method of payment ▶	25	
	26	**Overpayment.** If line 23d is larger than the total of lines 22c and 24, enter amount overpaid ▶	26	
	27	Enter amount of line 26 you want: **Credited to 1994 estimated tax** ▶ ____ **Refunded** ▶	27	

Please Sign Here

Under penalties of perjury, I declare that I have examined this return, including accompanying schedules and statements, and to the best of my knowledge and belief, it is true, correct, and complete. Declaration of preparer (other than taxpayer) is based on all information of which preparer has any knowledge.

▶ Signature of officer — Date — ▶ Title

Paid Preparer's Use Only

Preparer's signature ▶	Date	Check if self-employed ▶ ☐	Preparer's social security number
Firm's name (or yours if self-employed) and address ▶		E.I. No. ▶	
		ZIP code ▶	

For Paperwork Reduction Act Notice, see page 1 of separate instructions. Cat. No. 11510H Form **1120S** (1993)

Schedule A Cost of Goods Sold (See instructions.)

1	Inventory at beginning of year	1	
2	Purchases	2	
3	Cost of labor	3	
4	Additional section 263A costs (see instructions) *(attach schedule)*	4	
5	Other costs *(attach schedule)*	5	
6	**Total.** Add lines 1 through 5	6	
7	Inventory at end of year	7	
8	**Cost of goods sold.** Subtract line 7 from line 6. Enter here and on page 1, line 2	8	

9a Check all methods used for valuing closing inventory:
- (i) ☐ Cost
- (ii) ☐ Lower of cost or market as described in Regulations section 1.471-4
- (iii) ☐ Writedown of "subnormal" goods as described in Regulations section 1.471-2(c)
- (iv) ☐ Other (specify method used and attach explanation) ▶ ....

b Check if the LIFO inventory method was adopted this tax year for any goods *(if checked, attach Form 970)* ▶ ☐

c If the LIFO inventory method was used for this tax year, enter percentage (or amounts) of closing inventory computed under LIFO . . . **9c** ______

d Do the rules of section 263A (for property produced or acquired for resale) apply to the corporation? ☐ Yes ☐ No

e Was there any change in determining quantities, cost, or valuations between opening and closing inventory? ☐ Yes ☐ No
If "Yes," attach explanation.

Schedule B Other Information

		Yes	No
1	Check method of accounting: **(a)** ☐ Cash **(b)** ☐ Accrual **(c)** ☐ Other (specify) ▶		
2	Refer to the list in the instructions and state the corporation's principal: **(a)** Business activity ▶ .... **(b)** Product or service ▶		
3	Did the corporation at the end of the tax year own, directly or indirectly, 50% or more of the voting stock of a domestic corporation? (For rules of attribution, see section 267(c).) If "Yes," attach a schedule showing: **(a)** name, address, and employer identification number and **(b)** percentage owned		
4	Was the corporation a member of a controlled group subject to the provisions of section 1561?		
5	At any time during calendar year 1993, did the corporation have an interest in or a signature or other authority over a financial account in a foreign country (such as a bank account, securities account, or other financial account)? (See instructions for exceptions and filing requirements for Form TD F 90-22.1.)		
	If "Yes," enter the name of the foreign country ▶		
6	Was the corporation the grantor of, or transferor to, a foreign trust that existed during the current tax year, whether or not the corporation has any beneficial interest in it? If "Yes," the corporation may have to file Forms 3520, 3520-A, or 926		
7	Check this box if the corporation has filed or is required to file **Form 8264,** Application for Registration of a Tax Shelter ▶ ☐		
8	Check this box if the corporation issued publicly offered debt instruments with original issue discount ▶ ☐ If so, the corporation may have to file **Form 8281,** Information Return for Publicly Offered Original Issue Discount Instruments.		
9	If the corporation: **(a)** filed its election to be an S corporation after 1986, **(b)** was a C corporation before it elected to be an S corporation **or** the corporation acquired an asset with a basis determined by reference to its basis (or the basis of any other property) in the hands of a C corporation, and **(c)** has net unrealized built-in gain (defined in section 1374(d)(1)) in excess of the net recognized built-in gain from prior years, enter the net unrealized built-in gain reduced by net recognized built-in gain from prior years (see instructions) ▶ $		
10	Check this box if the corporation had subchapter C earnings and profits at the close of the tax year (see instructions) ▶ ☐		

Designation of Tax Matters Person (See instructions.)

Enter below the shareholder designated as the tax matters person (TMP) for the tax year of this return:

Name of designated TMP ▶ __________ Identifying number of TMP ▶ __________

Address of designated TMP ▶ __________

Schedule K Shareholders' Shares of Income, Credits, Deductions, etc.

	(a) Pro rata share items		(b) Total amount
Income (Loss)	1 Ordinary income (loss) from trade or business activities (page 1, line 21)	1	
	2 Net income (loss) from rental real estate activities *(attach Form 8825)*	2	
	3a Gross income from other rental activities . . . 3a		
	b Expenses from other rental activities *(attach schedule)*. . 3b		
	c Net income (loss) from other rental activities. Subtract line 3b from line 3a	3c	
	4 Portfolio income (loss):		
	a Interest income	4a	
	b Dividend income	4b	
	c Royalty income	4c	
	d Net short-term capital gain (loss) *(attach Schedule D (Form 1120S))*	4d	
	e Net long-term capital gain (loss) *(attach Schedule D (Form 1120S))*	4e	
	f Other portfolio income (loss) *(attach schedule)*	4f	
	5 Net gain (loss) under section 1231 (other than due to casualty or theft) *(attach Form 4797)*	5	
	6 Other income (loss) *(attach schedule)*	6	
Deductions	7 Charitable contributions (see instructions) *(attach schedule)*	7	
	8 Section 179 expense deduction *(attach Form 4562)*	8	
	9 Deductions related to portfolio income (loss) (see instructions) (itemize)	9	
	10 Other deductions *(attach schedule)*	10	
Investment Interest	11a Interest expense on investment debts	11a	
	b (1) Investment income included on lines 4a, 4b, 4c, and 4f above	11b(1)	
	(2) Investment expenses included on line 9 above	11b(2)	
Credits	12a Credit for alcohol used as a fuel *(attach Form 6478)*	12a	
	b Low-income housing credit (see instructions):		
	(1) From partnerships to which section 42(j)(5) applies for property placed in service before 1990	12b(1)	
	(2) Other than on line 12b(1) for property placed in service before 1990	12b(2)	
	(3) From partnerships to which section 42(j)(5) applies for property placed in service after 1989	12b(3)	
	(4) Other than on line 12b(3) for property placed in service after 1989	12b(4)	
	c Qualified rehabilitation expenditures related to rental real estate activities *(attach Form 3468)*	12c	
	d Credits (other than credits shown on lines 12b and 12c) related to rental real estate activities (see instructions)	12d	
	e Credits related to other rental activities (see instructions)	12e	
	13 Other credits (see instructions)	13	
Adjustments and Tax Preference Items	14a Depreciation adjustment on property placed in service after 1986	14a	
	b Adjusted gain or loss	14b	
	c Depletion (other than oil and gas)	14c	
	d (1) Gross income from oil, gas, or geothermal properties	14d(1)	
	(2) Deductions allocable to oil, gas, or geothermal properties	14d(2)	
	e Other adjustments and tax preference items *(attach schedule)*	14e	
Foreign Taxes	15a Type of income ▶		
	b Name of foreign country or U.S. possession ▶		
	c Total gross income from sources outside the United States *(attach schedule)*	15c	
	d Total applicable deductions and losses *(attach schedule)*	15d	
	e Total foreign taxes (check one): ▶ ☐ Paid ☐ Accrued	15e	
	f Reduction in taxes available for credit *(attach schedule)*	15f	
	g Other foreign tax information *(attach schedule)*	15g	
Other	16a Total expenditures to which a section 59(e) election may apply	16a	
	b Type of expenditures ▶		
	17 Tax-exempt interest income	17	
	18 Other tax-exempt income	18	
	19 Nondeductible expenses	19	
	20 Total property distributions (including cash) other than dividends reported on line 22 below	20	
	21 Other items and amounts required to be reported separately to shareholders (see instructions) *(attach schedule)*		
	22 Total dividend distributions paid from accumulated earnings and profits	22	
	23 **Income (loss).** (Required only if Schedule M-1 must be completed.) Combine lines 1 through 6 in column (b). From the result, subtract the sum of lines 7 through 11a, 15e, and 16a	23	

Schedule L Balance Sheets

Assets	Beginning of tax year (a)	(b)	End of tax year (c)	(d)
1 Cash				
2a Trade notes and accounts receivable				
b Less allowance for bad debts				
3 Inventories				
4 U.S. Government obligations				
5 Tax-exempt securities				
6 Other current assets *(attach schedule)*				
7 Loans to shareholders				
8 Mortgage and real estate loans				
9 Other investments *(attach schedule)*				
10a Buildings and other depreciable assets				
b Less accumulated depreciation				
11a Depletable assets				
b Less accumulated depletion				
12 Land (net of any amortization)				
13a Intangible assets (amortizable only)				
b Less accumulated amortization				
14 Other assets *(attach schedule)*				
15 Total assets				
Liabilities and Shareholders' Equity				
16 Accounts payable				
17 Mortgages, notes, bonds payable in less than 1 year				
18 Other current liabilities *(attach schedule)*				
19 Loans from shareholders				
20 Mortgages, notes, bonds payable in 1 year or more				
21 Other liabilities *(attach schedule)*				
22 Capital stock				
23 Paid-in or capital surplus				
24 Retained earnings				
25 Less cost of treasury stock		( )		( )
26 Total liabilities and shareholders' equity				

Schedule M-1 Reconciliation of Income (Loss) per Books With Income (Loss) per Return (You are not required to complete this schedule if the total assets on line 15, column (d), of Schedule L are less than $25,000.)

1 Net income (loss) per books		5 Income recorded on books this year not included on Schedule K, lines 1 through 6 (itemize): a Tax-exempt interest $	
2 Income included on Schedule K, lines 1 through 6, not recorded on books this year (itemize):			
3 Expenses recorded on books this year not included on Schedule K, lines 1 through 11a, 15e, and 16a (itemize): a Depreciation $ b Travel and entertainment $		6 Deductions included on Schedule K, lines 1 through 11a, 15e, and 16a, not charged against book income this year (itemize): a Depreciation $	
		7 Add lines 5 and 6	
4 Add lines 1 through 3		8 Income (loss) (Schedule K, line 23). Line 4 less line 7	

Schedule M-2 Analysis of Accumulated Adjustments Account, Other Adjustments Account, and Shareholders' Undistributed Taxable Income Previously Taxed (See instructions.)

	(a) Accumulated adjustments account	(b) Other adjustments account	(c) Shareholders' undistributed taxable income previously taxed
1 Balance at beginning of tax year			
2 Ordinary income from page 1, line 21			
3 Other additions			
4 Loss from page 1, line 21	( )		
5 Other reductions	( )	( )	
6 Combine lines 1 through 5			
7 Distributions other than dividend distributions			
8 Balance at end of tax year. Subtract line 7 from line 6			

*U.S. Government Printing Office: 1994 — 301-628/00131

1993 

Instructions for Form 1120S

U.S. Income Tax Return for an S Corporation

Section references are to the Internal Revenue Code unless otherwise noted.

Paperwork Reduction Act Notice

We ask for the information on these forms to carry out the Internal Revenue laws of the United States. You are required to give us the information. We need it to ensure that you are complying with these laws and to allow us to figure and collect the right amount of tax.

The time needed to complete and file the following forms will vary depending on individual circumstances. The estimated average times are:

Form	Recordkeeping	Learning about the law or the form	Preparing the form	Copying, assembling, and sending the form to the IRS
1120S	62 hr., 40 min.	19 hr., 36 min.	35 hr., 16 min.	4 hr., 1 min.
Sch. D (1120S)	9 hr., 20 min.	4 hr., 13 min.	9 hr., 13 min.	1 hr., 20 min.
Sch. K-1 (1120S)	14 hr., 21 min.	9 hr., 55 min.	14 hr., 19 min.	1 hr., 4 min.

If you have comments concerning the accuracy of these time estimates or suggestions for making these forms more simple, we would be happy to hear from you. You can write to both the **Internal Revenue Service,** Attention: Reports Clearance Officer, PC:FP, Washington, DC 20224; and the **Office of Management and Budget,** Paperwork Reduction Project (1545-0130), Washington, DC 20503. **DO NOT** send the tax forms to either of these offices. Instead, see **Where To File,** beginning on page 2.

Contents

Voluntary Contributions To Reduce the Public Debt

Quite often, inquiries are received about how to make voluntary contributions to reduce the public debt. A corporation may contribute by enclosing with the tax return a check made payable to "Bureau of the Public Debt."

Changes To Note

The Revenue Reconciliation Act of 1993 made the following changes:

- For tax years beginning after 1993, the percentage of the current year's taxes required to be paid in installments during the tax year has been increased to 100%. See **Estimated Tax** on page 4 for details.

Note: *The following changes affect only fiscal year 1993–1994 S corporations. Calendar year S corporations are not impacted until 1994.*

- The deductible portion of business meal costs and entertainment expenses paid after 1993 has been reduced from 80% to 50% for tax years of shareholders beginning after 1993. See page 12 for more details.
- Generally, lobbying expenses paid or incurred after 1993 are no longer deductible. These expenses include amounts paid or incurred in connection with influencing Federal or state legislation (but not local legislation), or amounts paid or incurred in connection with any communication with certain Federal executive branch officials in an attempt to influence the official actions or positions of the officials. However, certain in-house expenditures that do not exceed $2,000 are still deductible. Charitable contributions made after 1993 to an organization that conducts lobbying activities are not deductible if the lobbying activities relate to matters of direct financial interest to the donor's trade or business, and a principal purpose of the contribution was to avoid Federal income tax by obtaining a deduction for activities that would have been nondeductible under the lobbying expense rules if conducted directly by the donor.
- No deduction is allowed for amounts paid or incurred for club dues after 1993. See page 13 for more information.
- No deduction is allowed for travel expenses paid or incurred after 1993 for an officer's or employee's spouse or dependent or other individual accompanying an officer or employee of the S corporation on business travel, unless that spouse, dependent, or other

Cat. No. 11515K

individual is an employee of the S corporation, and the travel is for a bona fide business purpose and would otherwise be deductible by that person.

- Generally, no deduction is allowed for any charitable contribution of $250 or more made after 1993, unless the corporation obtains a written acknowledgement from the charitable organization. See page 17 for more details.
- If an S corporation makes a qualified cash contribution to a community development corporation selected by the Secretary of Housing and Urban Development, 5% of the contribution may be claimed as a credit for each tax year during the 10-year period beginning with the year the contribution was made. Get **Form 8847,** Credit for Contributions to Certain Community Development Corporations, for more details.
- Employers may be able to claim a credit of 20% of a limited amount of the wages and health insurance costs paid or incurred after 1993 for services performed on an Indian reservation by certain enrolled members of an Indian tribe (or their spouses). Services performed in certain gaming activities or buildings housing those activities do not qualify for the credit. Get **Form 8845,** Indian Employment Credit, for details.
- Food and beverage establishments may claim a credit equal to the employer's social security tax obligation attributable to tips in excess of those treated as wages for purposes of Federal minimum wage laws. The credit is available for taxes paid after 1993. Get **Form 8846,** Credit for Employer Social Security Taxes Paid on Certain Employee Cash Tips, for more details.

General Instructions

Note: *In addition to the publications listed throughout these instructions, you may wish to get* ***Pub. 334,*** *Tax Guide for Small Business;* ***Pub. 535,*** *Business Expenses;* ***Pub. 550,*** *Investment Income and Expenses;* ***Pub. 556,*** *Examination of Returns, Appeal Rights, and Claims for Refund; and* ***Pub. 589,*** *Tax Information on S Corporations.*

These and other publications referenced throughout these instructions may be obtained at most IRS offices. To order publications and forms, call our toll-free number 1-800-TAX-FORM (1-800-829-3676).

Purpose of Form

Form 1120S is used to report the income, deductions, gains, losses, etc., of a domestic corporation that has elected to be an S corporation by filing **Form 2553,** Election by a Small Business Corporation, and whose election is in effect for the tax year.

Who Must File

A corporation must file Form 1120S if **(a)** it elected to be an S corporation by filing Form 2553, **(b)** the IRS accepted the election, and **(c)** the election remains in effect. Do not file Form 1120S until the corporation has been notified by the IRS that the election has been accepted.

Termination of Election

Once the election is made, it stays in effect until it is terminated. During the 5 years after the election is terminated, the corporation (or a successor corporation) may make another election on Form 2553 only with IRS consent. See Regulations section 1.1362-5 for more details.

An election terminates **automatically** in any of the following cases:

1. The corporation is no longer a small business corporation as defined in section 1361(b). The termination of an election in this manner is effective as of the day on which the corporation no longer meets the definition of a small business corporation. If the election terminates for this reason, attach to Form 1120S for the final year of the S corporation a statement notifying the IRS of the termination and the date it occurred.

2. The corporation, for each of three consecutive tax years, **(a)** has subchapter C earnings and profits and **(b)** derives more than 25% of its gross receipts from passive investment income as defined in section 1362(d)(3)(D). The election terminates on the first day of the first tax year beginning after the third consecutive tax year. The corporation must pay a tax for each year it has excess net passive income. See the instructions for line 22a for details on how to figure the tax.

3. The election is revoked. An election may be revoked only with the consent of shareholders who, at the time the revocation is made, hold more than 50% of the number of issued and outstanding shares of stock (including non-voting stock). The revocation may specify an effective revocation date that is on or after the day the revocation is filed. If no date is specified, the revocation is effective at the start of a tax year if the revocation is made on or before the 15th day of the 3rd month of that tax year. If no date is specified and the revocation is made after the 15th day of the 3rd month of the tax year, the revocation is effective at the start of the next tax year. To revoke the election, the corporation must file a statement with the service center where it filed its election to be an S corporation. In the statement, the corporation must notify the IRS that it is revoking its election to be an S corporation. The statement must be signed by each shareholder who consents to the revocation and contain the information required by Regulations section 1.1362-6(a)(3). A revocation may be rescinded before the revocation takes effect. See Regulations section 1.1362-6(a)(4) for details.

For rules on allocating income and deductions between an S short year and a C short year and other special rules that apply when an election is terminated, see section 1362(e) and Regulations section 1.1362-3.

If an election was terminated under **1** or **2** above, and the corporation believes the termination was inadvertent, the corporation may request permission from the IRS to continue to be treated as an S corporation. See Regulations section 1.1362-4 for the specific requirements that must be met to qualify for inadvertent termination relief.

When To File

In general, file Form 1120S by the 15th day of the 3rd month following the date the corporation's tax year ended as shown at the top of Form 1120S. For calendar year corporations, the due date is March 15, 1994. If the due date falls on a Saturday, Sunday, or legal holiday, file on the next business day. A business day is any day that is not a Saturday, Sunday, or legal holiday.

If the S election was terminated during the tax year, file Form 1120S for the S short year by the due date (including extensions) of the C short year return.

Extension

Use **Form 7004,** Application for Automatic Extension of Time To File Corporation Income Tax Return, to request an automatic 6-month extension of time to file Form 1120S.

Period Covered

File the 1993 return for calendar year 1993 and fiscal years beginning in 1993 and ending in 1994. If the return is for a fiscal year or a short tax year, fill in the tax year space at the top of the form.

Note: *The 1993 Form 1120S may also be used if* ***(a)*** *the corporation has a tax year of less than 12 months that begins and ends in 1994 and* ***(b)*** *the 1994 Form 1120S is not available by the time the corporation is required to file its return. However, the corporation must show its 1994 tax year on the 1993 Form 1120S and incorporate any tax law changes that are effective for tax years beginning after December 31, 1993.*

Where To File

Use the preaddressed envelope. If you do not have the envelope, file your return at the applicable IRS address listed below.

If the corporation's principal business, office, or agency is located in	Use the following Internal Revenue Service Center address
New Jersey, New York (New York City and counties of Nassau, Rockland, Suffolk, and Westchester)	Holtsville, NY 00501
New York (all other counties), Connecticut, Maine, Massachusetts, New Hampshire, Rhode Island, Vermont	Andover, MA 05501
Florida, Georgia, South Carolina	Atlanta, GA 39901

Indiana, Kentucky, Michigan, Ohio, West Virginia	Cincinnati, OH 45999
Kansas, New Mexico, Oklahoma, Texas	Austin, TX 73301
Alaska, Arizona, California (counties of Alpine, Amador, Butte, Calaveras, Colusa, Contra Costa, Del Norte, El Dorado, Glenn, Humboldt, Lake, Lassen, Marin, Mendocino, Modoc, Napa, Nevada, Placer, Plumas, Sacramento, San Joaquin, Shasta, Sierra, Siskiyou, Solano, Sonoma, Sutter, Tehama, Trinity, Yolo, and Yuba), Colorado, Idaho, Montana, Nebraska, Nevada, North Dakota, Oregon, South Dakota, Utah, Washington, Wyoming	Ogden, UT 84201
California (all other counties), Hawaii	Fresno, CA 93888
Illinois, Iowa, Minnesota, Missouri, Wisconsin	Kansas City, MO 64999
Alabama, Arkansas, Louisiana, Mississippi, North Carolina, Tennessee	Memphis, TN 37501
Delaware, District of Columbia, Maryland, Pennsylvania, Virginia	Philadelphia, PA 19255

Who Must Sign

The return must be signed and dated by the president, vice president, treasurer, assistant treasurer, chief accounting officer, or any other corporate officer (such as tax officer) authorized to sign. A receiver, trustee, or assignee must sign and date any return he or she is required to file on behalf of a corporation.

If a corporate officer filled in Form 1120S, the Paid Preparer's space under "Signature of officer" should remain blank. If someone prepares Form 1120S and does not charge the corporation, that person should not sign the return. Certain others who prepare Form 1120S should not sign. For example, a regular, full-time employee of the corporation such as a clerk, secretary, etc., should not sign.

Generally, anyone paid to prepare Form 1120S must sign the return and fill in the other blanks in the Paid Preparer's Use Only area of the return.

The preparer required to sign the return MUST complete the required preparer information and:

- Sign it, by hand, in the space provided for the preparer's signature. (Signature stamps or labels are not acceptable.)
- Give a copy of Form 1120S to the taxpayer in addition to the copy filed with the IRS.

Accounting Methods

Ordinary income must be computed using the method of accounting regularly used in keeping the corporation's books and records. Generally, permissible methods include the cash method, the accrual method, or any other method permitted by the Internal Revenue Code. In all cases, the method adopted must clearly reflect income.

Generally, an S corporation may not use the cash method of accounting if the corporation is a tax shelter (as defined in section 448(d)(3)). See section 448 for details.

Under the accrual method, an amount is includible in income when all the events have occurred that fix the right to receive the income and the amount can be determined with reasonable accuracy. See Regulations section 1.451-1(a) for details.

Generally, an accrual basis taxpayer can deduct accrued expenses in the tax year in which all events that determine liability have occurred, the amount of the liability can be figured with reasonable accuracy, and economic performance takes place with respect to the expense. There are exceptions for recurring items and items involving transactions between related taxpayers described in section 267.

Except for real property construction contracts, long-term contracts must generally be accounted for using the percentage of completion method described in section 460.

Dealers in securities must use the "mark-to-market" accounting method described in new section 475 for tax years ending on or after December 31, 1993. Under the new rules, any security that is inventory to the dealer must be included in inventory at its fair market value. Any security that is not inventory and that is held at the close of the tax year is treated as sold at its fair market value on the last business day of the tax year, and any gain or loss must be taken into account in determining gross income. The gain or loss taken into account is generally treated as ordinary gain or loss.

Dealers who change their accounting method to comply with the new law are treated as having initiated the change in accounting method and as having received the consent of the IRS to the change. Generally, the net amount of the section 481(a) adjustment (reported on line 5) is taken into account ratably over a 5-year period, beginning with the first tax year ending on or after December 31, 1993.

For details, including exceptions, see new section 475.

Generally, the corporation may change its method of accounting used to report taxable income (for income as a whole or for any material item) only by getting consent on **Form 3115,** Application for Change in Accounting Method. For more information, get **Pub. 538,** Accounting Periods and Methods.

Accounting Periods

Generally, an S corporation may not change its accounting period to a tax year that is not a permitted year. A "permitted year" is a calendar year or any other accounting period for which the corporation can establish to the satisfaction of the IRS that there is a business purpose for the tax year.

To change an accounting period, see Regulations section 1.442-1 and **Form 1128,** Application to Adopt, Change, or Retain a Tax Year. Also see Pub. 538.

Election of a tax year other than a required year.—Under the provisions of section 444, an S corporation may elect to have a tax year other than a permitted year, but only if the deferral period of the tax year is not longer than 3 months. This election is made by filing **Form 8716,** Election To Have a Tax Year Other Than a Required Tax Year.

An S corporation may not make or continue an election under section 444 if it is a member of a tiered structure, other than a tiered structure that consists entirely of partnerships and S corporations that have the same tax year. For the S corporation to have a section 444 election in effect, it must make the payments required by section 7519 and file **Form 8752,** Required Payment or Refund Under Section 7519.

A section 444 election ends if an S corporation changes its accounting period to a calendar year or some other permitted year, it willfully fails to comply with the requirements of section 7519, or its S election is terminated (unless it immediately becomes a personal service corporation). If the termination results in a short tax year, type or legibly print at the top of the first page of Form 1120S for the short tax year, "SECTION 444 ELECTION TERMINATED."

Rounding Off to Whole Dollars

You may round off cents to whole dollars on your return and accompanying schedules. To do so, drop amounts under 50 cents and increase amounts from 50 to 99 cents to the next higher dollar.

Recordkeeping

The corporation's records must be kept as long as they may be needed for the administration of any provision of the Internal Revenue Code. Usually, records that support an item of income, deduction, or credit on the corporation's return must be kept for 3 years from the date the return is due or is filed, whichever is later. Keep records that verify the corporation's basis in property for as long as they are needed to figure the basis of the original or replacement property.

The corporation should also keep copies of any returns it has filed. They help in preparing future returns and in making computations when filing an amended return.

Depositary Method of Tax Payment

The corporation must pay the tax due in full no later than the 15th day of the 3rd month after the end of the tax year.

Deposit corporation income tax payments (and estimated tax payments) with **Form 8109,** Federal Tax Deposit Coupon. Do not submit deposits directly to an IRS office; otherwise, the corporation may have to pay a penalty. Mail or deliver the completed Form 8109 with the payment to a qualified depositary for Federal taxes or to the Federal Reserve bank (FRB) servicing your geographic area. Make your checks or money orders payable to that depositary or FRB.

To help ensure proper crediting, write the corporation's employer identification number, the tax period to which the deposit applies, and "Form 1120S" on your check or money order. Be sure to darken the "1120" box on the coupon. These records of deposit will be sent to the IRS.

For more information on deposits, see the instructions in the coupon booklet (Form 8109) and **Pub. 583,** Taxpayers Starting a Business.

Estimated Tax

Generally, the corporation must make estimated tax payments for the following taxes if the total of these taxes is $500 or more: **(a)** the tax on certain capital gains, **(b)** the tax on built-in gains, **(c)** the excess net passive income tax, and **(d)** the investment credit recapture tax.

For tax years beginning after 1993, the amount of estimated tax required to be paid annually is the lesser of **(a)** 100% of the above taxes shown on the return for the tax year (or if no return is filed, 100% of these taxes for the year); or **(b)** the sum of **(i)** 100% of the sum of the investment credit recapture tax and the built-in gains tax (or the tax on certain capital gains) shown on the return for the tax year (or if no return is filed, 100% of these taxes for the year), and **(ii)** 100% of any excess net passive income tax shown on the corporation's return for the preceding tax year. If the preceding tax year was less than 12 months, the estimated tax must be determined under **(a).**

The estimated tax is generally payable in four equal installments. However, the corporation may be able to lower the amount of one or more installments by using the annualized income installment method or adjusted seasonal installment method under section 6655(e).

For a calendar year corporation, the payments are due by April 15, June 15, September 15, and December 15. For a fiscal year corporation, they are due by the 15th day of the 4th, 6th, 9th, and 12th months of the fiscal year.

The payments are made using the depositary method described on page 3.

Interest and Penalties

Interest

Interest is charged on taxes not paid by the due date, even if an extension of time to file is granted. Interest is also charged from the due date (including extensions) to the date of payment on the failure to file penalty, the accuracy-related penalty, and the fraud penalty. The interest charge is figured at a rate determined under section 6621.

Late Filing of Return

A corporation that does not file its tax return by the due date, including extensions, may have to pay a penalty of 5% a month, or part of a month, up to a maximum of 25%, for each month the return is not filed. The penalty is imposed on the net amount due. The minimum penalty for filing a return more than 60 days late is the smaller of the tax due or $100. The penalty will not be imposed if the corporation can show that the failure to file on time was due to reasonable cause. If the failure is due to reasonable cause, attach an explanation to the return.

Late Payment of Tax

A corporation that does not pay the tax when due generally may have to pay a penalty of ½ of 1% a month or part of a month, up to a maximum of 25%, for each month the tax is not paid. The penalty is imposed on the net amount due.

The penalty will not be imposed if the corporation can show that failure to pay on time was due to reasonable cause.

Failure To Furnish Information Timely

Section 6037(b) requires an S corporation to furnish to each shareholder a copy of the information shown on Schedule K-1 (Form 1120S) that is attached to Form 1120S. Provide Schedule K-1 to each shareholder on or before the day on which the corporation files Form 1120S.

For each failure to furnish Schedule K-1 to a shareholder when due and each failure to include on Schedule K-1 all of the information required to be shown (or the inclusion of incorrect information), a penalty of $50 may be imposed with regard to each Schedule K-1 for which a failure occurs. If the requirement to report correct information is intentionally disregarded, each $50 penalty is increased to $100 or, if greater, 10% of the aggregate amount of items required to be reported. See sections 6722 and 6724 for more information.

The penalty will not be imposed if the corporation can show that not furnishing information timely was due to reasonable cause and not due to willful neglect.

Unresolved Tax Problems

The IRS has a Problem Resolution Program for taxpayers who have been unable to resolve their problems with the IRS. If the corporation has a tax problem it has been unable to resolve through normal channels, write to the corporation's local IRS District Director or call the corporation's local IRS office and ask for Problem Resolution assistance. Hearing-impaired persons who have access to TDD equipment may call 1-800-829-4059 to ask for help. The Problem Resolution office will ensure that your problem receives proper attention. Although the office cannot change the tax law or make technical decisions, it can help clear up problems that resulted from previous contacts.

Other Forms, Returns, Schedules, and Statements That May Be Required

- **Forms W-2** and **W-3,** Wage and Tax Statement; and Transmittal of Income and Tax Statements.
- **Form 720,** Quarterly Federal Excise Tax Return. Use Form 720 to report environmental excise taxes, communications and air transportation taxes, fuel taxes, luxury tax on passenger vehicles, manufacturers taxes, ship passenger tax, and certain other excise taxes.

Caution: *A trust fund recovery penalty may apply where certain excise taxes that should be collected are not collected or are not paid to the IRS. Under this penalty, certain officers or employees of the corporation become personally liable for payment of the taxes and may be penalized in an amount equal to the unpaid taxes. See the Instructions for Form 720 for more details.*

- **Form 940** or **Form 940-EZ,** Employer's Annual Federal Unemployment (FUTA) Tax Return. The corporation may be liable for FUTA tax and may have to file Form 940 or 940-EZ if it paid wages of $1,500 or more in any calendar quarter during the calendar year (or the preceding calendar year) or one or more employees worked for the corporation for some part of a day in any 20 different weeks during the calendar year (or the preceding calendar year). A corporate officer who performs substantial services is considered an employee. Except as provided in section 3306(a), reasonable compensation for these services is subject to FUTA tax, no matter what the corporation calls the payments.
- **Form 941,** Employer's Quarterly Federal Tax Return. Employers must file this form quarterly to report income tax withheld and employer and employee social security and Medicare taxes. A corporate officer who performs substantial services is considered an employee. Except as provided in sections 3121(a) and 3401(a), reasonable compensation for these services is subject to employer and employee social security and Medicare taxes and income tax withholding, no matter what the corporation calls the payments. Agricultural employers must file **Form 943,** Employer's Annual Tax Return for Agricultural Employees, instead of Form 941, to report income tax withheld and employer and employee social security and Medicare taxes on farmworkers.

Caution: *A trust fund recovery penalty may apply where income, social security, and Medicare taxes that should be withheld are not withheld or are not paid to the IRS. Under this penalty, certain officers or employees of the corporation become personally liable for payment of the taxes and may be penalized in an amount equal to the unpaid taxes. Get* **Circular E,**

Employer's Tax Guide (or **Circular A,** *Agricultural Employer's Tax Guide), for details.*

• **Form 966,** Corporate Dissolution or Liquidation.

• **Forms 1042** and **1042-S,** Annual Withholding Tax Return for U.S. Source Income of Foreign Persons; and Foreign Person's U.S. Source Income Subject to Withholding. Use these forms to report and transmit withheld tax on payments made to nonresident alien individuals, foreign partnerships, or foreign corporations to the extent such payments constitute gross income from sources within the United States (see sections 861 through 865). For more information, see sections 1441 and 1442, and **Pub. 515,** Withholding of Tax on Nonresident Aliens and Foreign Corporations.

• **Form 1096,** Annual Summary and Transmittal of U.S. Information Returns.

• **Form 1098,** Mortgage Interest Statement. Use this form to report the receipt from any individual of $600 or more of mortgage interest and points in the course of the corporation's trade or business.

• **Forms 1099-A, B, DIV, INT, MISC, OID, PATR, R,** and **S.** You may have to file these information returns to report abandonments; acquisitions through foreclosure; proceeds from broker and barter exchange transactions; certain dividends; interest payments; medical and dental health care payments; miscellaneous income payments; original issue discount; patronage dividends; distributions from pensions, annuities, retirement or profit-sharing plans, IRAs, insurance contracts, etc.; and proceeds from real estate transactions. Also use certain of these returns to report amounts that were received as a nominee on behalf of another person.

Use Form 1099-DIV to report actual dividends paid by the corporation. Only distributions from accumulated earnings and profits are classified as dividends. Do not issue Form 1099-DIV for dividends received by the corporation that are allocated to shareholders on line 4b of Schedule K-1.

For more information, see the separate **Instructions for Forms 1099, 1098, 5498, and W-2G.**

Note: *Every corporation must file Forms 1099-MISC if it makes payments of rents, commissions, or other fixed or determinable income (see section 6041) totaling $600 or more to any one person in the course of its trade or business during the calendar year.*

• **Form 5713,** International Boycott Report. Every corporation that had operations in, or related to, a "boycotting" country, company, or national of a country must file Form 5713. In addition, persons who participate in or cooperate with an international boycott may have to complete Schedule A or Schedule B and Schedule C of Form 5713 to compute their loss of the foreign tax credit, the deferral of earnings of a controlled foreign corporation, IC-DISC benefits, and FSC benefits.

• **Form 8264,** Application for Registration of a Tax Shelter, is used by tax shelter organizers to register tax shelters with the IRS for the purpose of receiving a tax shelter registration number.

• **Form 8271,** Investor Reporting of Tax Shelter Registration Number, is used by corporations that have acquired an interest in a tax shelter that is required to be registered to report the tax shelter's registration number. Form 8271 must be attached to any return on which a deduction, credit, loss, or other tax benefit attributable to a tax shelter is taken or any income attributable to a tax shelter is reported.

• **Form 8275,** Disclosure Statement. Form 8275 is used by taxpayers and income tax return preparers to disclose items or positions, except those contrary to a regulation, that are not otherwise adequately disclosed on a tax return. The disclosure is made to avoid the parts of the accuracy-related penalty imposed for negligence, disregard of rules, or substantial understatement of tax. Form 8275 is also used for disclosures relating to preparer penalties for understatements due to unrealistic positions or for willful or reckless conduct.

• **Form 8275-R,** Regulation Disclosure Statement, is used to disclose any item on a tax return for which a position has been taken that is contrary to Treasury regulations.

• **Form 8281,** Information Return for Publicly Offered Original Issue Discount Instruments. This form is used by issuers of publicly offered debt instruments having OID to provide the information required by section 1275(c).

• **Forms 8288** and **8288-A,** U.S. Withholding Tax Return for Dispositions by Foreign Persons of U.S. Real Property Interests; and Statement of Withholding on Dispositions by Foreign Persons of U.S. Real Property Interests. Use these forms to report and transmit withheld tax on the sale of U.S. real property by a foreign person. See section 1445 and the related regulations for additional information.

• **Form 8300,** Report of Cash Payments Over $10,000 Received in a Trade or Business. This form is used to report the receipt of more than $10,000 in cash or foreign currency in one transaction (or a series of related transactions).

• **Form 8594,** Asset Acquisition Statement, is to be filed by both the purchaser and seller of a group of assets constituting a trade or business if goodwill or a going concern value attaches, or could attach, to such assets and if the purchaser's basis in the assets is determined only by the amount paid for the assets.

• **Form 8697,** Interest Computation Under the Look-Back Method for Completed Long-Term Contracts. Certain S corporations that are not closely held may have to file Form 8697. Form 8697 is used to figure the interest due or to be refunded under the look-back method of section 460(b)(2) on certain long-term contracts that are accounted for under either the percentage of completion-capitalized cost method or the percentage of completion method. Closely held corporations should see the instructions on page 21 for line 23, item 10, of Schedule K-1 for details on the Form 8697 information they must provide to their shareholders.

Stock ownership in foreign corporations.—If the corporation owned at least 5% in value of the outstanding stock of a foreign personal holding company, and the corporation was required to include in its gross income any undistributed foreign personal holding company income, attach the statement required by section 551(c).

A corporation may have to file **Form 5471,** Information Return of U.S. Persons With Respect to Certain Foreign Corporations, if any of the following applies:

1. It controls a foreign corporation.

2. It acquires, disposes of, or owns 5% or more in value of the outstanding stock of a foreign corporation.

3. It is a 10%-or-more shareholder of a foreign personal holding company.

4. It owns stock in a controlled foreign corporation for an uninterrupted period of 30 days or more during any tax year of the foreign corporation, and it owned that stock on the last day of that year.

Transfers to a corporation controlled by the transferor.—If a person receives stock of a corporation in exchange for property, and no gain or loss is recognized under section 351, the transferor and transferee must each attach to their tax returns the information required by Regulations section 1.351-3.

Attachments

Attach **Form 4136,** Credit for Federal Tax Paid on Fuels, after page 4, Form 1120S. Attach schedules in alphabetical order and other forms in numerical order after Form 4136.

To assist us in processing the return, **please complete every applicable entry space on Form 1120S and Schedule K-1.** If you attach statements, do not write "See attached" instead of completing the entry spaces on Form 1120S and Schedule K-1.

If you need more space on the forms or schedules, attach separate sheets. Use the same size and format as on the printed forms. **But show the totals on the printed forms.** Attach these separate sheets after all the schedules and forms. Be sure to put the corporation's name and employer identification number (EIN) on each sheet.

Amended Return

To correct an error in a Form 1120S already filed, file an amended Form 1120S and check box F(4). If the amended return results in a change to income, or a change in the distribution of any income or other information provided to shareholders, an amended Schedule K-1 (Form 1120S) must also be filed with the amended Form 1120S and given to each shareholder. Be sure to check box D(2) on each Schedule K-1 to indicate that it is an amended Schedule K-1.

Note: *If an S corporation does not meet the small S corporation exception under Temporary Regulations section 301.6241-1T or if it is a small S corporation that has made the election described in Temporary Regulations section 301.6241-1T(c)(2)(v), and it files an amended return, the amended return will be a request for administrative adjustment and the tax matters person must file* ***Form 8082,*** *Notice of Inconsistent Treatment or Amended Return (Administrative Adjustment Request (AAR)). See the temporary regulations under section 6241 for more information.*

Passive Activity Limitations

In general, section 469 limits the amount of losses, deductions, and credits that shareholders may claim from "passive activities." The passive activity limitations do not apply to the corporation. Instead, they apply to each shareholder's share of any income or loss and credit attributable to a passive activity. Because the treatment of each shareholder's share of corporate income or loss and credit depends upon the nature of the activity that generated it, the corporation must report income or loss and credits separately for each activity.

The instructions below (pages 6 through 9) and the instructions for Schedules K and K-1 (pages 15 through 22) explain the applicable passive activity limitation rules and specify the type of information the corporation must provide to its shareholders for each activity. If the corporation had more than one activity, it must report information for each activity on an attachment to Schedules K and K-1.

Generally, passive activities include **(a)** activities that involve the conduct of a trade or business in which the shareholder does not materially participate and **(b)** any rental activity (see definition below) even if the shareholder materially participates. The level of each shareholder's participation in an activity must be determined by the shareholder.

The passive activity rules provide that losses and credits from passive activities can generally be applied only against income and tax from passive activities. Thus, passive losses and credits cannot be applied against income from salaries, wages, professional fees, or a business in which the shareholder materially participates; against "portfolio income" (see definition on page 7); or against the tax related to any of these types of income.

Special transitional rules apply to losses incurred by investors in qualified low-income housing projects. In addition, special rules require that net income from certain activities that would otherwise be treated as passive income must be recharacterized as nonpassive income for purposes of the passive activity limitations.

To allow each shareholder to apply the passive activity limitations at the individual level, the corporation must report income or loss and credits separately for each of the following: trade or business activities, rental real estate activities, rental activities other than rental real estate, and portfolio income. For definitions of each type of activity or income, see **Types of Activities and Income** below. For details on the special reporting requirements for passive activities, see **Passive Activity Reporting Requirements** on page 8.

Types of Activities and Income

Trade or business activities.—A trade or business activity is an activity (other than a rental activity or an activity treated as incidental to an activity of holding property for investment) that—

1. Involves the conduct of a trade or business (within the meaning of section 162),

2. Is conducted in anticipation of starting a trade or business, or

3. Involves research or experimental expenditures deductible under section 174 (or that would be if you chose to deduct rather than capitalize them).

If the shareholder does not materially participate in the activity, a trade or business activity of the corporation is a passive activity for the shareholder.

Note: *The section 469(c)(3) exception for a working interest in oil and gas properties is not applicable to an S corporation because state law generally limits the liability of corporate shareholders, including shareholders of an S corporation.*

Accordingly, the activity of holding a working interest in oil or gas properties is a trade or business activity and the material participation rules apply to determine if the activity is a passive activity. See Temporary Regulations section 1.469-1T(e)(4) and Regulations section 1.469-1(e)(4).

Each shareholder must determine if he or she materially participated in an activity. As a result, while the corporation's overall trade or business income (loss) is reported on page 1 of Form 1120S, the specific income and deductions from each separate trade or business activity must be reported on attachments to Form 1120S. Similarly, while each shareholder's allocable share of the corporation's overall trade or business income (loss) is reported on line 1 of Schedule K-1, each shareholder's allocable share of the income and deductions from each trade or business activity must be reported on attachments to each Schedule K-1. See **Passive Activity Reporting Requirements** on page 8 for more information.

Rental activities.—Generally, except as noted below, if the gross income from an activity consists of amounts paid principally for the use of real or personal tangible property held by the corporation, the activity is a rental activity.

There are several exceptions to this general rule. Under these exceptions, an activity involving the use of real or personal tangible property is not a rental activity if **(a)** the average period of customer use (see definition below) for such property is 7 days or less; **(b)** the average period of customer use for such property is 30 days or less and significant personal services (see definition below) are provided by or on behalf of the corporation; **(c)** extraordinary personal services (see definition on page 7) are provided by or on behalf of the corporation; **(d)** rental of the property is treated as incidental to a nonrental activity of the corporation under Temporary Regulations section 1.469-1T(e)(3)(vi) and Regulations section 1.469-1(e)(3)(vi); or **(e)** the corporation customarily makes the property available during defined business hours for nonexclusive use by various customers. In addition, if a corporation owns an interest in a partnership that conducts a nonrental activity, and the corporation provides property for use in that activity in the corporation's capacity as an owner of an interest in the partnership, the provision of the property is not a rental activity. Consequently, the corporation's distributive share of income from the activity is not income from a rental activity. A guaranteed payment described in section 707(c) is not income from a rental activity under any circumstances.

Whether the corporation provides property used in an activity of a partnership in the corporation's capacity as an owner of an interest in the partnership is based on all the facts and circumstances.

Average period of customer use.—The average period of customer use of property is computed by dividing the total number of days in all rental periods by the number of rentals during the tax year. If the activity involves renting more than one class of property, multiply the average period of customer use of each class by the ratio of the gross rental income from that class to the activity's total gross rental income. The activity's average period of customer use equals the sum of these class-by-class average periods weighted by gross income. See Regulations section 1.469-1(e)(3)(iii).

Significant personal services.—Personal services include only services performed by individuals. In determining whether personal services are significant personal services, all of the relevant facts and circumstances are considered. Relevant facts and circumstances include how often the services are provided, the type and amount of labor required to perform the services, and the value of the services in relation to the amount charged for the use of the property. The following services are excluded from consideration in determining whether personal services are significant: **(a)** services necessary to permit the lawful use of the rental property; **(b)** services performed in connection with improvements or repairs to the rental property that extend the useful life of the property substantially beyond the average rental period; and **(c)** services provided in connection with the use of any improved real property that are similar to those commonly provided in connection with long-term rentals of high-grade commercial or residential property (e.g., cleaning and maintenance of common areas, routine repairs, trash collection, elevator service, and security at entrances).

Extraordinary personal services.—Services provided in connection with making rental property available for customer use are extraordinary personal services only if the services are performed by individuals and the customers' use of the rental property is incidental to their receipt of the services. For example, a patient's use of a hospital room generally is incidental to the care that the patient receives from the hospital's medical staff. Similarly, a student's use of a dormitory room in a boarding school is incidental to the personal services provided by the school's teaching staff.

Rental property incidental to a nonrental activity.—An activity is not a rental activity if the rental of the property is incidental to a nonrental activity, such as the activity of holding property for investment, a trade or business activity, or the activity of dealing in property.

Rental property is incidental to an activity of holding property for investment if the main purpose for holding the property is to realize a gain from the appreciation of the property and the gross rental income from such property for the tax year is less than 2% of the smaller of the property's unadjusted basis or its fair market value.

Rental property is incidental to a trade or business activity if **(a)** the corporation owns an interest in the trade or business at all times during the year; **(b)** the rental property was mainly used in the trade or business activity during the tax year or during at least 2 of the 5 preceding tax years; and **(c)** the gross rental income from the property is less than 2% of the smaller of the property's unadjusted basis or its fair market value.

The sale or exchange of property that is also rented during the tax year (where the gain or loss is recognized) is treated as incidental to the activity of dealing in property if, at the time of the sale or exchange, the property was held primarily for sale to customers in the ordinary course of the corporation's trade or business.

See Temporary Regulations section 1.469-1T(e)(3) and Regulations section 1.469-1(e)(3) for more information on the definition of rental activities for purposes of the passive activity limitations.

Reporting of rental activities.—In reporting the corporation's income or losses and credits from rental activities, the corporation must separately report **(a)** rental real estate activities and **(b)** rental activities other than rental real estate activities.

Shareholders who actively participate in a rental real estate activity may be able to deduct part or all of their rental real estate losses (and the deduction equivalent of rental real estate credits) against income (or tax) from nonpassive activities. Generally, the combined amount of rental real estate losses and the deduction equivalent of rental real estate credits from all sources (including rental real estate activities not held through the corporation) that may be claimed is limited to $25,000.

Special transitional rules apply to investors in qualified low-income housing projects. See section 502 of the Tax Reform Act of 1986 and **Pub. 925,** Passive Activity and At-Risk Rules, for more information.

Rental real estate activity income (loss) is reported on **Form 8825,** Rental Real Estate Income and Expenses of a Partnership or an S Corporation, and on line 2 of Schedules K and K-1 rather than on page 1 of Form 1120S.

Credits related to rental real estate activities are reported on lines 12c and 12d of Schedules K and K-1. Low-income housing credits are reported on line 12b of Schedules K and K-1.

Income (loss) from rental activities other than rental real estate is reported on line 3 of Schedules K and K-1. Credits related to rental activities other than rental real estate are reported on line 12e of Schedules K and K-1.

Portfolio income.—Generally, portfolio income includes all gross income, other than income derived in the ordinary course of a trade or business, that is attributable to interest; dividends; royalties; income from a real estate investment trust, a regulated investment company, a real estate mortgage investment conduit, a common trust fund, a controlled foreign corporation, a qualified electing fund, or a cooperative; income from the disposition of property that produces income of a type defined as portfolio income; and income from the disposition of property held for investment.

Solely for purposes of the preceding paragraph, gross income derived in the ordinary course of a trade or business includes **(and portfolio income, therefore, does not include)** only the following types of income: **(a)** interest income on loans and investments made in the ordinary course of a trade or business of lending money; **(b)** interest on accounts receivable arising from the performance of services or the sale of property in the ordinary course of a trade or business of performing such services or selling such property, but only if credit is customarily offered to customers of the business; **(c)** income from investments made in the ordinary course of a trade or business of furnishing insurance or annuity contracts or reinsuring risks underwritten by insurance companies; **(d)** income or gain derived in the ordinary course of an activity of trading or dealing in any property if such activity constitutes a trade or business (unless the dealer held the property for investment at any time before such income or gain is recognized); **(e)** royalties derived by the taxpayer in the ordinary course of a trade or business of licensing intangible property; **(f)** amounts included in the gross income of a patron of a cooperative by reason of any payment or allocation to the patron based on patronage occurring with respect to a trade or business of the patron; and **(g)** other income identified by the IRS as income derived by the taxpayer in the ordinary course of a trade or business.

See Temporary Regulations section 1.469-2T(c)(3) for more information on portfolio income.

Portfolio income is reported on line 4 of Schedules K and K-1, rather than on page 1 of Form 1120S.

Expenses related to portfolio income are reported on line 9 of Schedules K and K-1.

Grouping Activities

Caution: *At the time these instructions went to print, former Temporary Regulations section 1.469-4T had expired and final regulations defining the term "activity" had not been issued. The following rules are based on Proposed Regulations section 1.469-4. When these regulations are finalized, the IRS will announce any changes made to the proposed rules.*

Generally, one or more trade or business activities or rental activities are treated as a single activity if the activities make up an appropriate economic unit for measurement of gain or loss for purposes of the passive activity rules. Whether activities are treated as a single activity depends on all the relevant facts and circumstances. The factors given the greatest weight in determining whether activities make up an appropriate economic unit are—

1. Similarities and differences in types of businesses,

2. The extent of common control,

3. The extent of common ownership,

4. Geographical location, and

5. Interdependencies among the activities.

Example: The corporation has a significant ownership interest in a bakery and a movie theater in Baltimore and in a bakery and a movie theater in Philadelphia. Depending on the relevant facts and circumstances, the corporation could group the movie theaters and bakeries into a single activity, into a movie theater activity and a bakery activity, into a Baltimore activity and a Philadelphia activity, or into four separate activities.

Once the corporation chooses a grouping under these rules, it must continue using that grouping in later tax years unless a material change in the facts and circumstances makes it clearly inappropriate.

The IRS may regroup the corporation's activities if the corporation's grouping fails to reflect one or more appropriate economic units and one of the primary purposes for the grouping is to circumvent the passive activity limitations.

Limitation on grouping certain activities.—The following activities may not be grouped together—

1. A rental activity with a trade or business activity (unless the rental activity is insubstantial in relation to the trade or business activity or vice versa),

2. An activity involving the rental of real property with an activity involving the rental of personal property (except for personal property provided in connection with real property), or

3. Any activity with another activity in which the corporation holds an interest as a limited partner or as a limited entrepreneur (as defined in section 464(e)(2)) if that other activity engages in holding, producing, or distributing motion picture films or videotapes; farming; leasing section 1245 property; or, exploring for (or exploiting) oil and gas resources or geothermal deposits. See Proposed Regulations section 1.469-4(f) for exceptions.

Activities conducted through partnerships.—Once a partnership determines its activities under these rules, the corporation as a partner uses these rules to group those activities with activities conducted directly by the corporation or through other partnerships.

Recharacterization of Passive Income

Under Temporary Regulations section 1.469-2T(f) and Regulations section 1.469-2(f), net passive income from certain passive activities must be treated as nonpassive income. Net passive income is the excess of an activity's passive activity gross income over its passive activity deductions (current year deductions and prior year unallowed losses).

Income from the following six sources is subject to recharacterization. Note that any net passive income recharacterized as nonpassive income is treated as investment income for purposes of computing investment interest expense limitations if it is from **(a)** an activity of renting substantially nondepreciable property from an equity-financed lending activity or **(b)** an activity related to an interest in a pass-through entity that licenses intangible property.

1. Significant participation passive activities.—A significant participation passive activity is any trade or business activity in which the shareholder both participates for more than 100 hours during the tax year and does not materially participate. Because each shareholder must determine his or her level of participation, the corporation will not be able to identify significant participation passive activities.

2. Certain nondepreciable rental property activities.—Net passive income from a rental activity is nonpassive income if less than 30% of the unadjusted basis of the property used or held for use by customers in the activity is subject to depreciation under section 167.

3. Passive equity-financed lending activities.—If the corporation has net income from a passive equity-financed lending activity, the lesser of the net passive income or equity-financed interest income from the activity is nonpassive income.

Note: *The amount of income from the activities in items **1** through **3** above that any shareholder will be required to recharacterize as nonpassive income may be limited under Temporary Regulations section 1.469-2T(f)(8). Because the corporation will not have information regarding all of a shareholder's activities, it must identify all corporate activities meeting the definitions in items **2** and **3** as activities that may be subject to recharacterization.*

4. Rental activities incidental to a development activity.—Net rental activity income is nonpassive income for a shareholder if all of the following apply: **(a)** the corporation recognizes gain from the sale, exchange, or other disposition of the rental property during the tax year; **(b)** the use of the item of property in the rental activity started less than 12 months before the date of disposition (the use of an item of rental property begins on the first day on which (i) the corporation owns an interest in the property, (ii) substantially all of the property is either rented or held out for rent and ready to be rented, and (iii) no significant value-enhancing services remain to be performed); and **(c)** the shareholder materially participated or significantly participated for any tax year in an activity that involved the performance of services for the purpose of enhancing the value of the property (or any other item of property, if the basis of the property disposed of is determined in whole or in part by reference to the basis of that item of property). Net rental activity income is the excess of passive activity gross income from renting or disposing of property over passive activity deductions (current year deductions and prior year unallowed losses) that are reasonably allocable to the rented property.

Because the corporation cannot determine a shareholder's level of participation, the corporation must identify net income from property described in items **(a)** and **(b)** above as income that may be subject to recharacterization.

5. Activities involving property rented to a nonpassive activity.—If a taxpayer rents property to a trade or business activity in which the taxpayer materially participates, the taxpayer's net rental activity income (defined above) from the property is nonpassive income.

6. Acquisition of an interest in a pass-through entity that licenses intangible property.—Generally, net royalty income from intangible property is nonpassive income if the taxpayer acquired an interest in the pass-through entity after it created the intangible property or performed substantial services or incurred substantial costs in developing or marketing the intangible property. Net royalty income is the excess of passive activity gross income from licensing or transferring any right in intangible property over passive activity deductions (current year deductions and prior year unallowed losses) that are reasonably allocable to the intangible property.

See Temporary Regulations section 1.469-2T(f)(7)(iii) for exceptions to this rule.

Passive Activity Reporting Requirements

To allow shareholders to correctly apply the passive activity loss and credit limitation rules, any corporation that carries on more than one activity must:

1. Provide an attachment for each activity conducted through the corporation that identifies the type of activity conducted (trade or business, rental real estate, rental activity other than rental real estate, or investment).

2. On the attachment for each activity, provide a schedule, using the same line numbers as shown on Schedule K-1, detailing the net income (loss), credits, and all items required to be separately stated under section 1366(a)(1) from each trade or business activity, from each rental real estate activity, from each rental activity other than a rental real estate activity, and from investments.

3. Identify the net income (loss) and the shareholder's share of corporation interest expense from each activity of renting a dwelling unit that the shareholder also uses for personal purposes during the year for more than the greater of 14 days or 10% of the number of days that the residence is rented at fair rental value.

4. Identify the net income (loss) and the shareholder's share of interest expense from each activity of trading personal property conducted through the corporation.

5. For any gain (loss) from the disposition of an interest in an activity or of an interest in property used in an activity (including dispositions before 1987 from which gain is being recognized after 1986):

a. Identify the activity in which the property was used at the time of disposition;

b. If the property was used in more than one activity during the 12 months preceding the disposition, identify the activities in which the property was used and the adjusted basis allocated to each activity; and

c. For gains only, if the property was substantially appreciated at the time of the disposition and the applicable holding period specified in Regulations section 1.469-2(c)(2)(iii)(A) was not satisfied, identify the amount of the nonpassive gain and indicate whether or not the gain is investment income under Regulations section 1.469-2(c)(2)(iii)(F).

6. Specify the amount of gross portfolio income, the interest expense properly allocable to portfolio income, and expenses other than interest expense that are clearly and directly allocable to portfolio income.

7. Identify the ratable portion of any section 481 adjustment (whether a net positive or a net negative adjustment) allocable to each corporate activity.

8. Identify any gross income from sources specifically excluded from passive activity gross income, including income from intangible property if the shareholder is an individual and the shareholder's personal efforts significantly contributed to the creation of the property; income from a qualified low-income housing project (as defined in section 502 of the Tax Reform Act of 1986) conducted through the corporation; income from state, local, or foreign income tax refunds; and income from a covenant not to compete (in the case of a shareholder who is an individual and who contributed the covenant to the corporation).

9. Identify any deductions that are not passive activity deductions.

10. If the corporation makes a full or partial disposition of its interest in another entity, identify the gain (loss) allocable to each activity conducted through the entity, and the gain allocable to a passive activity that would have been recharacterized as nonpassive gain had the corporation disposed of its interest in property used in the activity (because the property was substantially appreciated at the time of the disposition, and the gain represented more than 10% of the shareholder's total gain from the disposition).

11. Identify the following items that may be subject to the recharacterization rules under Temporary Regulations section 1.469-2T(f) and Regulations section 1.469-2(f):

a. Net income from an activity of renting substantially nondepreciable property;

b. The lesser of equity-financed interest income or net passive income from an equity-financed lending activity;

c. Net rental activity income from property developed (by the shareholder or the corporation), rented, and sold within 12 months after the rental of the property commenced;

d. Net rental activity income from the rental of property by the corporation to a trade or business activity in which the shareholder had an interest (either directly or indirectly); and

e. Net royalty income from intangible property if the shareholder acquired the shareholder's interest in the corporation after the corporation created the intangible property or performed substantial services or incurred substantial costs in developing or marketing the intangible property.

12. Identify separately the credits from each activity conducted by or through the corporation.

Specific Instructions

General Information

Name, Address, and Employer Identification Number

Use the label on the package that was mailed to the corporation. Cross out any errors and print the correct information on the label.

If the corporation did not receive a label, print or type the corporation's true name (as set forth in the corporate charter or other legal document creating it), address, and employer identification number on the appropriate lines.

Include the suite, room, or other unit number after the street address. If a preaddressed label is used, please include the information on the label. If the Post Office does not deliver to the street address and the corporation has a P.O. box, show the box number instead of the street address.

If the corporation changes its mailing address after filing its return, it can notify the IRS by filing **Form 8822,** Change of Address.

Item B—Business Code No.

See **Codes for Principal Business Activity** on page 24 of these instructions.

Item E—Total Assets

Enter the corporation's total assets at the end of the tax year, as determined by the accounting method regularly used in maintaining the corporation's books and records. If there are no assets at the end of the tax year, enter the total assets as of the beginning of the tax year.

Item F—Initial Return, Final Return, Change in Address, and Amended Return

If this is the corporation's first return, check box F(1). If the corporation has ceased to exist, check box F(2). Also check box D(1) on each Schedule K-1 to indicate that it is a final Schedule K-1. Indicate a change in address by checking box F(3). If this amends a previously filed return, check box F(4). If Schedules K-1 are also being amended, check box D(2) on each Schedule K-1.

Item G—Consolidated Audit Procedures

With certain exceptions, the tax treatment of S corporation items is determined at the corporate level in a consolidated audit proceeding, rather than in separate proceedings with individual shareholders. Check the box for item G if any of the following apply.

- The S corporation had more than five shareholders at any time during the tax year (for this purpose a husband and wife, and their estates, are treated as one shareholder).
- Any shareholder was other than a natural person or estate.
- The small S corporation (five or fewer shareholders) has elected as provided in Temporary Regulations section 301.6241-1T(c)(2)(v) to be subject to the rules for consolidated proceedings.

Note: *The S corporation does not make the section 301.6241-1T(c)(2)(v) election when it checks the box for item G. This election must be made separately.*

For more information on the consolidated audit procedures for S corporations, see sections 6241 through 6245, Temporary Regulations section 301.6241-1T, and **Pub. 556,** Examination of Returns, Appeal Rights, and Claims for Refund.

Income

Caution: *Report only trade or business activity income or loss on lines 1a through 6.* ***Do not report rental activity income or portfolio income or loss on these lines.*** *(See the instructions on* ***Passive Activity Limitations*** *beginning on page 6 for definitions of rental income and portfolio income.) Rental activity income and portfolio income are reported on Schedules K and K-1 (rental real estate activities are also reported on Form 8825).*

Do not include any tax-exempt income on lines 1 through 5. A corporation that receives any exempt income other than interest, or holds any property or engages in an activity that produces exempt income, reports the amount of this income on line 18 of Schedules K and K-1.

Tax-exempt interest income, including exempt-interest dividends received as a shareholder in a mutual fund or other regulated investment company, is reported on line 17 of Schedules K and K-1.

See **Deductions** on page 10 for information on how to report expenses related to tax-exempt income.

If the S corporation has had debt discharged resulting from a title 11 bankruptcy proceeding, or while insolvent, see **Form 982,** Reduction of Tax Attributes Due to Discharge of Indebtedness, and **Pub. 908,** Bankruptcy and Other Debt Cancellation.

Line 1—Gross Receipts or Sales

Enter gross receipts or sales from all trade or business operations except those you report on lines 4 and 5. For reporting advance payments, see Regulations section 1.451-5. To report income from long-term contracts, see section 460.

Installment sales.—Generally, the installment method cannot be used for dealer dispositions of property. A dealer disposition is any disposition of personal property by a person who regularly sells or otherwise disposes of property of the same type on the installment plan or any disposition of real property held for sale to customers in the ordinary course of the taxpayer's trade or business. The disposition of property used or produced in the farming business is not included as a dealer disposition. See section 453(l) for details and exceptions.

Enter on line 1a the gross profit on collections from installment sales for any of the following:

- Dealer dispositions of property before March 1, 1986.
- Dispositions of property used or produced in the trade or business of farming.
- Certain dispositions of timeshares and residential lots reported under the installment method.

Attach a schedule showing the following information for the current and the 3 preceding years: **(a)** gross sales, **(b)** cost of goods sold, **(c)** gross profits, **(d)** percentage of gross profits to gross sales, **(e)** amount collected, and **(f)** gross profit on the amount collected.

Line 2—Cost of Goods Sold

See the instructions for Schedule A.

Line 4—Net Gain (Loss) From Form 4797

Caution: *Include only ordinary gains or losses from the sale, exchange, or involuntary conversion of assets used in a trade or business activity. Ordinary gains or losses from the sale, exchange, or involuntary conversions of assets used in rental activities must be reported separately on Schedule K as part of the net income (loss) from the rental activity in which the property was used.*

A corporation that is a partner in a partnership must include on **Form 4797,** Sales of Business Property, its share of ordinary gains (losses) from sales, exchanges, or involuntary or compulsory conversions (other than casualties or thefts) of the partnership's trade or business assets.

Do not include any recapture of the section 179 expense deduction. See the instructions on page 21 for Schedule K-1, line 23, item 3, and the Instructions for Form 4797 for more information.

Line 5—Other Income (Loss)

Enter on line 5 trade or business income (loss) that is not included on lines 1a through 4. Examples of such income include:

1. Interest income derived in the ordinary course of the corporation's trade or business, such as interest charged on receivable balances;

2. Recoveries of bad debts deducted in earlier years under the specific charge-off method;

3. Taxable income from insurance proceeds;

4. The amount of credit figured on **Form 6478,** Credit for Alcohol Used as Fuel; and

5. All section 481 income adjustments resulting from changes in accounting methods.

Show the computation of the section 481 adjustment on an attached schedule.

The corporation must include as other income the recapture amount for section 280F if the business use of listed property drops to 50% or less. To figure the recapture amount, the corporation must complete Part IV of Form 4797.

The corporation must also include in other income the amount of any deduction previously taken under section 179A that is subject to recapture. The S corporation must recapture the benefit of any allowable deduction for qualified clean-fuel vehicle property (or clean-fuel vehicle refueling property), if, within 3 years after the date the property was placed in service, the property ceases to qualify for the deduction. See Pub. 535 for details on how to figure the recapture.

Do not include items requiring separate computations by shareholders that must be reported on Schedules K and K-1. See the instructions for Schedules K and K-1 beginning on page 15.

If "other income" consists of only one item, identify it by showing the account caption in parentheses on line 5. A separate schedule need not be attached to the return in this case.

Do not net any expense item (such as interest) with a similar income item. Report all trade or business expenses on lines 7 through 19.

Deductions

Caution: *Report **only** trade or business activity expenses on lines 7 through 19.*

Do not report rental activity expenses or deductions allocable to portfolio income on these lines. Rental activity expenses are separately reported on Form 8825 or line 3 of Schedules K and K-1. Deductions allocable to portfolio income are separately reported on line 9 of Schedules K and K-1. See **Passive Activity Limitations** beginning on page 6 for more information on rental activities and portfolio income.

Do not report any nondeductible amounts (such as expenses connected with the production of tax-exempt income) on lines 7 through 19. Instead, report nondeductible expenses on line 19 of Schedules K and K-1. If an expense is connected with both taxable income and nontaxable income, allocate a reasonable part of the expense to each kind of income.

Limitations on Deductions

Section 263A uniform capitalization rules.—The uniform capitalization rules of section 263A require corporations to capitalize or include in inventory certain costs incurred in connection with the production of real and personal tangible property held in inventory or held for sale in the ordinary course of business. Tangible personal property produced by a corporation includes a film, sound recording, video tape, book, or similar property. The rules also apply to personal property (tangible and intangible) acquired for resale. Corporations subject to the rules are required to capitalize not only direct costs but an allocable portion of most indirect costs (including taxes) that benefit the assets produced or acquired for resale. Interest expense paid or incurred during the production period of certain property must be capitalized and is governed by special rules. For more information, see Notice 88-99, 1988-2 C.B. 422. The uniform capitalization rules also apply to the production of property constructed or improved by a corporation for use in its trade or business or in an activity engaged in for profit.

Section 263A does not apply to personal property acquired for resale if the taxpayer's annual average gross receipts are $10 million or less. It does not apply to timber or to most property produced under a long-term contract. Special rules apply to certain corporations engaged in farming (see below). The rules do not apply to property produced for use by the taxpayer if substantial construction occurred before March 1, 1986.

In the case of inventory, some of the indirect costs that must be capitalized are administration expenses; taxes; depreciation; insurance; compensation paid to officers attributable to services; rework labor; and contributions to pension, stock bonus, and certain profit-sharing, annuity, or deferred compensation plans.

The costs required to be capitalized under section 263A are not deductible until the property to which the costs relate is sold, used, or otherwise disposed of by the corporation.

Research and experimental costs under section 174; intangible drilling costs for oil, gas, and geothermal property; and mining exploration and development costs are separately reported to shareholders for purposes of determinations under section 59(e). Temporary Regulations section 1.263A-1T specifies other indirect costs that may be currently deducted and those that must be capitalized with respect to production or resale activities. For more information, see Temporary Regulations section 1.263A-1T; Notice 88-86, 1988-2 C.B. 401; and Notice 89-67, 1989-1 C.B. 723.

Special rules for certain corporations engaged in farming.—For S corporations not required to use the accrual method of accounting, the rules of section 263A do **not** apply to expenses of raising any **(a)** animal or **(b)** plant that has a preproductive period of 2 years or less. Shareholders of S corporations not required to use the accrual method of accounting may elect to currently deduct the preproductive period expenses of certain plants that have a preproductive period of more than 2 years. Because the election to deduct these expenses is made by the shareholder, the farming corporation should not capitalize such preproductive expenses but should separately report these expenses on line 21 of Schedule K, and each shareholder's share on line 23 of Schedule K-1. See sections 263A(d) and (e) and Temporary Regulations section 1.263A-1T(c) for definitions and other details. Also see Notice 88-24, 1988-1 C.B. 491 and Notice 89-67.

Transactions between related taxpayers.—Generally, an accrual basis S corporation may deduct business expenses and interest owed to a related party (including any shareholder) **only** in the tax year of the corporation that includes the day on which the payment is includible in the income of the related party. See section 267 for details.

Section 291 limitations.—If the S corporation was a C corporation for any of the 3 immediately preceding years, the corporation may be required to adjust deductions allowed to the corporation for depletion of iron ore and coal, and the amortizable basis of pollution control facilities. See section 291 to determine the amount of the adjustment.

Business start-up expenses.—Business start-up expenses must be capitalized. An election may be made to amortize them over a period of not less than 60 months. See section 195.

Reducing certain expenses for which credits are allowable.—For each of the credits listed below, the corporation must reduce the otherwise allowable deductions for expenses used to figure the credit by the amount of the current year credit:

1. The orphan drug credit,
2. The credit for increasing research activities,
3. The enhanced oil recovery credit,
4. The disabled access credit,
5. The jobs credit,
6. The Indian employment credit, and
7. The employer social security credit.

If the corporation has any of these credits, be sure to figure each current year credit before figuring the deductions for expenses on which the credit is based.

Line 7—Compensation of Officers

Enter on line 7 the total compensation of all officers paid or incurred in the trade or business activities of the corporation, including fringe benefit expenditures made on behalf of officers owning more than 2% of the corporation's stock. Also report these fringe benefits as wages in box 1 of Form W-2. Do not include on line 7 amounts paid or incurred for fringe benefits of officers owning 2% or less of the corporation's stock. These amounts are reported on line 18, page 1, of Form 1120S. See the instructions for that line for information on the types of expenditures that are treated as fringe benefits and for the stock ownership rules.

Report amounts paid for health insurance coverage for a more than 2% shareholder (including that shareholder's spouse and dependents) as an information item in box 14 of that shareholder's Form W-2. A more than 2% shareholder may be allowed to deduct up to 25% of such amounts on Form 1040, line 26.

Do not include on line 7 compensation reported elsewhere on the return, such as amounts included in cost of goods sold, elective contributions to a section 401(k) cash or deferred arrangement, or amounts contributed under a salary reduction SEP agreement.

Line 8—Salaries and Wages

Enter on line 8a the amount of salaries and wages paid or incurred for the tax year, including fringe benefit expenditures made on behalf of employees (other than officers) owning more than 2% of the corporation's stock. Also report these fringe benefits as wages in box 1 of Form W-2. Do not include on line 8a amounts paid or incurred for fringe benefits of employees owning 2% or less of the corporation's stock. These amounts are reported on line 18, page 1, of Form 1120S. See the instructions for that line for information on the types of expenditures that are treated as fringe benefits and for the stock ownership rules.

Report amounts paid for health insurance coverage for a more than 2% shareholder (including that shareholder's spouse and dependents) as an information item in box 14 of that shareholder's Form W-2. A more than 2% shareholder may be allowed to deduct up to 25% of such amounts on Form 1040, line 26.

Do not include on line 8a salaries and wages reported elsewhere on the return, such as amounts included in cost of goods sold, elective contributions to a section 401(k) cash or deferred arrangement, or amounts contributed under a salary reduction SEP agreement.

Enter on line 8b the applicable employment credits from **Form 5884,** Jobs Credit, and **Form 8845,** Indian Employment Credit. See the instructions for these forms for more information.

If a shareholder or a member of the family of one or more shareholders of the corporation renders services or furnishes capital to the corporation for which reasonable compensation is not paid, the IRS may make adjustments in the items taken into account by such individuals and the value of such services or capital. See section 1366(e).

Line 9—Repairs and Maintenance

Enter the costs of incidental repairs and maintenance, such as labor and supplies, that do not add to the value of the property or appreciably prolong its life, but only to the extent that such costs relate to a trade or business activity and are not claimed elsewhere on the return. New buildings, machinery, or permanent improvements that increase the value of the property are not deductible. They are chargeable to capital accounts and may be depreciated or amortized.

Line 10—Bad Debts

Enter the total debts that became worthless in whole or in part during the year, but only to the extent such debts relate to a trade or business activity. Report deductible nonbusiness bad debts as a short-term capital loss on Schedule D (Form 1120S).

Caution: *Cash method taxpayers cannot take a bad debt deduction unless the amount was previously included in income.*

Line 11—Rents

If the corporation rented or leased a vehicle, enter the total annual rent or lease expense paid or incurred in the trade or business activities of the corporation. Also complete Part V of **Form 4562,** Depreciation and Amortization. If the corporation leased a vehicle for a term of 30 days or more, the deduction for vehicle lease expense may have to be reduced by an amount called the **inclusion amount.** The corporation may have an inclusion amount if—

The lease term began:	And the vehicle's fair market value on the first day of the lease exceeded:
After 12/31/92	$14,300
After 12/31/91 but before 1/1/93	$13,700
After 12/31/90 but before 1/1/92	$13,400
After 12/31/86 but before 1/1/91	$12,800

If the lease term began after June 18, 1984, but before January 1, 1987, get **Pub. 917,** Business Use of a Car, to find out if the corporation has an inclusion amount.

See Pub. 917 for instructions on figuring the inclusion amount.

Line 12—Taxes and Licenses

Enter taxes and licenses paid or incurred in the trade or business activities of the corporation, if not reflected in cost of goods sold. Federal import duties and Federal excise and stamp taxes are deductible only if paid or incurred in carrying on the trade or business of the corporation.

Do not deduct taxes, including state and local sales taxes, paid or accrued in connection with the acquisition or disposition of business property. These taxes must be added to the cost of the property, or in the case of a disposition, subtracted from the amount realized. See section 164.

Do not deduct taxes assessed against local benefits that increase the value of the property assessed (such as for paving, etc.), Federal income taxes, or taxes reported elsewhere on the return.

Do not deduct section 901 foreign taxes. These taxes are reported separately on line 15e, Schedule K.

Do not report on line 12 taxes allocable to portfolio income or to a rental activity. Taxes allocable to a rental real estate activity are reported on Form 8825. Taxes allocable to a rental activity other than a real estate rental activity are reported on line 3b of Schedule K. Taxes allocable to portfolio income are reported on line 9 of Schedules K and K-1.

Do not deduct on line 12 taxes paid or incurred for the production or collection of income, or for the management, conservation, or maintenance of property held to produce income. Report these taxes separately on line 10 of Schedules K and K-1.

See section 263A(a) for information on capitalization of allocable costs (including taxes) for any property.

Line 13—Interest

Include on line 13 only interest incurred in the trade or business activities of the corporation that is not claimed elsewhere on the return.

Do not include interest expense on debt used to purchase rental property or debt used in a rental activity. Interest allocable to a rental real estate activity is reported on Form 8825 and is used in arriving at net income (loss) from rental real estate activities on line 2 of Schedules K and K-1. Interest allocable to a rental activity other than a rental real estate activity is included on line 3b of Schedule K and is used in arriving at net income (loss) from a rental activity (other than a rental real estate activity). This net amount is reported on line 3c of Schedule K and line 3 of Schedule K-1.

Do not include interest expense clearly and directly allocable to portfolio or investment income. This interest expense is reported separately on line 11a of Schedule K.

Do not include interest on debt proceeds allocated to distributions made to shareholders during the tax year. Instead, report such interest on line 10 of Schedules K and K-1. To determine the amount to allocate to distributions to shareholders, see Notice 89-35, 1989-1 C.B. 675.

Do not include interest expense on debt required to be allocated to the production of qualified property. Interest allocable to certain property produced by an S corporation for its own use or for sale must be capitalized. The corporation must also capitalize any interest on debt that is allocable to an asset used to produce the above property. A shareholder may have to capitalize interest that the shareholder incurs during the tax year for the production expenditures of the S corporation. Similarly, interest incurred by an S corporation may have to be capitalized by a shareholder for the shareholder's own production expenditures. The information required by the shareholder to properly capitalize interest for this purpose must be provided by the corporation in an attachment for line 23 of Schedule K-1 (see the instructions on page 22 for Schedule K-1, line 23, item 9). See section 263A(f) and Notice 88-99, 1988-2 C.B. 422, for additional information.

Temporary Regulations section 1.163-8T gives rules for allocating interest expense among activities so that the limitations on passive activity losses, investment interest, and personal interest can be properly figured. Generally, interest expense is allocated in the same manner as debt is allocated. Debt is allocated by tracing disbursements of the debt proceeds to specific expenditures. These regulations give rules for tracing debt proceeds to expenditures.

Generally, prepaid interest can only be deducted over the period to which the prepayment applies. See section 461(g) for details.

Line 14—Depreciation

Enter on line 14a only the depreciation claimed on assets used in a trade or business activity. See the Instructions for Form 4562 or **Pub. 534,** Depreciation, to figure the amount of depreciation to enter on this line. Complete and attach Form 4562 only if the corporation placed property in service during 1993 or claims depreciation on any car or other listed property.

Do not include any section 179 expense deduction on this line. This amount is not deductible by the corporation. Instead, it is passed through to the shareholders on line 8 of Schedule K-1.

Line 15—Depletion

If the corporation claims a deduction for timber depletion, complete and attach **Form T,** Forest Industries Schedules.

Caution: *Do not deduct depletion for oil and gas properties. Each shareholder figures depletion on these properties under section 613A(c)(11). See the instructions on page 21 for Schedule K-1, line 23, item 2, for information on oil and gas depletion that must be supplied to the shareholders by the corporation.*

Line 17—Pension, Profit-Sharing, etc., Plans

Enter the deductible contributions not claimed elsewhere on the return made by the corporation for its employees under a qualified pension, profit-sharing, annuity, or simplified employee pension (SEP) plan, and under any other deferred compensation plan.

If the corporation contributes to an individual retirement arrangement (IRA) for employees, include the contribution in salaries and wages on page 1, line 8a, or Schedule A, line 3, and not on line 17.

Employers who maintain a pension, profit-sharing, or other funded deferred compensation plan, whether or not qualified under the Internal Revenue Code and whether or not a deduction is claimed for the current tax year, generally are required to file one of the forms listed below:

Form 5500, Annual Return/Report of Employee Benefit Plan (with 100 or more participants).

Form 5500-C/R, Return/Report of Employee Benefit Plan (with fewer than 100 participants).

Form 5500-EZ, Annual Return of One-Participant (Owners and Their Spouses) Pension Benefit Plan. Complete this form for a one-participant plan.

There are penalties for failure to file these forms on time and for overstating the pension plan deduction.

Line 18—Employee Benefit Programs

Enter amounts for fringe benefits paid or incurred on behalf of employees owning 2% or less of the corporation's stock. These fringe benefits include **(a)** up to $5,000 paid by reason of an employee's death to his estate or beneficiary, **(b)** employer contributions to certain accident and health plans, **(c)** the cost of up to $50,000 of group-term life insurance on an employee's life, and **(d)** meals and lodging furnished for the employer's convenience.

Do not deduct amounts that are an incidental part of a pension, profit-sharing, etc., plan included on line 17 or amounts reported elsewhere on the return.

Report amounts paid on behalf of more than 2% shareholders on line 7 or 8, whichever applies. A shareholder is considered to own more than 2% of the corporation's stock if that person owns on any day during the tax year more than 2% of the outstanding stock of the corporation or stock possessing more than 2% of the combined voting power of all stock of the corporation. See section 318 for attribution rules.

Line 19—Other Deductions

Attach your own schedule listing by type and amount all allowable deductions related to a trade or business activity for which there is no separate line on page 1 of Form 1120S. Enter the total on this line. Do not include items that must be reported separately on Schedules K and K-1.

An S corporation may not take the deduction for net operating losses provided by section 172 or the special deductions in sections 241 through 249 (except the election to amortize organizational expenditures under section 248). Subject to limitations, the corporation's net operating loss is allowed as a deduction from the shareholders' gross income. See section 1366.

Do not include qualified expenditures to which an election under section 59(e) may apply. See instructions for lines 16a and 16b of Schedule K-1 for details on treatment of these items.

Include on line 19 the deduction taken for amortization. See instructions for Form 4562 for more information. Complete and attach Form 4562 if the corporation is claiming amortization of costs that begin during its 1993 tax year.

Section 464(f) limits the deduction for certain expenditures of S corporations engaged in farming that use the cash method of accounting, and whose prepaid expenses for feed, seed, fertilizer, and other farm supplies, and the cost of poultry are more than 50% of other deductible farming expenses. Generally, any excess (amount over 50%) may be deducted only in the tax year the items are actually used or consumed. See section 464(f) for more information.

Do not deduct amounts paid or incurred to participate or intervene in any political campaign on behalf of a candidate for public office, or to influence the general public regarding legislative matters, elections, or referendums. In addition, fiscal year corporations generally cannot deduct expenses paid or incurred after 1993 to influence Federal or state legislation, or to influence the actions or positions of certain Federal executive branch officials. However, certain in-house lobbying expenditures that do not exceed $2,000 are still deductible. See section 162(e) for more details.

Do not deduct fines or penalties paid to a government for violating any law.

Meals, travel, and entertainment.— Generally, the corporation can deduct only 80% of the amount otherwise allowable for meals and entertainment expenses paid or incurred before 1994 in its trade or business. In addition, meals must not be lavish or extravagant; a bona fide business discussion must occur during, immediately before, or immediately after the meal; and an employee of the corporation must be present at the meal. See section 274(k)(2) for exceptions.

Fiscal year corporations should deduct on line 19 80% of their meals and entertainment expenses not fully deductible under section 274(n)(2) that were paid or incurred before 1994. Do not deduct on line 19 these meals and entertainment expenses paid or incurred after 1993; instead, state them separately on line 10 of Schedule K. See the instructions for Schedule K, line 10, for more details. Only 50% of these 1994 meals and entertainment expenses are deductible by shareholders with tax years beginning after 1993. However, 80% of these expenses are still deductible by shareholders with tax years beginning before 1994.

Additional limitations apply to deductions for gifts, skybox rentals, luxury water travel, convention expenses, and entertainment tickets. See section 274 and **Pub. 463,** Travel, Entertainment, and Gift Expenses, for details.

Fiscal year corporations are not allowed to deduct amounts paid or incurred after 1993 for membership dues in any club organized for business, pleasure, recreation, or other social purpose. This rule applies to all types of clubs, including business, social, athletic, luncheon, sporting, airline, and hotel clubs. In addition, no deduction is allowed for travel expenses paid or incurred after 1993 for an officer's or employee's spouse or dependent or other individual accompanying an officer or employee of the corporation, unless that spouse, dependent, or other individual is an employee of the corporation, and that person's travel is for a bona fide business purpose and would otherwise be deductible by that person.

Generally, a corporation can deduct all other ordinary and necessary travel and entertainment expenses paid or incurred in its trade or business. However, it cannot deduct an expense paid or incurred for a facility (such as a yacht or hunting lodge) used for an activity usually considered entertainment, amusement, or recreation.

Note: *The corporation may be able to deduct otherwise nondeductible meals, travel, and entertainment expenses if the amounts are treated as compensation and reported on Form W-2 for an employee or on Form 1099-MISC for an independent contractor.*

See Pub. 463 for more details.

Deduction for clean-fuel vehicle property and certain refueling property.—A deduction is allowed for part of the cost of qualified clean-fuel vehicle property and qualified clean-fuel vehicle refueling property (defined below) placed in service after June 30, 1993.

Qualified clean-fuel vehicle property includes:

1. The part of the basis of a new vehicle designed to use a clean-burning fuel that is attributable to an engine that uses that fuel (and its related fuel storage, delivery, and exhaust systems), and

2. New retrofit parts and components used to convert a motor vehicle to operate on a clean-burning fuel.

Clean-burning fuels are natural gas, liquefied natural gas, liquefied petroleum (LP) gas, hydrogen, electricity, and fuels containing at least 85% alcohol (including methanol and ethanol) or ether.

The deduction for most motor vehicles is limited to $2,000 per vehicle. A motor vehicle is any vehicle that has at least 4 wheels and is made for use on public roads. The limit is $5,000 per vehicle for trucks and vans with a gross vehicle weight (GVW) over 10,000 pounds but not over 26,000 pounds. For trucks and vans with a GVW over 26,000 pounds and buses that seat at least 20 adult passengers, the limit is $50,000 per vehicle.

Qualified clean-fuel vehicle refueling property is new depreciable property used to store or dispense clean-burning fuels (or to recharge an electric vehicle) that is located at the point where the fuel is delivered into the tank of the clean-fuel vehicle (or where the vehicle is recharged). The deduction for this property is limited to $100,000 per location.

For more details, see section 179A.

Line 21—Ordinary Income (Loss)

This is nonseparately computed income or loss as defined in section 1366(a)(2) attributable to trade or business activities of the corporation. This income or loss is entered on line 1 of Schedule K.

Line 21 income is not used in figuring the tax on line 22a or 22b. See the instructions for line 22a for figuring taxable income for purposes of line 22a or 22b tax.

Line 22a—Excess Net Passive Income Tax

Note: *The Revenue Reconciliation Act of 1993 increased the tax rate on excess net passive income from 34% to 35%.*

If the corporation has always been an S corporation, the excess net passive income tax does not apply. If the corporation has subchapter C earnings and profits (defined in section 1362(d)(3)(B)) at the close of its tax year, has passive investment income for the tax year that is in excess of 25% of gross receipts, **and** has taxable income at year end, the corporation must pay a tax on the excess net passive income. Complete lines 1 through 3 and line 9 of the worksheet below to make this determination. If line 2 is greater than line 3 and the corporation has taxable income (see instructions for line 9 of worksheet), it must pay the tax. Complete a separate schedule using the format of lines 1 through 11 of the worksheet below to figure the tax. Enter the tax on line 22a, page 1, Form 1120S, and attach the computation schedule to Form 1120S.

Reduce each item of passive income passed through to shareholders by its portion of tax on line 22a. See section 1366(f)(3).

Line 22b—Tax From Schedule D (Form 1120S)

If the corporation elected to be an S corporation before 1987 (or elected to be an S corporation during 1987 or 1988 and qualifies for transitional relief from the built-in gains tax), see instructions for Part III of Schedule D (Form 1120S) to determine if the corporation is liable for the capital gains tax.

Worksheet for Line 22a

1. Enter gross receipts for the tax year (see section 1362(d)(3)(C) for gross receipts from the sale of capital assets)* . . . . ________
2. Enter passive investment income as defined in Regulations section 1.1362-2(c)(5)* . . . . ________
3. Enter 25% of line 1 (If line 2 is less than line 3, stop here. You are not liable for this tax.) . . . . ________
4. Excess passive investment income—Subtract line 3 from line 2 . . . . ________
5. Enter deductions directly connected with the production of income on line 2 (see section 1375(b)(2))* . . . . ________
6. Net passive income—Subtract line 5 from line 2 . . . . ________
7. Divide amount on line 4 by amount on line 2 . . . . ________ %
8. Excess net passive income—Multiply line 6 by line 7 . . . . . . ________
9. Enter taxable income (see instructions for taxable income below) . . . ________
10. Enter smaller of line 8 or line 9 . . ________
11. Excess net passive income tax—Enter 35% of line 10. Enter here and on line 22a, page 1, Form 1120S . . . ________

*Income and deductions on lines 1, 2, and 5 are from total operations for the tax year. This includes applicable income and expenses from page 1, Form 1120S, as well as those reported separately on Schedule K. See section 1375(b)(4) for an exception regarding lines 2 and 5.

Line 9 of Worksheet—Taxable income

Line 9 taxable income is defined in Regulations section 1.1374-1(d). Figure this income by completing lines 1 through 28 of **Form 1120,** U.S. Corporation Income Tax Return. Include the Form 1120 computation with the worksheet computation you attach to Form 1120S. You do not have to attach the schedules, etc., called for on Form 1120. However, you may want to complete certain Form 1120 schedules, such as Schedule D (Form 1120), if you have capital gains or losses.

If the corporation made its election to be an S corporation after 1986, see the instructions for Part IV of Schedule D to determine if the corporation is liable for the built-in gains tax.

Note: *For purposes of line 19 of Part III and line 25 of Part IV of Schedule D, taxable income is defined in section 1375(b)(1)(B) and is generally figured in the same manner as taxable income for line 9 of the line 22a worksheet on page 13.*

Line 22c

Include in the total for line 22c the following:

Investment credit recapture tax.—Section 1371(d) provides that an S corporation is liable for investment credit recapture attributable to credits allowed for tax years for which the corporation was not an S corporation.

Figure the corporation's investment credit recapture tax by completing **Form 4255,** Recapture of Investment Credit. Include the tax in the total amount to be entered on line 22c. Write to the left of the line 22c total the amount of recapture tax and the words "Tax From Form 4255," and attach Form 4255 to Form 1120S.

LIFO recapture tax.—If the corporation used the LIFO inventory pricing method for its last tax year as a C corporation, the corporation may be liable for the additional tax due to LIFO recapture under section 1363(d).

The LIFO recapture tax is figured for the last tax year the corporation was a C corporation. See the Instructions for Forms 1120 and 1120-A for details. The LIFO tax is paid in four equal installments. The first installment is due with the corporation's Form 1120 (or 1120-A) for the corporation's last tax year as a C corporation, and each of the remaining installments is paid with the corporation's Form 1120S for the 3 succeeding tax years. Include this year's installment in the total amount to be entered on line 22c. Write to the left of the total on line 22c the installment amount and the words "LIFO tax."

Interest due under the look-back method for completed long-term contracts.—If the corporation completed **Form 8697,** Interest Computation Under the Look-Back Method for Completed Long-Term Contracts, and owes interest, write to the left of the line 22c total the amount of interest and "From Form 8697." Attach the completed form to Form 1120S.

Line 23d

If the S corporation is a beneficiary of a trust and the trust makes a section 643(g) election to credit its estimated tax overpayments to its beneficiaries, include the corporation's share of the overpayment (reported to the corporation on Schedule K-1 (Form 1041)) in the total amount entered on line 23d. Also, to the left of line 23d, write "T" and the amount of the overpayment.

Line 24—Estimated Tax Penalty

A corporation that fails to make estimated tax payments when due may be subject to an underpayment penalty for the period of underpayment. Use **Form 2220,** Underpayment of Estimated Tax by Corporations, to see if the corporation owes a penalty and to figure the amount of the penalty. If you attach Form 2220 to Form 1120S, be sure to check the box on line 24 and enter the amount of any penalty on this line.

Schedule A—Cost of Goods Sold

Section 263A Uniform Capitalization Rules

The uniform capitalization rules of section 263A are discussed under **Limitations on Deductions** on page 10. See those instructions before completing Schedule A.

Line 4—Additional Section 263A Costs

An entry is required on this line only for corporations that have elected a simplified method of accounting. For corporations that have elected the simplified production method, additional section 263A costs are generally those costs, other than interest, that were not capitalized or included in inventory costs under the corporation's method of accounting immediately prior to the effective date in Temporary Regulations section 1.263A-1T that are now required to be capitalized under section 263A.

For corporations that have elected a simplified resale method, additional section 263A costs are generally those costs incurred with respect to the following categories: off-site storage or warehousing; purchasing; handling, processing, assembly, and repackaging; and general and administrative costs (mixed service costs). Enter on line 4 the balance of section 263A costs paid or incurred during the tax year not included on lines 2, 3, and 5. See Temporary Regulations section 1.263A-1T for more information.

Line 5—Other Costs

Enter on line 5 any other inventoriable costs paid or incurred during the tax year not entered on lines 2 through 4.

Line 7—Inventory at End of Year

See Temporary Regulations section 1.263A-1T for details on figuring the amount of additional section 263A costs to be capitalized and added to ending inventory.

Lines 9a through 9e—Inventory Valuation Methods

Inventories can be valued at **(a)** cost, **(b)** cost or market value (whichever is lower), or **(c)** any other method approved by the IRS that conforms to the provisions of the applicable regulations.

Corporations that use erroneous valuation methods must change to a method permitted for Federal income tax purposes. To make this change, use Form 3115.

On line 9a, check the method(s) used for valuing inventories. Under "lower of cost or market," *market* generally applies to normal market conditions when there is a current bid price prevailing at the date the inventory is valued. When no regular open market exists or when quotations are nominal because of inactive market conditions, use fair market prices from the most reliable sales or purchase transactions that occurred near the date the inventory is valued.

Inventory may be valued below cost when the merchandise is unsalable at normal prices or unusable in the normal way because the goods are "subnormal" due to damage, imperfections, shop wear, etc., within the meaning of Regulations section 1.471-2(c). These goods may be valued at a current bona fide selling price minus direct cost of disposition (but not less than scrap value) if such a price can be established.

If this is the first year the last-in, first-out (LIFO) inventory method was either adopted or extended to inventory goods not previously valued under the LIFO method provided in section 472, attach **Form 970,** Application To Use LIFO Inventory Method, or a statement with the information required by Form 970. Also check the LIFO box on line 9b. On line 9c, enter the amount or the percent of total closing inventories covered under section 472. Estimates are acceptable.

If the corporation changed or extended its inventory method to LIFO and has had to "write up" its opening inventory to cost in the year of election, report the effect of this write-up as income (line 5, page 1) proportionately over a 3-year period that begins with the tax year of the election (section 472(d)).

See Pub. 538 for more information on inventory valuation methods.

Schedule B—Other Information

Be sure to answer the questions and provide other information in items 1 through 10.

Line 5—Foreign Financial Accounts

Answer "Yes" to question 5 if either **1** or **2** below applies to the corporation. Otherwise, check the "No" box.

1. At any time during calendar year 1993, the corporation had an interest in or signature or other authority over a bank account, securities account, or other financial account in a foreign country; AND

- The combined value of the accounts was more than $10,000 during the calendar year; AND

• The accounts were NOT with a U.S. military banking facility operated by a U.S. financial institution.

2. The corporation owns more than 50% of the stock in any corporation that would answer the question "Yes" based on item **1** above.

Get **Form TD F 90-22.1,** Report of Foreign Bank and Financial Accounts, to see if the corporation is considered to have an interest in or signature or other authority over a bank account, securities account, or other financial account in a foreign country.

If you answered "Yes" to question 5, file Form TD F 90-22.1 by June 30, 1994, with the Department of the Treasury at the address shown on the form. Form TD F 90-22.1 is not a tax return, so do not file it with Form 1120S. Form TD F 90-22.1 may be ordered by calling our toll-free number, 1-800-829-3676.

Line 9

Complete line 9 if the corporation **(a)** filed its election to be an S corporation after 1986; **(b)** was a C corporation before it elected to be an S corporation **or** the corporation acquired an asset with a basis determined by reference to its basis (or the basis of any other property) in the hands of a C corporation; and **(c)** has net unrealized built-in gain (defined below) in excess of the net recognized built-in gain from prior years.

The corporation is liable for section 1374 tax if **(a), (b),** and **(c)** above apply and it has a net recognized built-in gain (section 1374(d)(2)) for its tax year.

Section 633(d)(8) of the Tax Reform Act of 1986 provides transitional relief from the built-in gains tax for certain corporations that elected to be S corporations in 1987 or 1988. However, the relief rule does **not** apply to ordinary gains or losses (determined without regard to section 1239), gains or losses from the disposition of capital assets held 6 months or less, and gains from the disposition of any asset acquired by the corporation with a substituted basis if a principal purpose for acquiring the asset was to secure transitional relief from the built-in gains tax. See the instructions for Part IV of Schedule D (Form 1120S) for more information.

The corporation's net unrealized built-in gain is the amount, if any, by which the fair market value of the assets of the corporation at the beginning of its first S corporation year (or as of the date the assets were acquired, for any asset with a basis determined by reference to its basis (or the basis of any other property) in the hands of a C corporation) exceeds the aggregate adjusted basis of such assets at that time.

Enter on line 9 the corporation's net unrealized built-in gain reduced by the net recognized built-in gain for prior years. See sections 1374(c)(2) and (d)(1).

Line 10

Check the box on line 10 if the corporation was a C corporation in a prior year and has subchapter C earnings and profits (E&P) at the close of its 1993 tax year. For this purpose, subchapter C E&P is E&P of any corporation for any tax year when it was not an S corporation. See sections 1362(d)(3)(B) and 312 for other details. If the corporation has subchapter C E&P, it may be liable for tax imposed on excess net passive income. See the instructions for line 22a, page 1, of Form 1120S for details on this tax.

Designation of Tax Matters Person (TMP)

If the S corporation is subject to sections 6241 through 6245 (consolidated audit procedures), it may designate a shareholder as the TMP for the tax year for which the return is filed by completing the **Designation of Tax Matters Person** section at the bottom of page 2 of Form 1120S. Temporary Regulations section 301.6241-1T provides an exception to the consolidated provisions for small S corporations with five or fewer shareholders each of whom is a natural person or an estate. See **Item G—Consolidated Audit Procedures** on page 9 for other details.

General Instructions for Schedules K and K-1—Shareholders' Shares of Income, Credits, Deductions, etc.

Purpose of Schedules

The corporation is liable for taxes on lines 22a, b, and c, page 1, Form 1120S. Shareholders are liable for income tax on their shares of the corporation's income (reduced by any taxes paid by the corporation on income) and must include their share of the income on their tax return whether or not it is distributed to them. Unlike most partnership income, S corporation income is **not** self-employment income and is not subject to self-employment tax.

Schedule K is a summary schedule of all the shareholders' shares of the corporation's income, deductions, credits, etc. Schedule K-1 shows each shareholder's separate share. A copy of each shareholder's Schedule K-1 must be attached to the Form 1120S filed with the IRS. A copy is kept as a part of the corporation's records, and the corporation must give each shareholder a separate copy.

The total pro rata share items (column (b)) of all Schedules K-1 should equal the amount reported on the same line of Schedule K. Lines 1 through 20 of Schedule K correspond to lines 1 through 20 of Schedule K-1. Other lines do not correspond, but instructions will explain the differences.

Be sure to give each shareholder a copy of the Shareholder's Instructions for Schedule K-1 (Form 1120S). These instructions are available separately from Schedule K-1 at most IRS offices.

Note: *Instructions that apply only to line items reported on Schedule K-1 may be prepared and given to each shareholder instead of the instructions printed by the IRS.*

Substitute Forms

The corporation **does not** need IRS approval to use a substitute Schedule K-1 if it is an exact copy of the IRS schedule, **or** if it contains only those lines the taxpayer is required to use, and the lines have the same numbers and titles and are in the same order as on the IRS Schedule K-1. In either case, the substitute schedule must include the OMB number and either **(a)** the Shareholder's Instructions for Schedule K-1 (Form 1120S) or **(b)** instructions that apply to the items reported on Schedule K-1 (Form 1120S).

The corporation must request IRS approval to use other substitute Schedules K-1. To request approval by U.S. mail, write to Internal Revenue Service, Attention: Substitute Forms Program Coordinator, T:I:F, P.O. Box 969, Oxon Hill, MD 20750. Requests sent by other carriers (e.g., Federal Express, United Parcel Service) should be addressed to: Internal Revenue Service, Attention: Substitute Forms Program Coordinator, T:I:F, 6710 Oxon Hill Road, 4th Floor, Oxon Hill, MD 20745.

The corporation may be subject to a penalty if it files a substitute Schedule K-1 that does not conform to the specifications of Rev. Proc. 92-21, 1992-1 C.B. 709.

Shareholder's Pro Rata Share Items

Items of income, loss, deductions, etc., are allocated to a shareholder on a daily basis, according to the number of shares of stock held by the shareholder on each day during the tax year of the corporation. See **Item A** on page 16.

A transferee shareholder (rather than the transferor) is considered to be the owner of stock on the day it is transferred.

Special rule.—If a shareholder terminates his or her interest in a corporation during the tax year, the corporation, with the consent of all shareholders (including the one whose interest is terminated), may elect to allocate income and expenses, etc., as if the corporation's tax year consisted of 2 tax years, the first of which ends on the date of the shareholder's termination. To make the election, the corporation must file a statement of election with the return for the tax year of election and attach a statement of consent signed by all shareholders. If the election is made, write "Section 1377(a)(2) Election Made" at the top of each Schedule K-1.

See section 1377(a)(2) and Temporary Regulations section 18.1377-1 for details.

Specific Instructions (Schedule K Only)

Enter the total pro rata share amount for each applicable line item on Schedule K.

Specific Instructions (Schedule K-1 Only)

General Information

On each Schedule K-1, complete the date spaces at the top; enter the names, addresses, and identifying numbers of the shareholder and corporation; complete items A through D; and enter the shareholder's pro rata share of each item. **Schedule K-1 must be prepared and given to each shareholder on or before the day on which Form 1120S is filed.**

Note: *Space has been provided on line 23 (Supplemental Information) of Schedule K-1 for the corporation to provide additional information to shareholders. This space, if sufficient, should be used in place of any attached schedules required for any lines on Schedule K-1, or other amounts not shown on lines 1 through 22 of Schedule K-1. Please be sure to identify the applicable line number next to the information entered below line 23.*

Special Reporting Requirements for Corporations With Multiple Activities

If items of income, loss, deduction, or credit from more than one activity (determined for purposes of the passive activity loss and credit limitations) are reported on lines 1, 2, or 3 of Schedule K-1, the corporation must provide information for each activity to its shareholders. See **Passive Activity Reporting Requirements** on page 8 for details on the reporting requirements.

Special Reporting Requirements for At-Risk Activities

If the corporation is involved in one or more at-risk activities for which a loss is reported on Schedule K-1, the corporation must report information separately for each at-risk activity. See section 465(c) for a definition of at-risk activities.

For each at-risk activity, the following information must be provided on an attachment to Schedule K-1:

1. A statement that the information is a breakdown of at-risk activity loss amounts.

2. The identity of the at-risk activity; the loss amount for the activity; other income and deductions; and other information that relates to the activity.

Specific Items

Item A

If there was no change in shareholders or in the relative interest in stock the shareholders owned during the tax year, enter the percentage of total stock owned by each shareholder during the tax year. For example, if shareholders X and Y each owned 50% for the entire tax year, enter 50% in item A for each shareholder. Each shareholder's pro rata share items (lines 1 through 20 of Schedule K-1) are figured by multiplying the Schedule K amount on the corresponding line of Schedule K by the percentage in item A.

If there was a change in shareholders or in the relative interest in stock the shareholders owned during the tax year, each shareholder's percentage of ownership is weighted for the number of days in the tax year that stock was owned. For example, A and B each held 50% for half the tax year and A, B, and C held 40%, 40%, and 20%, respectively, for the remaining half of the tax year. The percentage of ownership for the year for A, B, and C is figured as follows and is then entered in item A.

	a	b	c (a × b)	
	% of total stock owned	% of tax year held	% of ownership for the year	
A	50 40	50 50	25 +20	45
B	50 40	50 50	25 +20	45
C	20	50	10	10
Total				100%

If there was a change in shareholders or in the relative interest in stock the shareholders owned during the tax year, each shareholder's pro rata share items can also be figured on a daily basis, based on the percentage of stock held by the shareholder on each day. See sections 1377(a)(1) and (2) for details.

Item B

Enter the Internal Revenue Service Center address where the Form 1120S, to which a copy of this K-1 was attached, was or will be filed.

Item C

If the corporation is a registration-required tax shelter, it must enter its tax shelter registration number in item C. If the corporation invested in a registration-required shelter, the corporation must also furnish a copy of its Form 8271 to its shareholders. See Form 8271 for more information.

Specific Instructions (Schedules K and K-1, Except as Noted)

Income (Loss)

Reminder: Before entering income items on Schedule K or K-1, be sure to reduce the items of income for the following:

1. Built-in gains tax (Schedule D, Part IV, line 31).—Each recognized built-in gain item (within the meaning of section 1374(d)(3)) is reduced by its proportionate share of the built-in gains tax.

2. Capital gains tax (Schedule D, Part III, line 23).—The section 1231 gain included on line 5 or 6 of Schedule K is reduced by this tax.

3. Excess net passive income tax (line 22a, page 1, Form 1120S).—Each item of passive investment income (within the meaning of Regulations section 1.1362-2(c)(5)) is reduced by its proportionate share of the net passive income tax.

Line 1—Ordinary Income (Loss) From Trade or Business Activities

Enter the amount from line 21, page 1. Enter the income or loss without reference to **(a)** shareholders' basis in the stock of the corporation and in any indebtedness of the corporation to the shareholders (section 1366(d)), **(b)** shareholders' at-risk limitations, and **(c)** shareholders' passive activity limitations. These limitations, if applicable, are determined at the shareholder level.

If the corporation is involved in more than one trade or business activity, see **Passive Activity Reporting Requirements** on page 8 for details on the information to be reported for each activity. If an at-risk activity loss is reported on line 1, see **Special Reporting Requirements for At-Risk Activities** above.

Line 2—Net Income (Loss) From Rental Real Estate Activities

Enter the net income or loss from rental real estate activities of the corporation from **Form 8825,** Rental Real Estate Income and Expenses of a Partnership or an S Corporation. Each Form 8825 has space for reporting the income and expenses of up to eight properties.

If the corporation has income or loss from more than one rental real estate activity reported on line 2, see **Passive Activity Reporting Requirements** on page 8 for details on the information to be reported for each activity. If an at-risk activity loss is reported on line 2, see **Special Reporting Requirements for At-Risk Activities** above.

If a loss from a qualified low-income housing project is reported on line 2, identify this loss on a statement attached to the Schedule K-1 of each shareholder who is a qualified investor in the project. Any loss sustained by a qualified investor in a qualified low-income housing project for any tax year in the relief period is not subject to the passive activity loss limitations under section 502 of the Tax Reform Act of 1986. See Act section 502 for definitions and other information on qualified low-income housing projects.

Line 3—Income and Expenses of Other Rental Activities

Enter on lines 3a and 3b of Schedule K (line 3 of Schedule K-1) the income and expenses of rental activities other than the income and expenses reported on Form 8825. If the corporation has more than one rental activity reported on line 3, see **Passive Activity Reporting Requirements** on page 8 for details on the information to be reported for each activity. If an at-risk activity loss is reported on line 3, see **Special Reporting Requirements for At-Risk Activities** on page 16. Also see **Rental activities** on page 6 for a definition and other details on other rental activities.

Lines 4a Through 4f—Portfolio Income (Loss)

Enter portfolio income (loss) on lines 4a through 4f. See **Portfolio income** on page 7 for a definition of portfolio income. Do not reduce portfolio income by deductions allocated to it. Such deductions (other than interest expense) are reported on line 9 of Schedules K and K-1. Interest expense allocable to portfolio income is generally investment interest expense and is reported on line 11a of Schedules K and K-1.

Lines 4a and 4b.—Enter only taxable interest and dividends that are portfolio income. Interest income derived in the ordinary course of the corporation's trade or business, such as interest charged on receivable balances, is reported on line 5, page 1, Form 1120S. See Temporary Regulations section 1.469-2T(c)(3).

Lines 4d and 4e.—Enter on line 4d the net short-term capital gain or loss from line 6 of Schedule D (Form 1120S) that is portfolio income. Enter on line 4e the net long-term capital gain or loss from line 12 of Schedule D (Form 1120S) that is portfolio income. If any gain or loss from lines 6 and 12 of Schedule D is not portfolio income (e.g., gain or loss from the disposition of nondepreciable personal property used in a trade or business), do not report this income or loss on lines 4d and 4e. Instead, report it on line 6 of Schedules K and K-1. If the income or loss is attributable to more than one activity, report the income or loss amount separately for each activity on an attachment to Schedule K-1 and identify the activity to which the income or loss relates.

Line 4f.—Enter any other portfolio income not reported on lines 4a through 4e.

If the corporation holds a residual interest in a REMIC, report on an attachment for line 4f each shareholder's share of taxable income (net loss) from the REMIC (line 1b of Schedule Q (Form 1066)); excess inclusion (line 2c of Schedule Q (Form 1066)); and section 212 expenses (line 3b of Schedule Q (Form 1066)). Because Schedule Q (Form 1066) is a quarterly statement, the corporation must follow the Schedule Q (Form 1066) Instructions for Residual Interest Holder to figure the amounts to report to shareholders for the corporation's tax year.

Line 5—Net Gain (Loss) Under Section 1231 (Other Than Due to Casualty or Theft)

Enter the gain (loss) under section 1231 shown on line 8 of Form 4797. Do not include net gains or losses from involuntary conversions due to casualties or thefts on this line. Instead, report them on line 6.

Line 6—Other Income (Loss)

Enter any other item of income or loss not included on lines 1 through 5, such as:

1. Recoveries of tax benefit items (section 111).

2. Gambling gains and losses (section 165(d)).

3. Net gain (loss) from involuntary conversions due to casualty or theft. The amount for this item is shown on **Form 4684,** Casualties and Thefts, line 38a or 38b.

4. Any net gain or loss from section 1256 contracts from **Form 6781,** Gains and Losses From Section 1256 Contracts and Straddles.

Deductions

Line 7—Charitable Contributions

Enter the amount of charitable contributions paid by the corporation during its tax year. On an attachment to Schedules K and K-1, show separately the dollar amount of contributions subject to each of the 50%, 30%, and 20% of adjusted gross income limits.

Generally, no deduction is allowed for any contribution of $250 or more made after 1993 unless the corporation obtains a written acknowledgement from the charitable organization by the due date (including extensions) of the corporation's return, or if earlier, the date the corporation files its return. For details, see section 170(f)(8).

Certain contributions made to an organization conducting lobbying activities are not deductible. See section 170(f)(9) for more details.

If the corporation contributes property other than cash and the deduction claimed for such property exceeds $500, complete **Form 8283,** Noncash Charitable Contributions, and attach it to Form 1120S. The corporation must give a copy of its Form 8283 to every shareholder if the deduction for any item or group of similar items of contributed property exceeds $5,000, even if the amount allocated to any shareholder is $5,000 or less.

If the deduction for an item or group of similar items of contributed property is $5,000 or less, the corporation must report each shareholder's pro rata share of the amount of noncash contributions to enable individual shareholders to complete their own Forms 8283. See the Instructions for Form 8283 for more information.

If the corporation made a qualified conservation contribution under section 170(h), also include the fair market value of the underlying property before and after the donation, as well as the type of legal interest contributed, and describe the conservation purpose furthered by the donation. Give a copy of this information to each shareholder.

Line 8—Section 179 Expense Deduction

An S corporation may elect to expense part of the cost of certain tangible property that the corporation purchased during the tax year for use in its trade or business or certain rental activities. See the Instructions for Form 4562 for more information.

Complete Part I of Form 4562 to figure the corporation's section 179 expense deduction. The corporation does not deduct the expense itself but passes the expense through to its shareholders. Attach Form 4562 to Form 1120S and show the total section 179 expense deduction on Schedule K, line 8. Report each individual shareholder's pro rata share on Schedule K-1, line 8. Do not complete line 8 of Schedule K-1 for any shareholder that is an estate or trust.

See the instructions for line 23 of Schedule K-1, item 3, for any recapture of a section 179 amount.

Line 9—Deductions Related to Portfolio Income (Loss)

Enter on line 9 the deductions clearly and directly allocable to portfolio income (other than interest expense). Interest expense related to portfolio income is investment interest expense and is reported on line 11a of Schedules K and K-1. Generally, the line 9 expenses are section 212 expenses and are subject to section 212 limitations at the shareholder level.

Note: *No deduction is allowed under section 212 for expenses allocable to a convention, seminar, or similar meeting. Because these expenses are not deductible by shareholders, the corporation does not report these expenses on line 9 or line 10. The expenses are nondeductible and are reported as such on line 19 of Schedules K and K-1.*

Line 10—Other Deductions

Enter any other deductions not included on lines 7, 8, 9, and 15e. On an attachment, identify the deduction and amount, and if the corporation has more than one activity, the activity to which the deduction relates.

Examples of items to be reported on an attachment to line 10 include:

- Amounts (other than investment interest required to be reported on line 11a of Schedules K and K-1) paid by the corporation that would be allowed as itemized deductions on a shareholder's income tax return if they were paid directly by a shareholder for the same purpose. These amounts include, but are not limited to, expenses under section 212 for the production of income other than from the corporation's trade or business.

- Any penalty on early withdrawal of savings not reported on line 9 because the corporation withdrew funds from its time savings deposit before its maturity.
- Soil and water conservation expenditures (section 175).
- Expenditures paid or incurred for the removal of architectural and transportation barriers to the elderly and disabled that the corporation has elected to treat as a current expense. See section 190.
- Interest expense allocated to debt-financed distributions. See Notice 89-35, 1989-1 C.B. 675, for more information.
- If there was a gain (loss) from a casualty or theft to property not used in a trade or business or for income producing purposes, provide each shareholder with the needed information to complete Form 4684.
- Meals and entertainment expenses paid or incurred after 1993 not fully deductible under section 274(n)(2). Identify these expenses as "1994 meals and entertainment expenses."

Investment Interest

Lines 11a and 11b must be completed for all shareholders.

Line 11a—Investment Interest Expense

Include on this line the interest properly allocable to debt on property held for investment purposes. Property held for investment includes property that produces income (unless derived in the ordinary course of a trade or business) from interest, dividends, annuities, or royalties; and gains from the disposition of property that produces those types of income or is held for investment.

Investment interest expense **does not** include interest expense allocable to a passive activity.

Report investment interest expense only on line 11a of Schedules K and K-1.

The amount on line 11a will be deducted by individual shareholders on Form 1040 after applying the investment interest expense limitations of section 163(d).

For more information, see **Form 4952,** Investment Interest Expense Deduction.

Lines 11b(1) and 11b(2)—Investment Income and Expenses

Enter on line 11b(1) only the investment income included on lines 4a, b, c, and f of Schedule K-1. Do not include other portfolio gains or losses on this line.

Enter on line 11b(2) only the investment expense included on line 9 of Schedule K-1.

If there are other items of investment income or expense included in the amounts that are required to be passed through separately to the shareholders on Schedule K-1, such as net short-term capital gain or loss, net long-term capital gain or loss, and other portfolio gains or losses, give each shareholder a schedule identifying these amounts.

Investment income includes gross income from property held for investment, the excess of net gain attributable to the disposition of property held for investment over net capital gain from the disposition of property held for investment, and any net capital gain from the disposition of property held for investment that each shareholder elects to include in investment income under section 163(d)(4)(B)(iii). Generally, investment income and investment expenses do not include any income or expenses from a passive activity. See Regulations section 1.469-2(f)(10) for exceptions.

Property subject to a net lease is not treated as investment property because it is subject to the passive loss rules. Do not reduce investment income by losses from passive activities.

Investment expenses are deductible expenses (other than interest) directly connected with the production of investment income. See the Instructions for Form 4952 for more information on investment income and expenses.

Credits

Note: *If the corporation has credits from more than one trade or business activity on line 12a or 13, or from more than one rental activity on line 12b, 12c, 12d, or 12e, it must report separately on an attachment to Schedule K-1, the amount of each credit and provide any other applicable activity information listed in **Passive Activity Reporting Requirements** on page 8.*

Line 12a—Credit for Alcohol Used as Fuel

Enter on line 12a of Schedule K the credit for alcohol used as fuel attributable to trade or business activities. Enter on line 12d or 12e the credit for alcohol used as fuel attributable to rental activities. Figure the credit on **Form 6478,** Credit for Alcohol Used as Fuel, and attach it to Form 1120S. The credit must be included in income on page 1, line 5, of Form 1120S. See section 40(f) for an election the corporation can make to have the credit not apply.

Enter each shareholder's share of the credit for alcohol used as fuel on line 12a, 12d, or 12e of Schedule K-1.

If this credit includes the small ethanol producer credit, identify on a statement attached to each Schedule K-1 **(a)** the amount of the small producer credit included in the total credit allocated to the shareholder, **(b)** the number of gallons of qualified ethanol fuel production allocated to the shareholder, and **(c)** the shareholder's pro rata share in gallons of the corporation's productive capacity for alcohol.

Line 12b—Low-Income Housing Credit

Section 42 provides for a low-income housing credit that may be claimed by owners of low-income residential rental buildings. If shareholders are eligible to claim the low-income housing credit, complete the applicable parts of **Form 8586,** Low-Income Housing Credit, and attach it to Form 1120S. Enter the credit figured by the corporation on Form 8586, and any low-income housing credit received from other entities in which the corporation is allowed to invest, on the applicable line as explained below. The corporation must also complete and attach **Form 8609,** Low-Income Housing Credit Allocation Certification, and **Schedule A (Form 8609),** Annual Statement, to Form 1120S. See the Instructions for Form 8586 and Form 8609 for information on completing these forms.

Note: *No credit may be claimed for any building in a qualified low-income housing project for which any person was allowed to claim a loss from the project by reason of not being subject to the passive activity limitations (see section 502 of the Tax Reform Act of 1986 for details).*

Line 12b(1).—If the corporation invested in a partnership to which the provisions of section 42(j)(5) apply, report on line 12b(1) the credit the partnership reported to the corporation on line 13b(1) of Schedule K-1 (Form 1065). If the corporation invested **before 1990** in a section 42(j)(5) partnership, also include on this line any credit the partnership reported to the corporation on line 13b(3) of Schedule K-1 (Form 1065).

Line 12b(2).—Report on line 12b(2) any low-income housing credit for property placed in service before 1990 and not reported on line 12b(1). This includes any credit from a building placed in service before 1990 in a project owned by the corporation and any credit from a partnership reported to the corporation on line 13b(2) of Schedule K-1 (Form 1065). Also include on this line any credit from a partnership reported to the corporation on line 13b(4) of Schedule K-1 (Form 1065), if the corporation invested in that partnership **before 1990.**

Line 12b(3).—If the corporation invested **after 1989** in a partnership to which the provisions of section 42(j)(5) apply, report on line 12b(3) the credit the partnership reported to the corporation on line 13b(3) of Schedule K-1 (Form 1065).

Line 12b(4).—Report on line 12b(4) any low-income housing credit for property placed in service after 1989 and not reported on any other line. This includes any credit from a building placed in service after 1989 in a project owned by the corporation and any credit from a partnership reported to the corporation on line 13b(4) of Schedule K-1 (Form 1065), if the corporation invested in that partnership **after 1989.**

Line 12c—Qualified Rehabilitation Expenditures Related to Rental Real Estate Activities

Enter total qualified rehabilitation expenditures related to rental real estate activities of the corporation. For line 12c of Schedule K, complete the applicable lines of **Form 3468,** Investment Credit, that apply to qualified rehabilitation expenditures for property related to rental real estate activities of the corporation for which income or loss is reported on line 2 of Schedule K. See Form 3468 for details on qualified rehabilitation expenditures. Attach Form 3468 to Form 1120S.

For line 12c of Schedule K-1, enter each shareholder's pro rata share of the expenditures. On the dotted line to the left of the entry space for line 12c, enter the line number of Form 3468 on which the shareholder should report the expenditures. If there is more than one type of expenditure, or the expenditures are from more than one line 2 activity, report this information separately for each expenditure or activity on an attachment to Schedules K and K-1.

Note: *Qualified rehabilitation expenditures **not** related to rental real estate activities must be listed separately on line 23 of Schedule K-1.*

Line 12d—Credits (Other Than Credits Shown on Lines 12b and 12c) Related to Rental Real Estate Activities

Enter on line 12d any other credit (other than credits on lines 12b and 12c) related to rental real estate activities. On the dotted line to the left of the entry space for line 12d, identify the type of credit. If there is more than one type of credit or the credit is from more than one line 2 activity, report this information separately for each credit or activity on an attachment to Schedules K and K-1. These credits may include any type of credit listed in the instructions for line 13.

Line 12e—Credits Related to Other Rental Activities

Enter on line 12e any credit related to other rental activities for which income or loss is reported on line 3 of Schedules K and K-1. On the dotted line to the left of the entry space for line 12e, identify the type of credit. If there is more than one type of credit or the credit is from more than one line 3 activity, report this information separately for each credit or activity on an attachment to Schedules K and K-1. These credits may include any type of credit listed in the instructions for line 13.

Line 13—Other Credits

Enter on line 13 any other credit (other than credits or expenditures shown or listed for lines 12a through 12e of Schedules K and K-1). On the dotted line to the left of the entry space for line 13, identify the type of credit. If there is more than one type of credit or the credit is from more than one activity, report this information separately for each credit or activity on an attachment to Schedules K and K-1.

The credits to be reported on line 13 and other required attachments follow:

- **Nonconventional source fuel credit.** Figure this credit on a separate schedule and attach it to Form 1120S. See section 29 for rules on figuring the credit.
- **Unused investment credit from cooperatives.** If the corporation is a member of a cooperative that passes an unused investment credit through to its members, the credit is in turn passed through to the corporation's shareholders.
- **Credit for backup withholding on dividends, interest, or patronage dividends.**
- **Credit for increasing research activities and orphan drug credit.** Complete and attach **Form 6765,** Credit for Increasing Research Activities (or for claiming the orphan drug credit), to Form 1120S.
- **Jobs credit.** Complete and attach **Form 5884,** Jobs Credit, to Form 1120S.
- **Disabled access credit.** Complete and attach **Form 8826,** Disabled Access Credit, to Form 1120S.
- **Enhanced oil recovery credit.** Complete and attach **Form 8830,** Enhanced Oil Recovery Credit, to Form 1120S.
- **Qualified electric vehicle credit.** Complete and attach **Form 8834,** Qualified Electric Vehicle Credit, to Form 1120S.
- **Renewable electricity production credit.** Complete and attach **Form 8835,** Renewable Electricity Production Credit, to Form 1120S.
- **Indian employment credit.** Complete and attach **Form 8845,** Indian Employment Credit, to Form 1120S.
- **Employer social security credit.** Complete and attach **Form 8846,** Credit for Employer Social Security Taxes Paid on Certain Employee Cash Tips, to Form 1120S.
- **Credit for contributions to certain community development corporations.** Complete and attach **Form 8847,** Credit for Contributions to Certain Community Development Corporations, to Form 1120S.

See the instructions for line 21 (Schedule K) and line 23 (Schedule K-1) to report expenditures qualifying for the **(a)** rehabilitation credit not related to rental real estate activities, **(b)** energy credit, or **(c)** reforestation credit.

Adjustments and Tax Preference Items

Lines 14a through 14e must be completed for all shareholders.

Enter items of income and deductions that are adjustments or tax preference items. Get **Form 6251,** Alternative Minimum Tax—Individuals, Schedule H of **Form 1041,** U.S. Fiduciary Income Tax Return, and **Pub. 909,** Alternative Minimum Tax for Individuals, to determine the amounts to enter and for other information.

Do not include as a tax preference item any qualified expenditures to which an election under section 59(e) may apply. Because these expenditures are subject to an election by each shareholder, the corporation cannot compute the amount of any tax preference related to them. Instead, the corporation must pass through to each shareholder on lines 16a and 16b of Schedule K-1 the information needed to compute the deduction.

Line 14a—Depreciation Adjustment on Property Placed in Service After 1986

Figure the adjustment for line 14a based only on tangible property placed in service after 1986 (and tangible property placed in service after July 31, 1986, and before 1987 for which the corporation elected to use the General Depreciation System). **Do not** make an adjustment for motion picture films, videotapes, sound recordings, certain public utility property (as defined in section 168(f)(2)), or property depreciated under the unit-of-production method (or any other method not expressed in a term of years).

Using the same convention the corporation used for regular tax purposes, refigure depreciation as follows:

- For property that is neither real property nor property depreciated using the straight line method, use the 150% declining balance method over the property's class life (instead of the recovery period), switching to straight line for the first tax year that method gives a better result. See Pub. 534 for a table of class lives. For property having no class life, use 12 years.
- For property depreciated using the straight line method (other than real property), use the straight line method over the property's class life (instead of the recovery period). For property having no class life, use 12 years.
- For residential rental and nonresidential real property, use the straight line method over 40 years.

Determine the depreciation adjustment by subtracting the recomputed depreciation from the depreciation claimed on Form 4562. If the recomputed depreciation exceeds the depreciation claimed on Form 4562, enter the difference as a negative amount. See the instructions for Form 6251 and Form 4562 for more information.

Line 14b—Adjusted Gain or Loss

If the corporation disposed of any tangible property placed in service after 1986 (or after July 31, 1986, if an election was made to use the General Depreciation System), or if it disposed of a certified pollution control facility placed in service after 1986, refigure the gain or loss from the disposition using the adjusted basis for alternative minimum tax (AMT) purposes. The property's adjusted basis for AMT purposes is its cost or other basis minus all depreciation or amortization deductions allowed or allowable for AMT purposes during the current tax year and previous tax years. Enter on this line the difference between the gain (or loss) reported for regular tax purposes and the gain (or loss) recomputed for AMT purposes. If the gain recomputed for AMT purposes is less than the gain computed for regular tax purposes, OR if the loss recomputed for AMT purposes is more than the loss computed for regular tax purposes, OR if there is a loss for AMT purposes and a gain for regular tax purposes, enter the difference as a negative amount.

Line 14c—Depletion (Other Than Oil and Gas)

Do not include any depletion on oil and gas wells. The shareholders must compute their depletion deductions separately under section 613A.

In the case of mines, wells, and other natural deposits, other than oil and gas wells, enter the amount by which the deduction for depletion under section 611 (including percentage depletion for geothermal deposits) is more than the adjusted basis of such property at the end of the tax year. Figure the adjusted basis without regard to the depletion deduction and figure the excess separately for each property.

Lines 14d(1) and 14d(2)

Generally, the amounts to be entered on these lines are only the income and deductions for oil, gas, and geothermal properties that are used to figure the amount on line 21, page 1, Form 1120S.

If there are any items of income or deductions for oil, gas, and geothermal properties included in the amounts that are required to be passed through separately to the shareholders on Schedule K-1, give each shareholder a schedule that shows, for the line on which the income or deduction is included, the amount of income or deductions included in the total amount for that line. Do not include any of these direct passthrough amounts on line 14d(1) or 14d(2). The shareholder is told in the Shareholder's Instructions for Schedule K-1 (Form 1120S) to adjust the amounts on lines 14d(1) and 14d(2) for any other income or deductions from oil, gas, or geothermal properties included on lines 2 through 10 and 23 of Schedule K-1 in order to determine the total income and deductions from oil, gas, and geothermal properties for the corporation.

Figure the amounts for lines 14d(1) and 14d(2) separately for oil and gas properties which are not geothermal deposits and for all properties that are geothermal deposits.

Give the shareholders a schedule that shows the separate amounts included in the computation of the amounts on lines 14d(1) and 14d(2).

Line 14d(1). Gross income from oil, gas, and geothermal properties.—Enter the total amount of gross income (within the meaning of section 613(a)) from all oil, gas, and geothermal properties received or accrued during the tax year and included on page 1, Form 1120S.

Line 14d(2). Deductions allocable to oil, gas, and geothermal properties.—Enter the amount of any deductions allocable to oil, gas, and geothermal properties reduced by the excess intangible drilling costs included on page 1, Form 1120S, on properties for which the corporation made an election to expense intangible drilling costs in tax years beginning before 1983. Do not include nonproductive well costs included on page 1.

Figure excess intangible drilling costs as follows: From the allowable intangible drilling and development costs (except for costs in drilling a nonproductive well), subtract the amount that would have been allowable if the corporation had capitalized these costs and either amortized them over the 120 months that started when production began, or treated them according to any election the corporation made under section 57(b)(2).

See section 57(a)(2) for more information.

Line 14e—Other Adjustments and Tax Preference Items

Attach a schedule that shows each shareholder's share of other items not shown on lines 14a through 14d(2) that are adjustments or tax preference items or that the shareholder needs to complete Form 6251 or Schedule H of Form 1041. See these forms and their instructions to determine the amount to enter. Other adjustments or tax preference items include the following:

- Accelerated depreciation of real property under pre-1987 rules.
- Accelerated depreciation of leased personal property under pre-1987 rules.
- Amortization of certified pollution control facilities. The deduction allowable under section 169 for any facility placed in service after 1986 must be refigured using the alternative depreciation system under section 168(g).
- Long-term contracts entered into after February 28, 1986. Except for certain home construction contracts, the taxable income from these contracts must be figured using the percentage of completion method of accounting for alternative minimum tax purposes.
- Installment sales after March 1, 1986, of property held primarily for sale to customers in the ordinary course of the corporation's trade or business. Generally, the installment method may not be used for these sales in computing alternative minimum taxable income.
- Losses from tax shelter farm activities. No loss from any tax shelter farm activity is allowed for alternative minimum tax purposes.

Foreign Taxes

Lines 15a through 15g must be completed whether or not a shareholder is eligible for the foreign tax credit, if the corporation has foreign income, deductions, or losses, or has paid or accrued foreign taxes.

In addition to the instructions below, see **Form 1116,** Foreign Tax Credit (Individual, Fiduciary, or Nonresident Alien Individual), and the related instructions.

Line 15a—Type of Income

Enter the type of income from outside the United States as follows:

- Passive income.
- High withholding tax interest.
- Financial services income.
- Shipping income.
- Dividends from a DISC or former DISC.
- Certain distributions from a foreign sales corporation (FSC) or former FSC.
- Dividends from each noncontrolled section 902 corporation.
- Taxable income attributable to foreign trade income (within the meaning of section 923(b)).
- General limitation income (all other income from sources outside the United States, including income from sources within U.S. possessions).

If, for the country or U.S. possession shown on line 15b, the corporation had more than one type of income, enter "See attached" and attach a schedule for each type of income for lines 15c through 15g.

Line 15b—Foreign Country or U.S. Possession

Enter the name of the foreign country or U.S. possession. If, for the type of income shown on line 15a, the corporation had income from, or paid taxes to, more than one foreign country or U.S. possession, enter "See attached" and attach a schedule for each country for lines 15a and 15c through 15g.

Line 15c—Total Gross Income From Sources Outside the United States

Enter in U.S. dollars the total gross income from sources outside the United States. Attach a schedule that shows each type of income listed in the instructions for line 15a.

Line 15d—Total Applicable Deductions and Losses

Enter in U.S. dollars the total applicable deductions and losses attributable to income on line 15c. Attach a schedule that shows each type of deduction or loss as follows:

- Expenses directly allocable to each type of income listed above.
- Pro rata share of all other deductions not directly allocable to specific items of income.
- Pro rata share of losses from other separate limitation categories.

Line 15e—Total Foreign Taxes

Enter in U.S. dollars the total foreign taxes (described in section 901) paid or accrued by the corporation to foreign countries or U.S. possessions. Attach a schedule that shows the dates the taxes were paid or accrued, and the amount in both foreign currency and in U.S. dollars, as follows:

- Taxes withheld at source on dividends.
- Taxes withheld at source on rents and royalties.
- Other foreign taxes paid or accrued.

Line 15f—Reduction in Taxes Available for Credit

Enter in U.S. dollars the total reduction in taxes available for credit. Attach a schedule that shows separately the:

- Reduction for foreign mineral income.
- Reduction for failure to furnish returns required under section 6038.
- Reduction for taxes attributable to boycott operations (section 908).
- Reduction for foreign oil and gas extraction income (section 907(a)).
- Reduction for any other items (specify).

Line 15g—Other Foreign Tax Information

Enter in U.S. dollars any items not covered on lines 15c through 15f that shareholders need to complete Form 1116 (e.g., gross income from all sources).

Other

Lines 16a and 16b

Generally, section 59(e) allows each shareholder to make an election to deduct the shareholder's pro rata share of the corporation's otherwise deductible qualified expenditures ratably over 10 years (3 years for circulation expenditures), beginning with the tax year in which the expenditures were made (or for intangible drilling and development costs, over the 60-month period beginning with the month in which such costs were paid or incurred). The term "qualified expenditures" includes only the following types of expenditures paid or incurred during the tax year: circulation expenditures, research and experimental expenditures, intangible drilling and development costs, and mining exploration and development costs. If a shareholder makes this election, these items are not treated as tax preference items.

Because the shareholders are generally allowed to make this election, the corporation cannot deduct these amounts or include them as adjustments or tax preference items on Schedule K-1. Instead, on lines 16a and 16b of Schedule K-1, the corporation passes through the information the shareholders need to compute their separate deductions.

Enter on line 16a the qualified expenditures paid or incurred during the tax year to which an election under section 59(e) may apply. Enter this amount for all shareholders whether or not any shareholder makes an election under section 59(e). On line 16b, enter the type of expenditure claimed on line 16a. If the expenditure is for intangible drilling and development costs, enter the month in which the expenditure was paid or incurred (after the type of expenditure on line 16b). If there is more than one type of expenditure included in the total shown on line 16a (or intangible drilling and development costs were paid or incurred for more than 1 month), report this information separately for each type of expenditure (or month) on an attachment to Schedules K and K-1.

Line 17—Tax-Exempt Interest Income

Enter on line 17 tax-exempt interest income, including any exempt-interest dividends received from a mutual fund or other regulated investment company. This information must be reported by individuals on line 8b of Form 1040. Generally, the basis of the shareholder's stock is increased by the amount shown on this line under section 1367(a)(1)(A).

Line 18—Other Tax-Exempt Income

Enter on line 18 all income of the corporation exempt from tax other than tax-exempt interest (e.g., life insurance proceeds). Generally, the basis of the shareholder's stock is increased by the amount shown on this line under section 1367(a)(1)(A).

Line 19—Nondeductible Expenses

Enter on line 19 nondeductible expenses paid or incurred by the corporation. Do not include separately stated deductions shown elsewhere on Schedules K and K-1, capital expenditures, or items the deduction for which is deferred to a later tax year. Generally, the basis of the shareholder's stock is decreased by the amount shown on this line under section 1367(a)(2)(D).

Line 20

Enter total distributions made to each shareholder other than dividends reported on line 22 of Schedule K. Noncash distributions of appreciated property are valued at fair market value. See Schedule M-2 instructions for ordering rules on distributions.

Line 21 (Schedule K Only)

Attach a statement to Schedule K to report the corporation's total income, expenditures, or other information for items 1 through 14 of the line 23 (Schedule K-1 Only) instruction below.

Line 22 (Schedule K Only)

Enter total dividends paid to shareholders from accumulated earnings and profits. Report these dividends to shareholders on Form 1099-DIV. Do not report them on Schedule K-1.

Lines 22a and 22b (Schedule K-1 Only)—Recapture of Low-Income Housing Credit

If recapture of part or all of the low-income housing credit is required because **(a)** prior year qualified basis of a building decreased or **(b)** the corporation disposed of a building or part of its interest in a building, get **Form 8611,** Recapture of Low-Income Housing Credit. The instructions for Form 8611 indicate when Form 8611 is completed by the corporation and what information is provided to shareholders when recapture is required.

Note: *If a shareholder's ownership interest in a building decreased because of a transaction at the shareholder level, the corporation must provide the necessary information to the shareholder to enable the shareholder to compute the recapture.*

If the corporation posted a bond as provided in section 42(j)(6) to avoid recapture of the low-income housing credit, no entry should be made on line 22 of Schedule K-1.

See Form 8586, Form 8611, and section 42 for more information.

Supplemental Information

Line 23 (Schedule K-1 Only)

Enter in the line 23 Supplemental Information space of Schedule K-1, or on an attached schedule if more space is needed, each shareholder's share of any information asked for on lines 1 through 22 that is required to be reported in detail, and items **1** through **14** below. Please identify the applicable line number next to the information entered in the Supplemental Information space. Show income or gains as a positive number. Show losses in parentheses.

1. Taxes paid on undistributed capital gains by a regulated investment company. As a shareholder of a regulated investment company, the corporation will receive notice on **Form 2439,** Notice to Shareholder of Undistributed Long-Term Capital Gains, that the company paid tax on undistributed capital gains.

2. Gross income and other information relating to oil and gas well properties that are reported to shareholders to allow them to figure the depletion deduction for oil and gas well properties. See section 613A(c)(11) for details.

The corporation cannot deduct depletion on oil and gas wells. Each shareholder must determine the allowable amount to report on his or her return. See Pub. 535 for more information.

3. Recapture of section 179 expense deduction. For property placed in service after 1986, the section 179 deduction is recaptured at any time the business use of property drops to 50% or less. Enter the amount originally passed through and the corporation's tax year in which it was passed through. Inform the shareholder if the recapture amount was caused by the disposition of the section 179 property. See section 179(d)(10) for more information. Do not include this amount on line 4 or 5, page 1, Form 1120S.

4. Recapture of certain mining exploration expenditures (section 617).

5. Any information or statements the corporation is required to furnish to shareholders to allow them to comply with requirements under section 6111 (registration of tax shelters) or section 6662(d)(2)(B)(ii) (regarding adequate disclosure of items that may cause an understatement of income tax).

6. If the corporation is involved in farming or fishing activities, report the gross income from these activities to shareholders.

7. Any information needed by a shareholder to compute the interest due under section 453(l)(3). If the corporation elected to report the dispositions of certain timeshares and residential lots on the installment method, each shareholder's tax liability must be increased by the shareholder's pro rata share of the interest on tax attributable to the installment payments received during the tax year.

8. Any information needed by a shareholder to compute the interest due under section 453A(c). If an obligation arising from the disposition of property to which section 453A applies is outstanding at the close of the year, each shareholder's tax liability must be increased by the tax due under section 453A(c) on the shareholder's pro rata share of the tax deferred under the installment method.

9. Any information needed by a shareholder to properly capitalize interest as required by section 263A(f). See **Section 263A uniform capitalization rules** on page 10 for additional information. See Notice 88-99, 1988-2 C.B. 422, for more information.

10. If the corporation is a closely held S corporation (defined in section 460(b)) and it entered into any long-term contracts after February 28, 1986, that are accounted for under either the percentage of completion-capitalized cost method or the percentage of completion method, it must attach a schedule to Form 1120S showing the information required in items (a) and (b) of the instructions for lines 1 and 3 of Part II for **Form 8697,** Interest Computation Under the Look-Back Method for Completed Long-Term Contracts. It must also report the amounts for Part II, lines 1 and 3, to its shareholders. See the instructions for Form 8697 for more information.

11. Expenditures qualifying for the **(a)** rehabilitation credit not related to rental real estate activities, **(b)** energy credit, or **(c)** reforestation credit. Complete and attach Form 3468 to Form 1120S. See Form 3468 and related instructions for information on eligible property and the lines on Form 3468 to complete. Do not include that part of the cost of the property the corporation has elected to expense under section 179. Attach to each Schedule K-1 a separate schedule in a format similar to that shown on Form 3468 detailing each shareholder's pro rata share of qualified expenditures. Also indicate the lines of Form 3468 on which the shareholders should report these amounts.

12. Recapture of investment credit. Complete and attach **Form 4255,** Recapture of Investment Credit, when investment credit property is disposed of, or it no longer qualifies for the credit, before the end of the recapture period or the useful life applicable to the property. State the kind of property at the top of Form 4255, and complete lines 2, 3, 4, and 8, whether or not any shareholder is subject to recapture of the credit. Attach to each Schedule K-1 a separate schedule providing the information the corporation is required to show on Form 4255, but list only the shareholder's pro rata share of the cost of the property subject to recapture. Also indicate the lines of Form 4255 on which the shareholders should report these amounts.

The corporation itself is liable for investment credit recapture in certain cases. See the instructions for line 22c, page 1, Form 1120S, for details.

13. Any information needed by a shareholder to compute the recapture of the qualified electric vehicle credit. See Pub. 535 for more information.

14. Any other information the shareholders need to prepare their tax returns.

Specific Instructions

Schedule L—Balance Sheets

The balance sheets should agree with the corporation's books and records. Include certificates of deposit as cash on line 1 of Schedule L.

Line 5—Tax-Exempt Securities

Include on this line—

1. State and local government obligations, the interest on which is excludible from gross income under section 103(a), and

2. Stock in a mutual fund or other regulated investment company that distributed exempt-interest dividends during the tax year of the corporation.

Line 24—Retained Earnings

If the corporation maintains separate accounts for appropriated and unappropriated retained earnings, it may want to continue such accounting for purposes of preparing its financial balance sheet. Also, if the corporation converts to C corporation status in a subsequent year, it will be required to report its appropriated and unappropriated retained earnings on separate lines of Schedule L of Form 1120.

Schedule M-1—Reconciliation of Income (Loss) per Books With Income (Loss) per Return

Line 3b—Travel and Entertainment

Include on this line 20% of meals and entertainment paid or incurred before 1994 not allowed under section 274(n); expenses for the use of an entertainment facility; the part of business gifts in excess of $25; expenses of an individual allocable to conventions on cruise ships in excess of $2,000; employee achievement awards in excess of $400; the cost of entertainment tickets in excess of face value (also subject to 20% disallowance); the cost of skyboxes in excess of the face value of nonluxury box seat tickets; the part of the cost of luxury water travel not allowed under section 274(m); expenses for travel as a form of education; nondeductible club dues; and other travel and entertainment expenses not allowed as a deduction.

Schedule M-2—Analysis of Accumulated Adjustments Account, Other Adjustments Account, and Shareholders' Undistributed Taxable Income Previously Taxed

Column (a)—Accumulated Adjustments Account

The accumulated adjustments account (AAA) is an account of the S corporation that generally reflects the accumulated undistributed net income of the corporation for the corporation's post-1982 years. S corporations with accumulated earnings and profits must maintain the AAA to determine the tax effect of distributions during S years and the post-termination transition period. An S corporation without accumulated earnings and profits does not need to maintain the AAA in order to determine the tax effect of distributions. Nevertheless, if an S corporation without accumulated earnings and profits engages in certain transactions to which section 381(a) applies, such as a merger into an S corporation with accumulated earnings and profits, the S corporation must be able to calculate its AAA at the time of the merger for purposes of determining the tax effect of post-merger distributions. Therefore, it is recommended that the AAA be maintained by all S corporations.

At the end of the tax year, the AAA is determined by taking into account the taxable income, deductible losses and expenses, and nondeductible losses and expenses for the tax year. Adjustments for nontaxable income are made to the other adjustments account as explained in the column (b) instruction below. See section 1368. After the year-end income and expense adjustments are made, the AAA is reduced by distributions made during the tax year. See **Distributions** on page 23 for distribution rules.

Note: *The AAA may have a negative balance at year end. See section 1368(e).*

Column (b)—Other Adjustments Account

The other adjustments account is adjusted for tax-exempt income (and related expenses) of the corporation. See section 1368. After adjusting for tax-exempt income, the account is reduced for any distributions made during the year. See **Distributions** on page 23.

Column (c)—Shareholders' Undistributed Taxable Income Previously Taxed

The shareholders' undistributed taxable income previously taxed account, also called previously taxed income (PTI), is maintained only if the corporation had a balance in this account at the start of its 1993 tax year. If there is a beginning balance for the 1993 tax year, no adjustments are made to the account except to reduce the account for distributions made under section 1375(d) (as in effect before the enactment of the Subchapter S Revision Act of 1982). See **Distributions** below for the order of distributions from the account.

Each shareholder's right to nontaxable distributions from PTI is personal and cannot be transferred to another person. The corporation is required to keep records of each shareholder's net share of PTI.

Distributions

Generally, property distributions (including cash) are applied in the following order to reduce accounts of the S corporation that are used to compute the tax effect of distributions made by the corporation to its shareholders:

1. Reduce AAA (but not below zero). If distributions during the tax year exceed the AAA at the close of the tax year, the AAA is allocated pro rata to each distribution made during the tax year. See section 1368(c).

2. Reduce shareholders' PTI account for any section 1375(d) (as in effect before 1983) distributions. A distribution from the PTI account is tax free to the extent of a shareholder's basis in his or her stock in the corporation.

3. Reduce accumulated E&P. Generally, the S corporation has accumulated E&P only if it has not distributed E&P accumulated in prior years when the S corporation was a C corporation (section 1361(a)(2)) or a small business corporation prior to 1983 (section 1371 of prior law). See section 312 for information on E&P. The only adjustments that can be made to the accumulated E&P of an S corporation are **(a)** reductions for dividend distributions; **(b)** adjustments for redemptions, liquidations, reorganizations, etc.; and **(c)** reductions for investment credit recapture tax for which the corporation is liable. See sections 1371(c) and (d)(3).

4. Reduce the other adjustments account.

5. Reduce any remaining shareholders' equity accounts.

If the corporation has accumulated E&P and wants to distribute this E&P before making distributions from the AAA, it may elect to do so with the consent of all its affected shareholders (section 1368(e)(3)). If the corporation has PTI and wants to make distributions from retained earnings before making distributions from PTI, it may elect to do so with the consent of all its shareholders. The statement of election must be attached to a timely filed Form 1120S for the tax year during which the distributions are made. The election must be made separately for each tax year.

In the case of either election, after all accumulated E&P in the retained earnings are distributed, the above general order of distributions applies except that item **3** is eliminated.

Example

The following example shows how the Schedule M-2 accounts are adjusted for items of income (loss), deductions, and distributions reported on Form 1120S.

Items per return are:

1. Page 1, line 21 income—$219,000

2. Schedule K, line 2 loss—($3,000)

3. Schedule K, line 4a income—$4,000

4. Schedule K, line 4b income—$16,000

5. Schedule K, line 7 deduction—$24,000

6. Schedule K, line 8 deduction— $3,000

7. Schedule K, line 13 jobs credit—$6,000

8. Schedule K, line 17 tax-exempt interest—$5,000

9. Schedule K, line 19 nondeductible expenses—$6,000 (reduction in salaries and wages for jobs credit), and

10. Schedule K, line 20 distributions—$65,000.

Based on return items 1 through 10 and starting balances of zero, the columns for the AAA and the other adjustments account are completed as shown in the Schedule M-2 Worksheet below.

Note: *For the AAA account, the worksheet line 3—$20,000 amount is the total of the Schedule K, lines 4a and 4b incomes of $4,000 and $16,000. The worksheet line 5—$36,000 amount is the total of the Schedule K, line 2 loss of ($3,000), line 7 deduction of $24,000, line 8 deduction of $3,000, and the line 19 nondeductible expenses of $6,000. For the other adjustments account, the worksheet line 3 amount is the Schedule K, line 17, tax-exempt interest income of $5,000. Other worksheet amounts are self-explanatory.*

Schedule M-2 Worksheet

		(a) Accumulated adjustments account	(b) Other adjustments account	(c) Shareholders' undistributed taxable income previously taxed
1	Balance at beginning of tax year	-0-	-0-	
2	Ordinary income from page 1, line 21	219,000		
3	Other additions	20,000	5,000	
4	Loss from page 1, line 21	( )		
5	Other reductions	(36,000)	( )	
6	Combine lines 1 through 5	203,000	5,000	
7	Distributions other than dividend distributions	65,000	-0-	
8	Balance at end of tax year. Subtract line 7 from line 6	138,000	5,000	

Codes for Principal Business Activity

These codes for the Principal Business Activity are designed to classify enterprises by the type of activity in which they are engaged to facilitate the administration of the Internal Revenue Code. Though similar in format and structure to the Standard Industrial Classification (SIC) codes, they should not be used as SIC codes.

Using the list below, enter on page 1, under B, the code number for the specific industry group from which the largest percentage of "total receipts" is derived. Total receipts means the total of: gross receipts on line 1a, page 1; all other income on lines 4 and 5, page 1; all income on lines 2, 19, and 20a of Form 8825; and income (receipts only) on lines 3a and 4a through 4f of Schedule K.

On page 2, Schedule B, line 2, state the principal business activity and principal product or service that account for the largest percentage of total receipts. For example, if the principal business activity is "Grain mill products," the principal product or service may be "Cereal preparations."

If, as its principal business activity, the corporation: (1) purchases raw materials, (2) subcontracts out for labor to make a finished product from the raw materials, and (3) retains title to the goods, the corporation is considered to be a manufacturer and must enter one of the codes (2010–3998) under "Manufacturing."

Agriculture, Forestry, and Fishing

Code

- 0400 Agricultural production.
- 0600 Agricultural services (except veterinarians), forestry, fishing, hunting, and trapping.

Mining

Metal mining:

- 1010 Iron ores.
- 1070 Copper, lead and zinc, gold and silver ores.
- 1098 Other metal mining.
- 1150 Coal mining.

Oil and gas extraction:

- 1330 Crude petroleum, natural gas, and natural gas liquids.
- 1380 Oil and gas field services.

Nonmetallic minerals, except fuels:

- 1430 Dimension, crushed and broken stone; sand and gravel.
- 1498 Other nonmetallic minerals, except fuels.

Construction

General building contractors and operative builders:

- 1510 General building contractors.
- 1531 Operative builders.

1600 Heavy construction contractors.

Special trade contractors:

- 1711 Plumbing, heating, and air conditioning.
- 1731 Electrical work.
- 1798 Other special trade contractors.

Manufacturing

Food and kindred products:

- 2010 Meat products.
- 2020 Dairy products.
- 2030 Preserved fruits and vegetables.
- 2040 Grain mill products.
- 2050 Bakery products.
- 2060 Sugar and confectionery products.
- 2081 Malt liquors and malt.
- 2088 Alcoholic beverages, except malt liquors and malt.
- 2089 Bottled soft drinks, and flavorings.
- 2096 Other food and kindred products.

2100 Tobacco manufacturers.

Textile mill products:

- 2228 Weaving mills and textile finishing.
- 2250 Knitting mills.
- 2298 Other textile mill products.

Apparel and other textile products:

- 2315 Men's and boys' clothing.
- 2345 Women's and children's clothing.
- 2388 Other apparel and accessories.
- 2390 Miscellaneous fabricated textile products.

Lumber and wood products:

- 2415 Logging, sawmills, and planing mills.
- 2430 Millwork, plywood, and related products.
- 2498 Other wood products, including wood buildings and mobile homes.

2500 Furniture and fixtures.

Paper and allied products:

- 2625 Pulp, paper, and board mills.
- 2699 Other paper products.

Printing and publishing:

- 2710 Newspapers.
- 2720 Periodicals.
- 2735 Books, greeting cards, and miscellaneous publishing.
- 2799 Commercial and other printing, and printing trade services.

Code

Chemicals and allied products:

- 2815 Industrial chemicals, plastics materials and synthetics.
- 2830 Drugs.
- 2840 Soap, cleaners, and toilet goods.
- 2850 Paints and allied products.
- 2898 Agricultural and other chemical products.

Petroleum refining and related industries (including those integrated with extraction):

- 2910 Petroleum refining (including integrated).
- 2998 Other petroleum and coal products.

Rubber and misc. plastics products:

- 3050 Rubber products: plastics footwear, hose, and belting.
- 3070 Misc. plastics products.

Leather and leather products:

- 3140 Footwear, except rubber.
- 3198 Other leather and leather products.

Stone, clay, and glass products:

- 3225 Glass products.
- 3240 Cement, hydraulic.
- 3270 Concrete, gypsum, and plaster products.
- 3298 Other nonmetallic mineral products.

Primary metal industries:

- 3370 Ferrous metal industries; misc. primary metal products.
- 3380 Nonferrous metal industries.

Fabricated metal products:

- 3410 Metal cans and shipping containers.
- 3428 Cutlery, hand tools, and hardware; screw machine products, bolts, and similar products.
- 3430 Plumbing and heating, except electric and warm air.
- 3440 Fabricated structural metal products.
- 3460 Metal forgings and stampings.
- 3470 Coating, engraving, and allied services.
- 3480 Ordnance and accessories, except vehicles and guided missiles.
- 3490 Misc. fabricated metal products.

Machinery, except electrical:

- 3520 Farm machinery.
- 3530 Construction and related machinery.
- 3540 Metalworking machinery.
- 3550 Special industry machinery.
- 3560 General industrial machinery.
- 3570 Office, computing, and accounting machines.
- 3598 Other machinery except electrical.

Electrical and electronic equipment:

- 3630 Household appliances.
- 3665 Radio, television, and communications equipment.
- 3670 Electronic components and accessories.
- 3698 Other electrical equipment.

3710 Motor vehicles and equipment.

Transportation equipment, except motor vehicles:

- 3725 Aircraft, guided missiles and parts.
- 3730 Ship and boat building and repairing.
- 3798 Other transportation equipment, except motor vehicles.

Instruments and related products:

- 3815 Scientific instruments and measuring devices; watches and clocks.
- 3845 Optical, medical, and ophthalmic goods.
- 3860 Photographic equipment and supplies.

3998 Other manufacturing products.

Transportation and Public Utilities

Code

Transportation:

- 4000 Railroad transportation.
- 4100 Local and interurban passenger transit.
- 4200 Trucking and warehousing.
- 4400 Water transportation.
- 4500 Transportation by air.
- 4600 Pipe lines, except natural gas.
- 4700 Miscellaneous transportation services.

Communication:

- 4825 Telephone, telegraph, and other communication services.
- 4830 Radio and television broadcasting.

Electric, gas, and sanitary services:

- 4910 Electric services.
- 4920 Gas production and distribution.
- 4930 Combination utility services.
- 4990 Water supply and other sanitary services.

Wholesale Trade

Durable:

- 5008 Machinery, equipment, and supplies.
- 5010 Motor vehicles and automotive equipment.
- 5020 Furniture and home furnishings.
- 5030 Lumber and construction materials.
- 5040 Sporting, recreational, photographic, and hobby goods, toys and supplies.
- 5050 Metals and minerals, except petroleum and scrap.
- 5060 Electrical goods.
- 5070 Hardware, plumbing and heating equipment and supplies.
- 5098 Other durable goods.

Nondurable:

- 5110 Paper and paper products.
- 5129 Drugs, drug proprietaries, and druggists' sundries.
- 5130 Apparel, piece goods, and notions.
- 5140 Groceries and related products.
- 5150 Farm-product raw materials.
- 5160 Chemicals and allied products.
- 5170 Petroleum and petroleum products.
- 5180 Alcoholic beverages.
- 5190 Misc. nondurable goods.

Retail Trade

Building materials, garden supplies, and mobile home dealers:

- 5220 Building materials dealers.
- 5251 Hardware stores.
- 5265 Garden supplies and mobile home dealers.

5300 General merchandise stores.

Food stores:

- 5410 Grocery stores.
- 5490 Other food stores.

Automotive dealers and service stations:

- 5515 Motor vehicle dealers.
- 5541 Gasoline service stations.
- 5598 Other automotive dealers.

5600 Apparel and accessory stores.

5700 Furniture and home furnishings stores.

5800 Eating and drinking places.

Misc. retail stores:

- 5912 Drug stores and proprietary stores.
- 5921 Liquor stores.
- 5995 Other retail stores.

Finance, Insurance, and Real Estate

Code

Banking:

- 6030 Mutual savings banks.
- 6060 Bank holding companies.
- 6090 Banks, except mutual savings banks and bank holding companies.

Credit agencies other than banks:

- 6120 Savings and loan associations.
- 6140 Personal credit institutions.
- 6150 Business credit institutions.
- 6199 Other credit agencies.

Security, commodity brokers and services:

- 6210 Security brokers, dealers, and flotation companies.
- 6299 Commodity contracts brokers and dealers; security and commodity exchanges; and allied services.

Insurance:

- 6355 Life Insurance.
- 6356 Mutual insurance, except life or marine and certain fire or flood insurance companies.
- 6359 Other insurance companies.
- 6411 Insurance agents, brokers, and service.

Real estate:

- 6511 Real estate operators and lessors of buildings.
- 6516 Lessors of mining, oil, and similar property.
- 6518 Lessors of railroad property and other real property.
- 6530 Condominium management and cooperative housing associations.
- 6550 Subdividers and developers.
- 6599 Other real estate.

Holding and other investment companies, except bank holding companies:

- 6744 Small business investment companies.
- 6749 Other holding and investment companies, except bank holding companies.

Services

7000 Hotels and other lodging places.

7200 Personal services.

Business services:

- 7310 Advertising.
- 7389 Business services, except advertising.

Auto repair; miscellaneous repair services:

- 7500 Auto repair and services.
- 7600 Misc. repair services.

Amusement and recreation services:

- 7812 Motion picture production, distribution, and services.
- 7830 Motion picture theaters.
- 7900 Amusement and recreation services, except motion pictures.

Other services:

- 8015 Offices of physicians, including osteopathic physicians.
- 8021 Offices of dentists.
- 8040 Offices of other health practitioners.
- 8050 Nursing and personal care facilities.
- 8060 Hospitals.
- 8071 Medical laboratories.
- 8099 Other medical services.
- 8111 Legal services.
- 8200 Educational services.
- 8300 Social services.
- 8600 Membership organizations.
- 8911 Architectural and engineering services.
- 8930 Accounting, auditing, and bookkeeping.
- 8980 Miscellaneous services (including veterinarians).

Form **4562**

Department of the Treasury
Internal Revenue Service (O)

Depreciation and Amortization

(Including Information on Listed Property)

▶ See separate instructions. ▶ Attach this form to your return.

OMB No. 1545-0172

1993

Attachment Sequence No. **67**

Name(s) shown on return

Identifying number

Business or activity to which this form relates

Part I Election To Expense Certain Tangible Property (Section 179) (Note: *If you have any "Listed Property," complete Part V before you complete Part I.*)

1	Maximum dollar limitation (If an enterprise zone business, see instructions.)	1	$17,500
2	Total cost of section 179 property placed in service during the tax year (see instructions)	2	
3	Threshold cost of section 179 property before reduction in limitation	3	$200,000
4	Reduction in limitation. Subtract line 3 from line 2, but do not enter less than -0-	4	
5	Dollar limitation for tax year. Subtract line 4 from line 1, but do not enter less than -0-. (If married filing separately, see instructions.)	5	

	(a) Description of property	(b) Cost	(c) Elected cost
6			
7	Listed property. Enter amount from line 26	7	

8	Total elected cost of section 179 property. Add amounts in column (c), lines 6 and 7	8	
9	Tentative deduction. Enter the smaller of line 5 or line 8	9	
10	Carryover of disallowed deduction from 1992 (see instructions)	10	
11	Taxable income limitation. Enter the smaller of taxable income or line 5 (see instructions)	11	
12	Section 179 expense deduction. Add lines 9 and 10, but do not enter more than line 11	12	
13	Carryover of disallowed deduction to 1994. Add lines 9 and 10, less line 12 ▶ 13		

Note: *Do not use Part II or Part III below for listed property (automobiles, certain other vehicles, cellular telephones, certain computers, or property used for entertainment, recreation, or amusement). Instead, use Part V for listed property.*

Part II MACRS Depreciation For Assets Placed in Service ONLY During Your 1993 Tax Year (Do Not Include Listed Property)

(a) Classification of property	(b) Month and year placed in service	(c) Basis for depreciation (business/investment use only—see instructions)	(d) Recovery period	(e) Convention	(f) Method	(g) Depreciation deduction
14 General Depreciation System (GDS) (see instructions):						
a 3-year property						
b 5-year property						
c 7-year property						
d 10-year property						
e 15-year property						
f 20-year property						
g Residential rental property			27.5 yrs.	MM	S/L	
			27.5 yrs.	MM	S/L	
h Nonresidential real property				MM	S/L	
				MM	S/L	
15 Alternative Depreciation System (ADS) (see instructions):						
a Class life					S/L	
b 12-year			12 yrs.		S/L	
c 40-year			40 yrs.	MM	S/L	

Part III Other Depreciation (Do Not Include Listed Property)

16	GDS and ADS deductions for assets placed in service in tax years beginning before 1993 (see instructions)	16	
17	Property subject to section 168(f)(1) election (see instructions)	17	
18	ACRS and other depreciation (see instructions)	18	

Part IV Summary

19	Listed property. Enter amount from line 25	19	
20	**Total.** Add deductions on line 12, lines 14 and 15 in column (g), and lines 16 through 19. Enter here and on the appropriate lines of your return. (Partnerships and S corporations—see instructions)	20	
21	For assets shown above and placed in service during the current year, enter the portion of the basis attributable to section 263A costs (see instructions) 21		

For Paperwork Reduction Act Notice, see page 1 of the separate instructions. Cat. No. 12906N Form **4562** (1993)

Part V Listed Property—Automobiles, Certain Other Vehicles, Cellular Telephones, Certain Computers, and Property Used for Entertainment, Recreation, or Amusement

*For any vehicle for which you are using the standard mileage rate or deducting lease expense, complete **only** 22a, 22b, columns (a) through (c) of Section A, all of Section B, and Section C if applicable.*

Section A—Depreciation and Other Information (Caution: *See instructions for limitations for automobiles.)*

22a Do you have evidence to support the business/investment use claimed? ☐ **Yes** ☐ **No** **22b** If "Yes," is the evidence written? ☐ **Yes** ☐ **No**

(a) Type of property (list vehicles first)	(b) Date placed in service	(c) Business/ investment use percentage	(d) Cost or other basis	(e) Basis for depreciation (business/investment use only)	(f) Recovery period	(g) Method/ Convention	(h) Depreciation deduction	(i) Elected section 179 cost
23 Property used more than 50% in a qualified business use (see instructions):								
		%						
		%						
		%						
24 Property used 50% or less in a qualified business use (see instructions):								
		%				S/L -		
		%				S/L -		
		%				S/L -		

25 Add amounts in column (h). Enter the total here and on line 19, page 1 . . . . . . **25**

26 Add amounts in column (i). Enter the total here and on line 7, page 1 . . . . **26**

Section B—Information Regarding Use of Vehicles—*If you deduct expenses for vehicles:*

- *Always complete this section for vehicles used by a sole proprietor, partner, or other "more than 5% owner," or related person.*
- *If you provided vehicles to your employees, first answer the questions in Section C to see if you meet an exception to completing this section for those vehicles.*

	(a) Vehicle 1		(b) Vehicle 2		(c) Vehicle 3		(d) Vehicle 4		(e) Vehicle 5		(f) Vehicle 6	
27 Total business/investment miles driven during the year (DO NOT include commuting miles)												
28 Total commuting miles driven during the year												
29 Total other personal (noncommuting) miles driven												
30 Total miles driven during the year. Add lines 27 through 29.												
	Yes	No	Yes	No	Yes	No	Yes	No	Yes	No	Yes	No
31 Was the vehicle available for personal use during off-duty hours?												
32 Was the vehicle used primarily by a more than 5% owner or related person?												
33 Is another vehicle available for personal use?												

Section C—Questions for Employers Who Provide Vehicles for Use by Their Employees

Answer these questions to determine if you meet an exception to completing Section B. **Note:** *Section B must always be completed for vehicles used by sole proprietors, partners, or other more than 5% owners or related persons.*

	Yes	No
34 Do you maintain a written policy statement that prohibits all personal use of vehicles, including commuting, by your employees?		
35 Do you maintain a written policy statement that prohibits personal use of vehicles, except commuting, by your employees? (See instructions for vehicles used by corporate officers, directors, or 1% or more owners.)		
36 Do you treat all use of vehicles by employees as personal use?		
37 Do you provide more than five vehicles to your employees and retain the information received from your employees concerning the use of the vehicles?		
38 Do you meet the requirements concerning qualified automobile demonstration use (see instructions)? . .		

Note: *If your answer to 34, 35, 36, 37, or 38 is "Yes," you need not complete Section B for the covered vehicles.*

Part VI Amortization

(a) Description of costs	(b) Date amortization begins	(c) Amortizable amount	(d) Code section	(e) Amortization period or percentage	(f) Amortization for this year
39 Amortization of costs that begins during your 1993 tax year:					

40 Amortization of costs that began before 1993 . . . . **40**

41 **Total.** Enter here and on "Other Deductions" or "Other Expenses" line of your return . . . **41**

*U.S. Government Printing Office: 1993 — 345-370

Instructions for Form 4562

Depreciation and Amortization (Including Information on Listed Property)

Section references are to the Internal Revenue Code, unless otherwise noted.

General Instructions

Paperwork Reduction Act Notice

We ask for the information on this form to carry out the Internal Revenue laws of the United States. You are required to give us the information. We need it to ensure that you are complying with these laws and to allow us to figure and collect the right amount of tax.

The time needed to complete and file this form will vary depending on individual circumstances. The estimated average time is:

Recordkeeping	36 hr., 50 min.
Learning about the law or the form	4 hr., 40 min.
Preparing and sending the form to the IRS	5 hr., 28 min.

If you have comments concerning the accuracy of these time estimates or suggestions for making this form more simple, we would be happy to hear from you. You can write to both the IRS and the Office of Management and Budget at the addresses listed in the instructions for the tax return with which this form is filed.

Changes To Note

The Revenue Reconciliation Act of 1993 made the following changes:

- Beginning in 1993, the maximum section 179 expense deduction for most taxpayers has been increased from $10,000 to $17,500. A larger section 179 expense deduction may be claimed by enterprise zone businesses placing qualified zone property in service after 1993. In addition, only 50% of the cost of section 179 property that is also qualified zone property is taken into account when figuring the reduction in the maximum section 179 expense deduction for an enterprise zone business. See the instructions for lines 1 and 2 for more details.
- The recovery period for nonresidential real property placed in service after May 12, 1993 (with limited exceptions), has been increased from 31.5 to 39 years. See the instructions for column (d) of lines 14a through 14h for more details.
- Certain computer software may now be depreciated using the straight line method over a 36-month period. See the instructions for line 18 for more details.
- Goodwill and certain other intangibles may now be amortized over a 15-year period. See the instructions for line 39 for more details.
- Shorter recovery periods apply to qualified Indian reservation property placed in service after 1993. See the instructions for column (d) of lines 14a through 14h for more details.

Purpose of Form

Use Form 4562 to claim your deduction for depreciation and amortization; to make the election to expense certain tangible property (section 179); and to provide information on the business/investment use of automobiles and other listed property.

Who Must File

Except as otherwise noted, complete and file Form 4562 if you are claiming:

- Depreciation for property placed in service during the 1993 tax year;
- A section 179 expense deduction (which may include a carryover from a previous year);
- Depreciation on any vehicle or other listed property (regardless of when it was placed in service);
- A deduction for any vehicle reported on a form other than **Schedule C (Form 1040),** Profit or Loss From Businesss, or **Schedule C-EZ (Form 1040),** Net Profit From Business;
- Any depreciation on a corporate income tax return (other than Form 1120S); or
- Amortization of costs that begins during the 1993 tax year.

However, **do not** file Form 4562 to report depreciation and information on the use of vehicles if you are an employee deducting job-related vehicle expenses using either the standard mileage rate or actual expenses. Instead, use **Form 2106,** Employee Business Expenses, for this purpose.

You should prepare and submit a separate Form 4562 for each business or activity on your return. If more space is needed, attach additional sheets. However, complete only one Part I in its entirety when computing your allowable section 179 expense deduction.

Definitions

Depreciation

Depreciation is the annual deduction allowed to recover the cost or other basis of business or income-producing property with a determinable useful life of more than 1 year. However, land is not depreciable.

Depreciation starts when you first use the property in your business or for the production of income. It ends when you take the property out of service, deduct all your depreciable cost or other basis, or no longer use the property in your business or for the production of income.

If you acquired depreciable property for the first time in 1993, get **Pub. 946,** How To Begin Depreciating Your Property. For a more comprehensive guide on depreciation, get **Pub. 534,** Depreciation. For information on claiming depreciation on a car, get **Pub. 917,** Business Use of a Car.

Amortization

Amortization is similar to the straight line method of depreciation in that an annual deduction is allowed to recover certain costs over a fixed period of time. You can amortize such items as the costs of starting a business, goodwill and certain other intangibles, reforestation, and pollution control facilities. For additional information, get **Pub. 535,** Business Expenses.

Listed Property

For a definition of "listed property" see **Part V—Listed Property** on page 5.

Recordkeeping

Except for Part V (relating to listed property), the IRS does not require you to submit detailed information with your return regarding the depreciation of assets placed in service in previous tax years. However, the information needed to compute your depreciation deduction (basis, method, etc.) must be part of your permanent records.

Because Form 4562 does not provide for permanent recordkeeping, you may use the depreciation worksheet on page 8 to assist you in maintaining depreciation records. However, the worksheet is designed only for Federal income tax purposes. You may need to keep additional records for accounting and state income tax purposes.

Certification of Business Use Requirement for Aircraft Exempt From Luxury Tax

If you purchased a new aircraft in 1991 or 1992 that was exempt from the 10% Federal luxury tax **solely** because at least 80% of your use of the aircraft (measured in hours of flight time) would be for business purposes, you must attach a statement to your income tax return for each of the 2 tax years ending after the date the aircraft was placed in service. On this statement, you must certify that at least 80% of your use of the aircraft during the tax year was in a trade or business. If you fail to make this certification, you must pay a tax equal to the luxury tax that would have been imposed on the purchase of the aircraft if the business use exemption had not applied. In addition, interest is imposed on the tax from the date of purchase of the aircraft.

If you do not pay the tax when due because you failed to meet this requirement, no depreciation may be claimed on the aircraft for any tax year.

See the instructions for **Form 720,** Quarterly Federal Excise Tax Return, for more information on paying the tax and interest due.

Specific Instructions

Part I—Election To Expense Certain Tangible Property (Section 179)

Note: *An estate or trust cannot make this election.*

You may elect to expense part of the cost of certain tangible personal property used in your trade or business and certain other property described in Pub. 534. To do so, you must have purchased the property (as defined in section 179(d)(2)) and placed it in service during the 1993 tax year.

The election must be made with:

1. The original return you file for the tax year the property was placed in service (whether or not you file your return on time), or

2. An amended return filed no later than the due date (including extensions) for your return for the tax year the property was placed in service.

Once made, the election (and the selection of the property you elect to expense) may not be revoked without IRS consent.

If you elect this deduction, reduce the amount on which you figure your depreciation or amortization deduction by the section 179 expense deduction.

Section 179 property does **not** include:

1. Property used 50% or less in your trade or business,

2. Property held for investment (section 212 property), or

3. Property you lease to others (if you are a noncorporate lessor) **unless (a)** you manufactured or produced the property or **(b)** the term of the lease is less than 50% of the property's class life, and for the first 12 months after the property is transferred to the lessee, the sum of the deductions related to the property that are allowed to you solely under section 162 (except rents and reimbursed amounts) is more than 15% of the rental income from the property.

The section 179 expense deduction is subject to two separate limitations, both of which are figured in Part I:

1. A dollar limitation and

2. A taxable income limitation.

In the case of a partnership, these limitations apply to the partnership and each partner. In the case of an S corporation, these limitations apply to the S corporation and each shareholder. In the case of a controlled group, all component members are treated as one taxpayer.

Line 1

For an enterprise zone business, the maximum section 179 expense deduction is increased by the **smaller** of **(a)** $20,000, or **(b)** the cost of section 179 property that is also qualified zone property (including such property placed in service by your spouse, even if you are filing a separate return). Cross out the preprinted entry on line 1 and enter in the margin the larger amount if your business is an enterprise zone business. For the definitions of enterprise zone business and qualified zone property, see sections 1397B and 1397C.

Line 2

Enter the cost of all section 179 property placed in service during the tax year. Be sure to include amounts from any listed property from Part V. Also include any section 179 property placed in service by your spouse, even if you are filing a separate return.

For an enterprise zone business, include on this line only 50% of the cost of section 179 property that is also qualified zone property.

Line 5

If line 5 is zero, you cannot elect to expense any property; skip lines 6 through 11, enter zero on line 12, and enter the carryover of disallowed deduction from 1992, if any, on line 13.

If you are married filing separately, you and your spouse must allocate the dollar limitation for the tax year between you. To do so, multiply the total limitation that you would otherwise enter on line 5 by 50%, unless you and your spouse elect a different allocation. If you and your spouse elect a different allocation, multiply the total limitation by the percentage you elect. If a different allocation is elected, the sum of the percentages you and your spouse elect must equal 100%. Do not enter on line 5 more than your share of the total dollar limitation.

Line 6

Caution: *Do not include any listed property on line 6.*

Column (a).—Enter a brief description of the property for which you are making the election (e.g., truck, office furniture, etc.).

Column (b).—Enter the cost of the property. If you acquired the property through a trade-in, do not include any undepreciated basis of the assets you traded in. Get **Pub. 551,** Basis of Assets, for more information.

Column (c).—Enter the amount that you elect to expense. You do not have to elect to expense the entire cost of the property. You can depreciate the amount you do not elect to expense. See the line 14 and line 15 instructions.

To report your share of a section 179 expense deduction from a partnership or an S corporation, instead of completing columns (a) and (b), write "from Schedule K-1 (Form 1065)" or "from Schedule K-1 (Form 1120S)" across the columns.

Line 9

The tentative deduction represents the amount you may expense in 1993 or carry over to 1994. If this amount is less than the taxable income limitation on line 11, you may expense the entire amount. If this amount is more than line 11, you may expense in 1993 only an amount equal to line 11. Any excess may be carried over to 1994.

Line 10

The carryover of disallowed deduction from 1992 is the amount of section 179 property, if any, elected to be expensed in previous years, but not allowed as a deduction due to the taxable income limitation. If you filed Form 4562 for 1992, enter the amount from line 13 of your 1992 Form 4562. For additional information, see Pub. 534.

Line 11

The section 179 expense deduction is further limited to the "taxable income" limitation under section 179(b)(3).

If you are an individual, enter the smaller of line 5 or the aggregate taxable income from any trade or business actively conducted by you, computed without regard to any section 179 expense deduction, the deduction for one-half of self-employment taxes under section 164(f), or any net operating loss deduction. Include in aggregate taxable income the wages, salaries, tips, and other compensation you earned as an employee (not reduced by unreimbursed employee business expenses). If you are married filing a joint return, combine the aggregate taxable incomes for both you and your spouse.

For a partnership, enter the smaller of line 5 or the aggregate of the partnership's items of income and expense described in section 702(a) from any trade or business actively conducted by the partnership (other than credits, tax-exempt income, the section 179 expense deduction, and guaranteed payments under section 707(c)).

For an S corporation, enter the smaller of line 5 or the aggregate of the corporation's items of income and expense described in section 1366(a) from any trade or business actively conducted by the corporation (other than credits, tax-exempt income, the section 179 expense deduction, and the deduction for compensation paid to the corporation's shareholder-employees).

For a corporation (other than an S corporation), enter the smaller of line 5 or the corporation's taxable income before the net operating loss deduction and special deductions (excluding items not derived from a trade or business actively conducted by the corporation).

If you have to apply another Code section that has a limitation based on taxable income, see Regulations section 1.179-2(c)(5) for rules for applying the taxable income limitation under section 179 in such a case.

You are considered to actively conduct a trade or business if you meaningfully participate in the management or operations of the trade or business. A mere passive investor is not considered to actively conduct a trade or business.

Line 12

The limitations on lines 5 and 11 apply to the taxpayer, and not to each separate business or activity. Therefore, if you have more than one business or activity, you may allocate your allowable section 179 expense deduction among them. To do so, write "Summary" at the top of Part I of the separate Form 4562 you are completing for the aggregate amounts from all businesses or activities. Do not complete the rest of that form. On line 12 of the Form 4562 you prepare for each separate business or activity, enter the amount allocated to the business or activity from the "Summary." No other entry is required in Part I of the separate Form 4562 prepared for each business or activity.

Part II—MACRS Depreciation For Assets Placed in Service ONLY During Your 1993 Tax Year

Note: *The term "Modified Accelerated Cost Recovery System" (MACRS) includes the General Depreciation System and the Alternative Depreciation System. Generally, MACRS is used to depreciate any tangible property placed in service after 1986. However, MACRS does not apply to films, videotapes, and sound recordings. See section 168(f) for other exceptions.*

Depreciation may be an adjustment for alternative minimum tax purposes. For details, get **Form 4626,** Alternative Minimum Tax—Corporations; **Form 6251,** Alternative Minimum Tax—Individuals; or Schedule H of **Form 1041,** U.S. Fiduciary Income Tax Return.

Lines 14a Through 14h—General Depreciation System (GDS)

Note: *Use lines 14a through 14h only for assets placed in service during the tax year beginning in 1993 and depreciated under the General Depreciation System, except for automobiles and other listed property (which are reported in Part V).*

Column (a).—Determine which property you acquired and placed in service during the tax year beginning in 1993. Then, sort that property according to its classification (3-year property, 5-year property, etc.) as shown in column (a) of lines 14a through 14h. The classifications for some property are shown below. For property not shown, see **Determining the classification** on page 3.

- **3-year property** includes **(a)** a race horse that is more than 2 years old at the time it is placed in service and **(b)** any horse (other than a race horse) that is more than 12 years old at the time it is placed in service.
- **5-year property** includes **(a)** automobiles; **(b)** light general purpose trucks; **(c)** typewriters, calculators, copiers, and duplicating equipment; **(d)** any semi-conductor manufacturing equipment; **(e)** any computer or peripheral equipment; **(f)** any section 1245 property used in connection with research and experimentation; and **(g)** certain energy property specified in section 168(e)(3)(B)(vi).

• **7-year property** includes **(a)** office furniture and equipment; **(b)** appliances, carpets, furniture, etc., used in residential rental property; **(c)** railroad track; and **(d)** any property that does not have a class life and is not otherwise classified.

• **10-year property** includes **(a)** vessels, barges, tugs, and similar water transportation equipment; **(b)** any single purpose agricultural or horticultural structure (see section 168(i)(13)); and **(c)** any tree or vine bearing fruit or nuts.

• **15-year property** includes **(a)** any municipal wastewater treatment plant and **(b)** any telephone distribution plant and comparable equipment used for 2-way exchange of voice and data communications.

• **20-year property** includes any municipal sewers.

• **Residential rental property** is a building in which 80% or more of the total rent is from dwelling units.

• **Nonresidential real property** is any real property that is neither residential rental property nor property with a class life of less than 27.5 years.

• **50-year property** includes any improvements necessary to construct or improve a roadbed or right-of-way for railroad track that qualifies as a railroad grading or tunnel bore under section 168(e)(4).

There is no separate line to report 50-year property. Therefore, attach a statement showing the same information as required in columns (a) through (g). Include the deduction in the line 20 "Total" and write "See attachment" in the bottom margin of the form.

Determining the classification.—If your depreciable property is **not** listed above, determine the classification as follows: First, find the property's class life. The class life of most property can be found in the Table of Class Lives and Recovery Periods in Pub. 534. Next, use the following table to find the classification in column (b) that corresponds to the class life of the property in column (a).

(a) Class life (in years) (See Pub. 534)	(b) Classification
4 or less	3-year property
More than 4 but less than 10	5-year property
10 or more but less than 16	7-year property
16 or more but less than 20	10-year property
20 or more but less than 25	15-year property
25 or more	20-year property

Column (b).—For lines 14g and 14h, enter the month and year the property was placed in service. If property held for personal use is converted to use in a trade or business or for the production of income, treat the property as being placed in service on the date of conversion.

Column (c).—To find the basis for depreciation, multiply the cost or other basis of the property by the percentage of business/investment use. From that result, subtract any section 179 expense deduction, deduction for removal of barriers to the disabled and the elderly, disabled access credit, and enhanced oil recovery credit. See section 50(c) to determine the basis adjustment for investment credit property.

Column (d).—Determine the recovery period from **Table 1** below, unless either **1** or **2** below applies:

1. You make an irrevocable election to use the 150% declining balance method of depreciation for 3-, 5-, 7-, or 10-year property (excluding any tree or vine bearing fruit or nuts). The election applies to all property within the classification for which it is made that was placed in service during the tax year. If you elect this method, you must use the recovery period under the Alternative Depreciation System (ADS) discussed in the line 15 instructions. You will not have an adjustment for alternative minimum tax purposes on the property for which you make this election.

2. You acquired qualified Indian reservation property (as defined in section 168(j)(4)) that you placed in service after 1993. Use **Table 2** for qualified Indian reservation property placed in service after 1993.

Note: *Qualified Indian reservation property does not include property placed in service for purposes of conducting class I, II, or III gaming activities.*

Table 1—Recovery Period for Most Property

In the case of:	The applicable recovery period is:
3-year property	3 yrs.
5-year property	5 yrs.
7-year property	7 yrs.
10-year property	10 yrs.
15-year property	15 yrs.
20-year property	20 yrs.
Residential rental property	27.5 yrs.
Nonresidential real property placed in service before May 13, 1993	31.5 yrs.
Nonresidential real property placed in service after May 12, 1993	*39 yrs.
Railroad gradings and tunnel bores	50 yrs.

*The recovery period is 31.5 years for property you placed in service before 1994, if you started construction on the property before May 13, 1993, or you had a binding written contract to buy or build it before that date.

Table 2—Recovery Period for Qualified Indian Reservation Property Placed in Service After 1993

In the case of:	The applicable recovery period is:
3-year property	2 yrs.
5-year property	3 yrs.
7-year property	4 yrs.
10-year property	6 yrs.
15-year property	9 yrs.
20-year property	12 yrs.
Nonresidential real property	22 yrs.

Column (e).—The applicable convention determines the portion of the tax year for which depreciation is allowable during a year property is either placed in service or disposed of. There are three types of conventions (discussed below). To select the correct convention, you must know when you placed the property in service and the type of property.

Half-year convention (HY).—This convention applies to all property reported on lines 14a through 14f, unless the mid-quarter convention applies. It does not apply to residential rental property, nonresidential real property, and railroad gradings and tunnel bores. It treats all property placed in service (or disposed of) during any tax year as placed in service (or disposed of) on the mid-point of such tax year.

Mid-quarter convention (MQ).—If the aggregate bases of property subject to depreciation under section 168 and placed in service during the last 3 months of your tax year exceed 40% of the aggregate bases of property subject to depreciation under section 168 and placed in service during the entire tax year, the mid-quarter, instead of the half-year, convention applies.

The mid-quarter convention treats all property placed in service (or disposed of) during any quarter as placed in service (or disposed of) on the mid-point of such quarter. However, no depreciation is allowed under this convention for property that is placed in service and disposed of within the same tax year.

In determining whether the mid-quarter convention applies, **do not** take into account:

• Property that is being depreciated under the pre-1987 rules;

• Any residential rental property, nonresidential real property, or railroad gradings and tunnel bores; and

• Property that is placed in service and disposed of within the same tax year.

Mid-month convention (MM).—This convention applies ONLY to residential rental property, nonresidential real property (lines 14g or 14h), and railroad gradings and tunnel bores. It treats all property placed in service (or disposed of) during any month as placed in service (or disposed of) on the mid-point of such month.

Enter "HY" for half-year; "MQ" for mid-quarter; or "MM" for mid-month convention.

Column (f).—Applicable depreciation methods are prescribed for each classification of property. Except for property for which you elected to use the 150% declining balance method and any tree or vine bearing fruit or nuts, the applicable method for 3-, 5-, 7-, and 10-year property is the 200% declining balance method, switching to the straight line method in the first tax year that maximizes the depreciation allowance.

For 15- and 20-year property, property used in a farming business, and property for which you elected to use the 150% declining balance method, the applicable method is the 150% declining balance method, switching to the straight line method in the first tax year that maximizes the depreciation allowance.

For residential rental property, nonresidential real property, any railroad grading or tunnel bore, or any tree or vine bearing fruit or nuts, the only applicable method is the straight line method.

You may also make an irrevocable election to use the straight line method for all property within a classification that is placed in service during the tax year.

Enter "200 DB" for 200% declining balance; "150 DB" for 150% declining balance; or "S/L" for straight line.

Column (g).—To compute the depreciation deduction you may use optional Tables A through E on page 7. To do this, multiply the applicable rate from the appropriate table by the property's **unadjusted** basis (column (c)) (see Pub. 534 for complete tables). Or you may compute the deduction yourself by completing the following steps:

Step 1.—Determine the depreciation rate as follows:

• If you are using the 200% or 150% declining balance method in column (f), divide the declining balance rate (use 2.00 for 200 DB or 1.50 for 150 DB) by the number of years in the recovery period in column (d). For example, for property depreciated using the 200 DB method over a recovery period of 5 years, divide 2.00 by 5 for a rate of 40%.

• If you are using the straight line method, divide 1.00 by the remaining number of years in the recovery period as of the beginning of the tax year (but not less than one). For example, if there are 6½ years remaining in the recovery period as of the beginning of the year, divide 1.00 by 6.5 for a rate of 15.38%.

Note: *If you are using the 200% or 150% DB method, be sure to switch to the straight line rate in the first year that the straight line rate exceeds the declining balance rate.*

Step 2.—Multiply the percentage rate determined in Step 1 by the property's unrecovered basis (basis for depreciation (as defined in column (c)) reduced by all prior year's depreciation).

Step 3.—For property placed in service or disposed of during the current tax year, multiply the result from Step 2 by the applicable decimal amount from the tables below (based on the convention shown in column (e)).

Half-year (HY) convention		0.5

Mid-quarter (MQ) convention

Placed in service (or disposed of) during the:	Placed in service	Disposed of
1st quarter	0.875	0.125
2nd quarter	0.625	0.375
3rd quarter	0.375	0.625
4th quarter	0.125	0.875

Mid-month (MM) convention

Placed in service (or disposed of) during the:	Placed in service	Disposed of
1st month	0.9583	0.0417
2nd month	0.8750	0.1250
3rd month	0.7917	0.2083
4th month	0.7083	0.2917
5th month	0.6250	0.3750
6th month	0.5417	0.4583
7th month	0.4583	0.5417
8th month	0.3750	0.6250
9th month	0.2917	0.7083
10th month	0.2083	0.7917
11th month	0.1250	0.8750
12th month	0.0417	0.9583

Short tax years.—See Pub. 534 for rules on how to compute the depreciation deduction for property placed in service in a short tax year.

Lines 15a Through 15c—Alternative Depreciation System (ADS)

Note: *Lines 15a through 15c should be completed for assets, other than automobiles and other listed property, placed in service ONLY during the tax year beginning in 1993 and depreciated under the Alternative Depreciation System. Depreciation on assets placed in service in prior years is reported on line 16.*

Under ADS, depreciation Is computed by using the applicable depreciation method, the applicable recovery period, and the applicable convention. The following types of property **must** be depreciated under ADS:

- Any tangible property used predominantly outside the United States,
- Any tax-exempt use property,
- Any tax-exempt bond financed property,
- Any imported property covered by an executive order of the President of the United States, and
- Any property used predominantly in a farming business and placed in service during any tax year in which you made an election under section 263A(d)(3).

Instead of depreciating property under GDS (line 14), you may make an irrevocable election with respect to any classification of property for any tax year to use ADS. For residential rental and nonresidential real property, you may make this election separately for each property.

Column (a).—Use the following rules to determine the classification of the property under ADS:

- **Class life.** Under ADS, the depreciation deduction for most property is based on the property's class life, which can be found in the Table of Class Lives and Recovery Periods in Pub. 534. Use line 15a for all property depreciated under ADS, except for property that does not have a class life, residential rental and nonresidential real property, and railroad gradings and tunnel bores.

Note: *See section 168(g)(3)(B) for a special rule for determining the class life for certain property.*

- **12-year.** Use line 15b for property that does not have a class life.
- **40-year.** Use line 15c for residential rental and nonresidential real property.
- **Railroad gradings and tunnel bores** are 50-year property under ADS. There is no separate line to report 50-year property. Therefore, attach a statement showing the same information as required in columns (a) through (g). Include the deduction in the line 20 "Total" and write "See attachment" in the bottom margin of the form.

Column (b).—For 40-year property, enter the month and year it was placed in service or was converted to use in a trade or business or for the production of income.

Column (c).—See the instructions for line 14, column (c).

Column (d).—On line 15a, enter the property's class life.

Column (e).—Under ADS, the applicable conventions are the same as those used under GDS. See the instructions for line 14, column (e).

Column (f).—Under ADS, the only applicable method is the straight line method.

Column (g).—The depreciation deduction is computed in the same manner as under GDS except you must apply the straight line method over the ADS recovery period and use the applicable convention.

Part III—Other Depreciation

Note: *Do not use Part III for automobiles and other listed property. Instead, report this property in Part V on page 2 of Form 4562.*

Line 16

For tangible property placed in service after 1986 and depreciated under MACRS (including tangible property placed in service after July 31, 1986, for which you elected to use MACRS), enter the GDS and ADS deductions for the current year. To compute the deductions, see the instructions for column (g), line 14.

Line 17

Report property that you elect, under section 168(f)(1), to depreciate under the unit-of-production method or any other method not based on a term of years (other than the retirement-replacement-betterment method).

Attach a separate sheet showing **(a)** a description of the property and the depreciation method you elect that excludes the property from ACRS or MACRS; and **(b)** the depreciable basis (cost or other basis reduced, if applicable, by salvage value, any section 179 expense deduction, deduction for removal of barriers to the disabled and the elderly, disabled access credit, and enhanced oil recovery credit). See section 50(c) to determine the basis adjustment for investment credit property.

Line 18

Enter the total depreciation you are claiming for the following types of property (except listed property and property subject to a section 168(f)(1) election):

- ACRS property (pre-1987 rules);
- Property placed in service before 1981;
- Certain public utility property, which does not meet certain normalization requirements;
- Certain property acquired from related persons;
- Property acquired in certain nonrecognition transactions;
- Certain sound recordings, movies, and videotapes; and
- Intangible property, other than section 197 intangibles, including:

1. Computer software. Use the straight line method over 36 months for software acquired after August 10, 1993. You may also elect this method for software acquired after July 25, 1991. The amortization of section 197 intangibles is also included in this election. See the line 39 instructions for more details.

2. Any right to receive tangible property or services under a contract or granted by a governmental unit (not acquired as part of a business).

3. Any interest in a patent or copyright (not acquired as part of a business).

4. Mortgage servicing rights. Use the straight line method over 108 months for rights acquired after August 10, 1993. You may also elect this method for rights acquired after July 25, 1991. The amortization of section 197 intangibles is also included in this election. See the line 39 instructions for more details.

See section 167(f) for more details.

For ACRS property, unless you use an alternate percentage, multiply the property's unadjusted basis by the applicable percentage as follows:

- 5-year property—4th and 5th years (21%);
- 10-year property—4th through 6th years (10%), 7th through 10th years (9%);
- 15-year public utility property—4th year (8%), 5th and 6th years (7%), 7th through 15th years (6%);
- 15-year, 18-year, and 19-year real property and low-income housing—Use the tables in Pub. 534.

If you elected an alternate percentage for any ACRS property, use the straight line method over the recovery period you chose in the prior year. See Pub. 534 for more information and tables.

Include any amounts attributable to the Class Life Asset Depreciation Range (CLADR) system. If you previously elected the CLADR system, you must continue to use it to depreciate assets left in your vintage accounts. You must continue to meet recordkeeping requirements.

Prior years' depreciation, plus current year's depreciation, can never exceed the depreciable basis of the property.

The basis and amounts claimed for depreciation should be part of your permanent books and records. **No attachment is necessary.**

Part IV—Summary

Line 20

A partnership or S corporation does not include any section 179 expense deduction (line 12) on this line. Any section 179 expense deduction is passed through separately to the partners and shareholders on the appropriate line of their Schedules K-1.

Line 21

If you are subject to the uniform capitalization rules of section 263A, enter the increase in basis from costs that are required to be capitalized. For a detailed discussion of who is subject to these rules, which costs must be capitalized, and allocation of costs among activities, see Temporary Regulations section 1.263A-1T.

Part V—Listed Property

Taxpayers claiming the standard mileage rate, actual vehicle expenses (including depreciation), or depreciation on other listed property must provide the information requested in Part V, regardless of the tax year the property was placed in service. However, filers of Form 2106 and Schedule C-EZ (Form 1040) report this information on those forms and not in Part V. Also Schedule C (Form 1040) filers who are claiming the standard mileage rate or actual vehicle expenses (except depreciation), and who are not required to file Form 4562 for any other reason, report vehicle information in Part IV of Schedule C and not on Form 4562.

Listed property generally includes, but is not limited to:

- Passenger automobiles weighing 6,000 pounds or less.
- Any other property used for transportation if the nature of the property lends itself to personal use, such as motorcycles, pick-up trucks, etc.
- Any property used for entertainment or recreational purposes (such as photographic, phonographic, communication, and video recording equipment).
- Cellular telephones (or other similar telecommunications equipment).
- Computers or peripheral equipment.

Exception. Listed property does not include **(a)** photographic, phonographic, communication, or video equipment used exclusively in a taxpayer's trade or business or at the taxpayer's regular business establishment; **(b)** any computer or peripheral equipment used exclusively at a regular business establishment and owned or leased by the person operating the establishment; or **(c)** an ambulance, hearse, or vehicle used for transporting persons or property for hire. For purposes of the preceding sentence, a portion of the taxpayer's home is treated as a regular business establishment only if that portion meets the requirements under section 280A(c)(1) for deducting expenses attributable to the business use of a home. (However, for any property listed under **(a)** above, the regular business establishment of an employee is his or her employer's regular business establishment.)

Section A—Depreciation and Other Information

Lines 23 and 24

Qualified business use.—For purposes of determining whether to use line 23 or line 24 to report your listed property, you must first determine the percentage of qualified business use for each property. Generally, a qualified business use is any use in your trade or business. However, it does not include:

- Any investment use;
- Leasing the property to a 5% owner or related person;
- The use of the property as compensation for services performed by a 5% owner or related person; or
- The use of the property as compensation for services performed by any person (who is not a 5% owner or related person), unless an amount is included in that person's income for the use of the property and, if required, income tax was withheld on that amount.

As an exception to the general rule, if at least 25% of the total use of any aircraft during the tax year is for a qualified business use, the leasing or compensatory use of the aircraft by a 5% owner or related person is considered a qualified business use.

Determine your percentage of qualified business use in a manner similar to that used to figure the business/investment use percentage in column (c). Your percentage of qualified business use may be smaller than the business/investment use percentage.

For more information, see Pub. 534.

Column (a).—List on a property-by-property basis all of your listed property in the following order:

1. Automobiles and other vehicles; and
2. Other listed property (computers and peripheral equipment, etc.).

In column (a), list the make and model of automobiles, and give a general description of other listed property.

If you have more than five vehicles used 100% for business/investment purposes, you may group them by tax year. Otherwise, list each vehicle separately.

Column (b).—Enter the date the property was placed in service. If property held for personal use is converted to business/investment use, treat the property as placed in service on the date of conversion.

Column (c).—Enter the percentage of business/investment use. For automobiles and other vehicles, this is determined by dividing the number of miles the vehicle is driven for trade or business purposes or for the production of income during the year (not to include any commuting mileage) by the total number of miles the vehicle is driven for all purposes. Treat vehicles used by employees as being used 100% for business/investment purposes if the value of personal use is included in the employees' gross income, or the employees reimburse the employer for the personal use.

Employers who report the amount of personal use of the vehicle in the employee's gross income, and withhold the appropriate taxes, should enter "100%" for the percentage of business/investment use. For more information, see Pub. 917. For listed property (such as computers or video equipment), allocate the use based on the most appropriate unit of time the property is actually used. See Temporary Regulations section 1.280F-6T.

If during the tax year you convert property used solely for personal purposes to business/investment use, figure the percentage of business/investment use only for the number of months the property is used in your business or for the production of income. Multiply that percentage by the number of months the property is used in your business or for the production of income, and divide the result by 12.

Column (d).—Enter the property's actual cost or other basis (unadjusted for prior years' depreciation). If you traded in old property, your basis is the adjusted basis of the old property (figured as if 100% of the property's use had been for business/investment purposes) plus any additional amount you paid for the new property. For a vehicle, reduce your basis by any diesel-powered highway vehicle credit, qualified electric vehicle credit, or deduction for clean-fuel vehicles you claimed. For property purchased after 1986, add to your basis any sales tax paid on the property.

If you converted the property from personal use to business/investment use, your basis for depreciation is the smaller of the property's adjusted basis or its fair market value on the date of conversion.

Column (e).—Multiply column (d) by the percentage in column (c). From that result, subtract any section 179 expense deduction and half of any investment credit taken before 1986 (unless you took the reduced credit). For automobiles and other listed property placed in service after 1985 (i.e., transition property), reduce the depreciable basis by the entire investment credit.

Column (f).—Enter the recovery period. For property placed in service after 1986 and used more than 50% in a qualified business use, use the table in the line 14, column (d) instructions. For property placed in service after 1986 and used 50% or less in a qualified business use, depreciate the property using the straight line method over its ADS recovery period. The ADS recovery period is 5 years for automobiles and computers.

Column (g).—Enter the method and convention used to figure your depreciation deduction. See the instructions for line 14, columns (e) and (f). Write "200 DB," "150 DB," or "S/L," for the depreciation method, and "HY," "MM," or "MQ," for half-year, mid-month, or mid-quarter conventions, respectively. For property placed in service before 1987, write "PRE" if you used the prescribed percentages under ACRS. If you elected an alternate percentage, enter "S/L."

Column (h).—See **Limitations for automobiles** below before entering an amount in column (h).

If the property is used more than 50% in a qualified business use (line 23), and the property was placed in service after 1986, figure column (h) by following the instructions for line 14, column (g). If placed in service before 1987, multiply column (e) by the applicable percentages given in the line 18 instructions for ACRS property. If the recovery period for the property ended before your tax year beginning in 1993, enter your unrecovered basis, if any, in column (h).

If the property is used 50% or less in a qualified business use (line 24), and the property was placed in service after 1986, figure column (h) by dividing column (e) by column (f) and using the same conventions as discussed in the instructions for line 14, column (e). The amount in column (h) cannot exceed the property's unrecovered basis. For automobiles placed in service after June 18, 1984, and before your tax year beginning in 1988, enter your unrecovered basis, if any, in column (h).

For computers placed in service after June 18, 1984, and before 1987, multiply column (e) by 8.333%.

For property placed in service before 1987 that was disposed of during the year, enter zero.

Limitations for automobiles.—The depreciation deduction plus section 179 expense deduction for automobiles is limited for any tax year. The limitation depends on when you placed the property in service. Use Table F on page 7 to determine the limitation. For any automobile you list on line 23 or 24, the total of columns (h) and (i) for that automobile cannot exceed the limit shown in Table F.

Note: *These limitations are further reduced when the business/investment use percentage (column (c)) is less than 100%. For example, if an automobile placed in service in 1993 is used*

60% for business/investment purposes, then the first year depreciation plus section 179 expense deduction is limited to 60% of $2,860, which is $1,716.

Column (i).—Enter the amount you choose to expense for section 179 property used more than 50% in a qualified business use (subject to the limitations for automobiles noted above). Refer to the Part I instructions to determine if the property qualifies under section 179. Be sure to include the total cost of such property (50% of the cost if qualified zone property placed in service by an enterprise zone business) on line 2, page 1.

Recapture of depreciation and section 179 expense deduction.—If any listed property was used more than 50% in a qualified business use in the year it was placed in service, and used 50% or less in a later year, you may have to recapture in the later year part of the depreciation and section 179 expense deduction. Use **Form 4797,** Sales of Business Property, to figure the recapture amount.

Section B—Information Regarding Use of Vehicles

The information requested in Questions 27 through 33 must be completed for each vehicle identified in Section A.

Employees must provide their employers with the information requested in Questions 27 through 33 for each automobile or vehicle provided for their use.

Employers providing more than five vehicles to their employees, who are not more than 5% owners or related persons, are not required to complete Questions 27 through 33 for such vehicles. Instead, they must obtain this information from their employees, check "Yes" to Question 37, and retain the information received as part of their permanent records.

Section C—Questions for Employers Who Provide Vehicles for Use by Their Employees

For employers providing vehicles to their employees, a written policy statement regarding the use of such vehicles, if initiated and kept by the employer, will relieve the employee of keeping separate records for substantiation.

Two types of written policy statements will satisfy the employer's substantiation requirements under section 274(d): **(a)** a policy statement that prohibits personal use including commuting; and **(b)** a policy statement that prohibits personal use except for commuting.

Line 34

A policy statement that prohibits personal use (including commuting) must meet the following conditions:

- The vehicle is owned or leased by the employer and is provided to one or more employees for use in the employer's trade or business;
- When the vehicle is not used in the employer's trade or business, it is kept on the employer's business premises, unless it is temporarily located elsewhere (e.g., for maintenance or because of a mechanical failure);
- No employee using the vehicle lives at the employer's business premises;
- No employee may use the vehicle for personal purposes, other than de minimis personal use (e.g., a stop for lunch between two business deliveries); and
- Except for de minimis use, the employer reasonably believes that no employee uses the vehicle for any personal purpose.

Line 35

A policy statement that prohibits personal use (except for commuting) is NOT available if the commuting employee is an officer, director, or 1% or more owner. This policy must meet the following conditions:

- The vehicle is owned or leased by the employer and is provided to one or more employees for use in the employer's trade or business and is used in the employer's trade or business;
- For bona fide noncompensatory business reasons, the employer requires the employee to commute to and/or from work in the vehicle;
- The employer establishes a written policy under which the employee may not use the vehicle for personal purposes, other than commuting or de minimis personal use (e.g., a stop for a personal errand between a business delivery and the employee's home);
- Except for de minimis use, the employer reasonably believes that the employee does not use the vehicle for any personal purpose other than commuting; and
- The employer accounts for the commuting use by including an appropriate amount in the employee's gross income.

For both written policy statements, there must be evidence that would enable the IRS to determine whether use of the vehicle meets the conditions stated above.

Line 38

An automobile is considered to have qualified demonstration use if the employer maintains a written policy statement that:

- Prohibits its use by individuals other than full-time automobile salesmen;
- Prohibits its use for personal vacation trips;
- Prohibits storage of personal possessions in the automobile; and
- Limits the total mileage outside the salesmen's normal working hours.

Part VI—Amortization

Each year you may elect to deduct part of certain capital costs over a fixed period. If you amortize property, the part you amortize does not qualify for the election to expense certain tangible property or depreciation.

For individuals reporting amortization of bond premium for bonds acquired before October 23, 1986, do not report the deduction here. See the instructions for Schedule A (Form 1040).

For taxpayers (other than corporations) claiming a deduction for amortization of bond premium for bonds acquired after October 22, 1986, but before January 1, 1988, the deduction is treated as interest expense and is subject to the investment interest limitations. Use **Form 4952,** Investment Interest Expense Deduction, to compute the allowable deduction.

For taxable bonds acquired after 1987, the amortization offsets the interest income. Get **Pub. 550,** Investment Income and Expenses.

Line 39

Complete line 39 only for those costs for which the amortization period begins during your tax year beginning in 1993.

Column (a).—Describe the costs you are amortizing. You may amortize:

- Pollution control facilities (section 169, limited by section 291 for corporations).
- Certain bond premiums (section 171).
- Research and experimental expenditures (section 174).
- The cost of acquiring a lease (section 178).
- Qualified forestation and reforestation costs (section 194).
- Business start-up expenditures (section 195).
- Organizational expenditures for a corporation (section 248) or partnership (section 709).
- Optional write-off of certain tax preferences over the period specified in section 59(e).
- Section 197 intangibles, which generally include:

1. Goodwill,

2. Going concern value,

3. Workforce in place,

4. Business books and records, operating systems, or any other information base,

5. Any patent, copyright, formula, process, design, pattern, knowhow, format, or similar item,

6. Any customer-based intangible (e.g., composition of market or market share),

7. Any supplier-based intangible,

8. Any license, permit, or other right granted by a governmental unit,

9. Any covenant not to compete entered into in connection with the acquisition of a business, and

10. Any franchise (other than a sports franchise), trademark, or trade name.

Section 197 intangibles acquired after August 10, 1993, must be amortized over 15 years starting with the month the intangibles were acquired. You may also elect to amortize section 197 intangibles acquired after July 25, 1991, over the same period. If you make this election, it applies to all property acquired after July 25, 1991. In addition to section 197 intangibles, the election requires that you depreciate computer software and mortgage servicing rights under the special rules in section 167(f) (as discussed in the line 18 instructions). Once made, the election may not be revoked without IRS consent.

Note: *Section 197 will not apply to an acquisition of property under a binding contract in effect on August 10, 1993, and all times thereafter until you acquired the property, if you elect to exclude the property from this provision.*

Column (b).—Enter the date the amortization period begins under the applicable Code section.

Column (c).—Enter the total amount you are amortizing. See the applicable Code section for limits on the amortizable amount.

Column (d).—Enter the Code section under which you amortize the costs.

Column (f).—Compute the amortization deduction by:

1. Dividing column (c) by the number of months over which the costs are to be amortized, and multiplying the result by the number of months in the amortization period included in your tax year beginning in 1993; or

2. Multiplying column (c) by the percentage in column (e).

Attach any other information the Code and regulations may require to make a valid election. See Pub. 535 for more information.

Line 40

Enter the amount of amortization attributable to those costs for which the amortization period began before 1993.

Table A—General Depreciation System **Method:** 200% declining balance switching to straight line **Convention:** Half-year

Year	If the recovery period is: 3 yrs.	5 yrs.	7 yrs.	10 yrs.
1	33.33%	20.00%	14.29%	10.00%
2	44.45%	32.00%	24.49%	18.00%
3	14.81%	19.20%	17.49%	14.40%
4	7.41%	11.52%	12.49%	11.52%
5		11.52%	8.93%	9.22%
6		5.76%	8.92%	7.37%
7			8.93%	6.55%
8			4.46%	6.55%

Table B—General and Alternative Depreciation System **Method:** 150% declining balance switching to straight line **Convention:** Half-year

Year	If the recovery period is: 5 yrs.	7 yrs.	10 yrs.	12 yrs.	15 yrs.	20 yrs.
1	15.00%	10.71%	7.50%	6.25%	5.00%	3.750%
2	25.50%	19.13%	13.88%	11.72%	9.50%	7.219%
3	17.85%	15.03%	11.79%	10.25%	8.55%	6.677%
4	16.66%	12.25%	10.02%	8.97%	7.70%	6.177%
5	16.66%	12.25%	8.74%	7.85%	6.93%	5.713%
6	8.33%	12.25%	8.74%	7.33%	6.23%	5.285%
7		12.25%	8.74%	7.33%	5.90%	4.888%
8		6.13%	8.74%	7.33%	5.90%	4.522%

Table C—General Depreciation System **Method:** Straight line **Convention:** Mid-month **Recovery period:** 27.5 years

Year	The month in the 1st recovery year the property is placed in service: 1	2	3	4	5	6	7	8	9	10	11	12
1	3.485%	3.182%	2.879%	2.576%	2.273%	1.970%	1.667%	1.364%	1.061%	0.758%	0.455%	0.152%
2–8	3.636%	3.636%	3.636%	3.636%	3.636%	3.636%	3.636%	3.636%	3.636%	3.636%	3.636%	3.636%

Table D—General Depreciation System **Method:** Straight line **Convention:** Mid-month **Recovery period:** 31.5 years

Year	The month in the 1st recovery year the property is placed in service: 1	2	3	4	5	6	7	8	9	10	11	12
1	3.042%	2.778%	2.513%	2.249%	1.984%	1.720%	1.455%	1.190%	0.926%	0.661%	0.397%	0.132%
2–7	3.175%	3.175%	3.175%	3.175%	3.175%	3.175%	3.175%	3.175%	3.175%	3.175%	3.175%	3.175%
8	3.175%	3.174%	3.175%	3.174%	3.175%	3.174%	3.175%	3.175%	3.175%	3.175%	3.175%	3.175%

Table E—General Depreciation System **Method:** Straight line **Convention:** Mid-month **Recovery period:** 39 years

Year	The month in the 1st recovery year the property is placed in service: 1	2	3	4	5	6	7	8	9	10	11	12
1	2.461%	2.247%	2.033%	1.819%	1.605%	1.391%	1.177%	0.963%	0.749%	0.535%	0.321%	0.107%
2–39	2.564%	2.564%	2.564%	2.564%	2.564%	2.564%	2.564%	2.564%	2.564%	2.564%	2.564%	2.564%

Table F—Limitations for Automobiles

Date Placed in Service	Year of Deduction: 1st Tax Year	2nd Tax Year	3rd Tax Year	4th & Later Tax Years
June 19–Dec. 31, 1984				$6,000
Jan. 1–April 2, 1985				$6,200
April 3, 1985–Dec. 31, 1986 . . .				$4,800
Jan. 1, 1987–Dec. 31, 1990 . . .				$1,475
Jan. 1–Dec. 31, 1991			$2,550	$1,575
Jan. 1–Dec. 31, 1992		$4,400	$2,650	$1,575
Jan. 1–Dec. 31, 1993	$2,860	$4,600	$2,750	$1,675
After Dec. 31, 1993	*	*	*	*

* The limitations for automobiles placed in service after Dec. 31, 1993, will be published in the Internal Revenue Bulletin. These amounts were not available at the time these instructions were printed.

Depreciation Worksheet

Description of Property	Date Placed in Service	Cost or Other Basis	Business/ Investment Use %	Section 179 Deduction	Depreciation Prior Years	Basis for Depreciation	Method/ Convention	Recovery Period	Rate or Table %	Depreciation Deduction

☆ U.S. GOVERNMENT PRINTING OFFICE: 1993 345-373

SCHEDULE K-1 (Form 1065)
Department of the Treasury
Internal Revenue Service

Partner's Share of Income, Credits, Deductions, etc.

► See separate instructions.

For calendar year 1993 or tax year beginning , 1993, and ending , 19

OMB No. 1545-0099

1993

Partner's identifying number ►

Partner's name, address, and ZIP code

Partnership's identifying number ►

Partnership's name, address, and ZIP code

A This partner is a ☐ general partner ☐ limited partner ☐ limited liability company member

B What type of entity is this partner? ► ....

C Is this partner a ☐ domestic or a ☐ foreign partner?

D Enter partner's percentage of:

	(i) Before change or termination	(ii) End of year
Profit sharing	%	%
Loss sharing	%	%
Ownership of capital	%	%

E IRS Center where partnership filed return:

F Partner's share of liabilities (see instructions):

Nonrecourse . . . . $ ....

Qualified nonrecourse financing . $ ....

Other . . . . $ ....

G Tax shelter registration number . ► ....

H Check here if this partnership is a publicly traded partnership as defined in section 469(k)(2) . . . . ☐

I Check applicable boxes: (1) ☐ Final K-1 (2) ☐ Amended K-1

J Analysis of partner's capital account:

(a) Capital account at beginning of year	(b) Capital contributed during year	(c) Partner's share of lines 3, 4, and 7, Form 1065, Schedule M-2	(d) Withdrawals and distributions	(e) Capital account at end of year (combine columns (a) through (d))
			( )	

	(a) Distributive share item		(b) Amount	(c) 1040 filers enter the amount in column (b) on:
Income (Loss)	1 Ordinary income (loss) from trade or business activities . . .	1		See Partner's Instructions for Schedule K-1 (Form 1065).
	2 Net income (loss) from rental real estate activities	2		
	3 Net income (loss) from other rental activities	3		
	4 Portfolio income (loss):			
	a Interest	4a		Sch. B, Part I, line 1
	b Dividends	4b		Sch. B, Part II, line 5
	c Royalties	4c		Sch. E, Part I, line 4
	d Net short-term capital gain (loss)	4d		Sch. D, line 5, col. (f) or (g)
	e Net long-term capital gain (loss)	4e		Sch. D, line 13, col. (f) or (g)
	f Other portfolio income (loss) *(attach schedule)*	4f		Enter on applicable line of your return.
	5 Guaranteed payments to partner	5		See Partner's Instructions for Schedule K-1 (Form 1065).
	6 Net gain (loss) under section 1231 (other than due to casualty or theft)	6		
	7 Other income (loss) *(attach schedule)*	7		Enter on applicable line of your return.
Deductions	8 Charitable contributions (see instructions) *(attach schedule)* . .	8		Sch. A, line 13 or 14
	9 Section 179 expense deduction	9		See Partner's Instructions for Schedule K-1 (Form 1065).
	10 Deductions related to portfolio income *(attach schedule)* . . .	10		
	11 Other deductions *(attach schedule)*	11		
Investment Interest	12a Interest expense on investment debts	12a		Form 4952, line 1
	b (1) Investment income included on lines 4a, 4b, 4c, and 4f above	b(1)		See Partner's Instructions for Schedule K-1 (Form 1065).
	(2) Investment expenses included on line 10 above	b(2)		
Credits	13a Credit for income tax withheld	13a		See Partner's Instructions for Schedule K-1 (Form 1065).
	b Low-income housing credit:			
	(1) From section 42(j)(5) partnerships for property placed in service before 1990	b(1)		Form 8586, line 5
	(2) Other than on line 13b(1) for property placed in service before 1990	b(2)		
	(3) From section 42(j)(5) partnerships for property placed in service after 1989	b(3)		
	(4) Other than on line 13b(3) for property placed in service after 1989	b(4)		
	c Qualified rehabilitation expenditures related to rental real estate activities (see instructions)	13c		See Partner's Instructions for Schedule K-1 (Form 1065).
	d Credits (other than credits shown on lines 13b and 13c) related to rental real estate activities (see instructions)	13d		
	e Credits related to other rental activities (see instructions) . . .	13e		
	14 Other credits (see instructions)	14		

For Paperwork Reduction Act Notice, see Instructions for Form 1065. Cat. No. 11394R **Schedule K-1 (Form 1065) 1993**

	(a) Distributive share item		(b) Amount	(c) 1040 filers enter the amount in column (b) on:
Self-employment	**15a** Net earnings (loss) from self-employment	15a		Sch. SE, Section A or B
	b Gross farming or fishing income	15b		See Partner's Instructions for Schedule K-1 (Form 1065).
	c Gross nonfarm income	15c		
Adjustments and Tax Preference Items	**16a** Depreciation adjustment on property placed in service after 1986	16a		See Partner's Instructions for Schedule K-1 (Form 1065) and Instructions for Form 6251.
	b Adjusted gain or loss	16b		
	c Depletion (other than oil and gas)	16c		
	d **(1)** Gross income from oil, gas, and geothermal properties	d(1)		
	(2) Deductions allocable to oil, gas, and geothermal properties	d(2)		
	e Other adjustments and tax preference items *(attach schedule)*	16e		
Foreign Taxes	**17a** Type of income ▶			Form 1116, check boxes
	b Name of foreign country or U.S. possession ▶			Form 1116, Part I
	c Total gross income from sources outside the United States *(attach schedule)*	17c		
	d Total applicable deductions and losses *(attach schedule)*	17d		
	e Total foreign taxes (check one): ▶ ☐ Paid ☐ Accrued	17e		Form 1116, Part II
	f Reduction in taxes available for credit *(attach schedule)*	17f		Form 1116, Part III
	g Other foreign tax information *(attach schedule)*	17g		See Instructions for Form 1116.
Other	**18a** Total expenditures to which a section 59(e) election may apply	18a		See Partner's Instructions for Schedule K-1 (Form 1065).
	b Type of expenditures ▶			
	19 Tax-exempt interest income	19		Form 1040, line 8b
	20 Other tax-exempt income	20		See Partner's Instructions for Schedule K-1 (Form 1065).
	21 Nondeductible expenses	21		
	22 Recapture of low-income housing credit:			
	a From section 42(j)(5) partnerships	22a		Form 8611, line 8
	b Other than on line 22a	22b		

Supplemental Information

23 Supplemental information required to be reported separately to each partner *(attach additional schedules if more space is needed)*:

1993 

Partner's Instructions for Schedule K-1 (Form 1065)

Partner's Share of Income, Credits, Deductions, etc.

(For Partner's Use Only)

Section references are to the Internal Revenue Code unless otherwise noted.

General Instructions

Purpose of Schedule K-1

The partnership uses Schedule K-1 to report your share of the partnership's income, credits, deductions, etc. **Keep it for your records. Do not file it with your tax return.** The partnership has filed a copy with the IRS.

Although the partnership is not subject to income tax, you are liable for tax on your share of the partnership income, whether or not distributed. Include your share on your tax return if a return is required. Use these instructions to help you report the items shown on Schedule K-1 on your tax return.

The amount of loss and deduction that you may claim on your tax return may be less than the amount reported on Schedule K-1. **It is the partner's responsibility to consider and apply any applicable limitations.** See **Limitations on Losses, Deductions, and Credits,** on page 2, for more information.

Where "attach schedule" appears beside a line item on Schedule K-1, see either the schedule that the partnership has attached for that line or line 23 of Schedule K-1.

Inconsistent Treatment of Items

Generally, you must report partnership items shown on your Schedule K-1 (and any attached schedules) the same way that the partnership treated the items on its return. This rule does not apply if your partnership is within the "small partnership exception" and does not elect to have the tax treatment of partnership items determined at the partnership level.

If the treatment on your original or amended return is inconsistent with the partnership's treatment, or if the partnership was required to but has not filed a return, you must file **Form 8082,** Notice of Inconsistent Treatment or Amended Return (Administrative Adjustment Request (AAR)), with your original or amended return to identify and explain any inconsistency (or to note that a partnership return has not been filed).

If you are required to file Form 8082 but fail to do so, you may be subject to the accuracy-related penalty. This penalty is in addition to any tax that results from making your amount or treatment of the item consistent with that shown on the partnership's return. Any deficiency that results from making the amounts consistent may be assessed immediately.

Errors

If you believe the partnership has made an error on your Schedule K-1, notify the partnership and ask for a corrected Schedule K-1. Do not change any items on your copy of Schedule K-1. Be sure that the partnership sends a copy of the corrected Schedule K-1 to the IRS. If you are a partner in a partnership that does not meet the small partnership exception and you report any partnership item on your return in a manner different from the way the partnership reported it, you must file Form 8082.

Sale or Exchange of Partnership Interest

Generally, a partner who sells or exchanges a partnership interest in a section 751(a) exchange must notify the partnership, in writing, within 30 days of the exchange (or, if earlier, by January 15 of the calendar year following the calendar year in which the exchange occurred). A "section 751(a) exchange" is any sale or exchange of a partnership interest in which any money or other property received by the partner in exchange for that partner's interest is attributable to unrealized receivables (as defined in section 751(c)) or substantially appreciated inventory items (as defined in section 751(d)).

The written notice to the partnership must include the names and addresses of both parties to the exchange, the identifying numbers of the transferor and (if known) of the transferee, and the exchange date.

An exception to this rule is made for sales or exchanges of publicly traded partnership interests for which a broker is required to file **Form 1099-B,** Proceeds From Broker and Barter Exchange Transactions.

If a partner is required to notify the partnership of a section 751(a) exchange but fails to do so, a $50 penalty may be imposed for each such failure. However, no penalty will be imposed if the partner can show that the failure was due to reasonable cause and not willful neglect.

Nominee Reporting

Generally, any person who holds, directly or indirectly, an interest in a partnership as a nominee for another person must furnish a written statement to the partnership by the last day of the month following the end of the partnership's tax year. This statement must include the name, address, and identifying number of the nominee and such other person, description of the partnership interest held as nominee for that person, and other information required under Temporary Regulations section 1.6031(c)-1T. Instead of this statement, the nominee may furnish to the person for whom the nominee holds the partnership interest a copy of Schedule K-1 and related information within 30 days of receiving it from the partnership.

Note: *A nominee who fails to furnish when due all the required information, or who furnishes incorrect information, is subject to a $50 penalty for each statement for which a failure occurs. The maximum penalty is $100,000 for all such failures during a calendar year. If the nominee intentionally disregards the requirement to report correct information, each $50 penalty increases to $100 or, if greater, 10% of the aggregate amount of items required to be reported (and the $100,000 maximum does not apply).*

Cat. No. 11396N

U.S. Persons With Interests in Foreign Partnerships

If you are a U.S. person in a foreign partnership that does not file a partnership return, you may be required to furnish information necessary to determine your correct income (loss) from the partnership.

International Boycotts

Every partnership that had operations in, or related to, a boycotting country, company, or a national of a country must file **Form 5713,** International Boycott Report.

If the partnership cooperated with an international boycott, it must give you a copy of its Form 5713. You must file your own Form 5713 to report the partnership's activities and any other boycott operations that you may have. You may lose certain tax benefits if the partnership participated in, or cooperated with, an international boycott. See Form 5713 and the instructions for more information.

Definitions

General Partner

A general partner is a partner who is personally liable for partnership debts.

Limited Partner

A limited partner is a partner whose potential personal liability for partnership debts is limited to the amount of money or other property that the partner contributed or is required to contribute to the partnership.

Nonrecourse Loans

Nonrecourse loans are those liabilities of the partnership for which no partner bears the economic risk of loss.

Elections

Generally, the partnership decides how to figure taxable income from its operations. However, certain elections are made by you separately on your income tax return and not by the partnership. These elections are made under the following code sections:

- Section 59(e) (deduction of certain qualified expenditures ratably over the period of time specified in that section. For more information, see the instructions for lines 18a and 18b of Schedule K-1);
- Section 108(b)(5) (income from the discharge of indebtedness);
- Section 617 (deduction and recapture of certain mining exploration expenditures); and
- Section 901 (foreign tax credit).

Additional Information

For more information on the treatment of partnership income, credits, deductions, etc., get **Pub. 541,** Tax Information on Partnerships; **Pub. 535,** Business Expenses; and **Pub. 556,** Examination of Returns, Appeal Rights, and Claims for Refund.

You can get the above publications and other publications referenced throughout these instructions at most IRS offices. To order publications and forms, call our toll-free number 1-800-TAX-FORM (1-800-829-3676).

Limitations on Losses, Deductions, and Credits

There are three separate potential limitations on the amount of partnership losses that you may deduct on your return. These limitations and the order in which you must apply them are as follows: the basis rules, the at-risk limitations, and the passive activity limitations. Each of these limitations is discussed separately below.

Note: *Other limitations may apply to specific deductions (e.g., the section 179 expense deduction). These limitations on specific deductions generally apply before the basis, at-risk, and passive loss limitations.*

Basis Rules

Generally, you may **not** claim your share of a partnership loss (including a capital loss) to the extent that it is greater than the adjusted basis of your partnership interest at the end of the partnership's tax year.

You can compute the adjusted basis of your partnership interest by adding items that increase your basis and then subtracting items that decrease your basis.

Items that **increase** your basis are:

- Money and your adjusted basis in property contributed to the partnership.
- Your share of the partnership's income.
- Your share of the increase in the partnership's liabilities (or your individual liabilities caused by your assumption of partnership liabilities).

Items that **decrease** your basis are:

- Money and the adjusted basis of property distributed to you.
- Your share of the partnership's losses.
- Your share of the decrease in the partnership's liabilities (or your individual liabilities assumed by the partnership).

The above is not a complete list of items and factors that determine basis. See Pub. 541 for more information.

At-Risk Limitations

Generally, if you have **(a)** a loss or other deduction from any activity carried on as a trade or business or for the production of income by the partnership, and **(b)** amounts in the activity for which you are not at risk, you will have to complete **Form 6198,** At-Risk Limitations, to figure your allowable loss.

The at-risk rules generally limit the amount of loss (including loss on the disposition of assets) and other deductions (such as the section 179 expense deduction) that you can claim to the amount you could actually lose in the activity. However, if you acquired your partnership interest before 1987, the at-risk rules do not apply to losses from an activity of holding real property placed in service before 1987 by the partnership. The activity of holding mineral property does not qualify for this exception. The partnership should identify on an attachment to Schedule K-1 the amount of any losses that are not subject to the at-risk limitations.

Generally, you are not at risk for amounts such as the following:

- Nonrecourse loans used to finance the activity, to acquire property used in the activity, or to acquire your interest in the activity, that are not secured by your own property (other than the property used in the activity). See **Item F,** on page 5, for the exception for qualified nonrecourse financing secured by real property.
- Cash, property, or borrowed amounts used in the activity (or contributed to the activity, or used to acquire your interest in the activity) that are protected against loss by a guarantee, stop-loss agreement, or other similar arrangement (excluding casualty insurance and insurance against tort liability).
- Amounts borrowed for use in the activity from a person who has an interest in the activity, other than as a creditor, or who is related, under section 465(b)(3), to a person (other than you) having such an interest.

To help you complete Form 6198, the partnership should specify on an attachment to Schedule K-1 your share of the total pre-1976 losses from a section 465(c)(1) activity for which there existed a corresponding amount of nonrecourse liability at the end of the year in which the losses occurred. Also, you should get a separate statement of income, expenses, etc., for each activity from the partnership.

Passive Activity Limitations

Section 469 provides rules that limit the deduction of certain losses and credits. These rules apply to partners who:

- Are individuals, estates, trusts, closely held corporations, or personal service corporations, and
- Have a passive activity loss or credit for the tax year.

Passive activities include:

1. Trade or business activities in which you do not materially participate, and

2. Activities that meet the definition of rental activities under Temporary Regulations section 1.469-1T(e)(3) and Regulations section 1.469-1(e)(3).

Passive activities **do not** include:

1. Trade or business activities in which you materially participate,

2. Working interests in oil or gas wells if you are a general partner,

3. Qualifying low-income housing activities, and

4. Activities of trading personal property for the account of owners of interests in the activities.

If you are an individual, an estate, or a trust, and you have a passive activity loss or credit, get **Form 8582,** Passive Activity Loss Limitations, to figure your allowable passive losses and **Form 8582-CR,** Passive Activity Credit Limitations, to figure your allowable passive credits. For a corporation, get **Form 8810,** Corporate Passive Activity Loss and Credit Limitations. See the instructions for these forms for more information.

If the partnership is conducting more than one activity, it will attach a statement to your Schedule K-1 that identifies each activity (trade or business activity, rental real estate activity, rental activity other than rental real estate, etc.) and specifies the income (loss), deductions, and credits from each activity.

Material participation in trade or business activities.—You must determine if you materially participated in each trade or business activity held through the partnership. **All determinations of material participation are made regarding your participation during the partnership's tax year.**

Material participation standards for partners who are individuals are listed below. Special rules apply to certain retired or disabled farmers and to the surviving spouses of farmers. See the Instructions for Form 8582 for details.

Corporations should refer to the Instructions for Form 8810 for the material participation standards that apply to them.

Individuals (other than limited partners).—If you are an individual (either a general partner or a limited partner who owned a general partnership interest at all times during the tax year), you materially participated in an activity only if:

1. You participated in the activity for more than 500 hours during the tax year; or

2. Your participation in the activity for the tax year constituted substantially all the participation in the activity of all individuals (including individuals who are not owners of interests in the activity); or

3. You participated in the activity for more than 100 hours during the tax year, and your participation in the activity for the tax year was not less than the participation in the activity of any other individual (including individuals who were not owners of interests in the activity) for the tax year; or

4. The activity was a significant participation activity for the tax year, and you participated in all significant participation activities (including activities outside the partnership) during the year for more than 500 hours. A "significant participation activity" is any trade or business activity in which you participated for more than 100 hours during the year and in which you did not materially participate under any of the material participation tests (other than this test **4**); or

5. You materially participated in the activity for any 5 tax years (whether or not consecutive) during the 10 tax years that immediately precede the tax year; or

6. The activity was a personal service activity and you materially participated in the activity for any 3 tax years (whether or not consecutive) preceding the tax year. A "personal service activity" involves the performance of personal services in the fields of health, law, engineering, architecture, accounting, actuarial science, performing arts, consulting, or any other trade or business in which capital is not a material income-producing factor; or

7. Based on all the facts and circumstances, you participated in the activity on a regular, continuous, and substantial basis during the tax year.

Limited partners.—If you are a limited partner, you do not materially participate in an activity unless you meet one of the tests in paragraphs **1, 5,** or **6** above.

Work counted toward material participation.—Generally, any work that you or your spouse does in connection with an activity held through a partnership (where you own your partnership interest at the time the work is done) is counted toward material participation. However, work in connection with the activity is not counted toward material participation if:

1. The work is not the sort of work that owners of the activity would usually do and one of the principal purposes of the work that you or your spouse does is to avoid the passive loss or credit limitations; or

2. You do the work in your capacity as an investor and you are not directly involved in the day-to-day operations of the activity. Examples of work done as an investor that would not count toward material participation include **(a)** studying and reviewing financial statements or reports on operations of the activity; **(b)** preparing or compiling summaries or analyses of the finances or operations of the activity for your own use; and **(c)** monitoring the finances or operations of the activity in a nonmanagerial capacity.

Effect of determination.—If you determine that you materially participated in a trade or business activity of the partnership, report the income (loss), deductions, and credits from that activity as indicated in either column (c) of Schedule K-1 or the instructions for each line.

If you determine that you did not materially participate in a trade or business activity of the partnership or if you have income (loss), deductions, or credits from a rental activity of the partnership, the amounts from that activity are passive. Report passive income (losses), deductions, and credits as follows:

1. If you have an overall gain (the excess of income over deductions and losses, including any prior year unallowed loss) from a passive activity, report the income, deductions, and losses from the activity as indicated on Schedule K-1 or in these instructions.

2. If you have an overall loss (the excess of deductions and losses, including any prior year unallowed loss, over income) or credits from a passive activity, report the income, deductions, losses, and credits from **all** passive activities following the Instructions for Form 8582 or Form 8582-CR (or Form 8810), to see if your deductions, losses, and credits are limited under the passive activity rules.

Publicly traded partnerships.—The passive activity limitations are applied separately for items (other than the low-income housing credit and the rehabilitation credit) from each publicly traded partnership (PTP). Thus, a net passive loss from a PTP may not be deducted from other passive income. Instead, a passive loss from a PTP is suspended and carried forward to be applied against passive income from the same PTP in later years. If the partner's entire interest in the PTP is completely disposed of, any unused losses are allowed in full in the year of disposition.

If you have an overall gain from a PTP, the net gain is nonpassive income. In addition, the nonpassive income is included in investment income to figure your investment interest expense deduction.

Do not report passive income, gains, or losses from a PTP on Form 8582. Instead, use the following rules to figure and report on the proper form or schedule your income, gains, and losses from passive activities that you held through each PTP you owned during the tax year:

1. Combine any current year income, gains and losses, and any prior year unallowed losses to see if you have an overall gain or loss from the PTP. Include only the same types of income and losses you would include in figuring your net income or loss from a non-PTP passive activity. Get **Pub. 925,** Passive Activity and At-Risk Rules, for more details.

2. If you have an overall gain, the net gain portion (total gain minus total losses) is nonpassive income. On the form or schedule you normally use, report the net gain portion as nonpassive income and the remaining income and the total losses as passive income and loss. Write to the left of the entry space, **"From PTP."** It is important to identify the nonpassive income because the nonpassive portion is included in modified adjusted gross income for purposes of figuring on Form 8582 the "special allowance" for active participation in a non-PTP rental real estate activity. In addition, the nonpassive income is included in investment income when figuring your investment interest expense deduction on Form 4952.

Example. If you have Schedule E income of $8,000, and a Form 4797 prior year unallowed loss of $3,500 from the passive activities of a particular PTP, you have a $4,500 overall gain ($8,000–$3,500). On Schedule E, Part II, report the $4,500 net gain as nonpassive income in column (k). In column (h), report the remaining Schedule E gain of $3,500 ($8,000–$4,500). On the appropriate line of Form 4797, report the prior year unallowed loss of $3,500. Be sure to write **"From PTP"** to the left of each entry space.

3. If you have an overall loss (but did not dispose of your entire interest in the PTP to an unrelated person in a fully taxable transaction during the year), the losses are allowed to the extent of the income, and the excess loss is carried forward to use in a future year when you have income to offset it. Report as a passive loss on the schedule or form you normally use the portion of the loss equal to the income. Report the income as passive income on the form or schedule you normally use.

Example. You have a Schedule E loss of $12,000 (current year losses plus prior year unallowed losses) and a Form 4797 gain of $7,200. Report the $7,200 gain on the appropriate line of Form 4797. On Schedule E, Part II, report $7,200 of the losses as a passive loss in column (g). Carry forward to 1994 the unallowed loss of $4,800 ($12,000–$7,200).

If you have unallowed losses from more than one activity of the PTP or from the same activity of the PTP that must be reported on different forms, you must allocate the unallowed losses on a pro rata basis to figure the amount allowed from each activity or on each form.

Tax tip. To allocate and keep a record of the unallowed losses, use Worksheets 4, 5, and 6 of Form 8582. List each activity of the PTP in Worksheet 4. Enter the overall loss from each activity in column (a). Complete column (b) of Worksheet 4 according to its instructions. Multiply the total unallowed loss from the PTP by each ratio in column (b) and enter the result in column (c) of Worksheet 4. Then complete Worksheet 5 if all of the loss from the same activity is to be reported on one form or schedule. Use Worksheet 6 instead of Worksheet 5 if you have more than one loss to be reported on different forms or schedules for the same activity. Enter the net loss plus any prior year unallowed losses in column (a) of Worksheet 5 (or Worksheet 6 if applicable). The losses in column (c) of Worksheet 5 (column (e) of Worksheet 6) are the allowed losses to report on the forms or schedules. Report both these losses and any income from the PTP on the forms and schedules you normally use.

4. If you have an overall loss and you disposed of your entire interest in the PTP to an unrelated person in a fully taxable transaction during the year, your losses (including prior year unallowed losses) allocable to the activity for the year are not limited by the passive loss rules. A fully taxable transaction is one in which you recognize all your realized gain or loss. Report the income and losses on the forms and schedules you normally use.

Note: *For rules on the disposition of an entire interest reported using the installment method, see the Instructions for Form 8582.*

Active participation in a rental real estate activity.—If you actively participated in a rental real estate activity, you may be able to deduct up to $25,000 of the loss from the activity from nonpassive income. This "special allowance" is an exception to the general rule disallowing losses in excess of income from passive activities. The special allowance is not available if you were married, file a separate return for the year, and did not live apart from your spouse at all times during the year.

Only individuals and qualifying estates can actively participate in a rental real estate activity. Estates (other than qualifying estates), trusts, and corporations cannot actively participate. Limited partners cannot actively participate unless future regulations provide an exception.

You are not considered to actively participate in a rental real estate activity if at any time during the tax year your interest (including your spouse's interest) in the activity was less than 10% (by value) of all interests in the activity.

Active participation is a less stringent requirement than material participation. You may be treated as actively participating if you participated, for example, in making management decisions or arranging for others to provide services (such as repairs) in a significant and bona fide sense. Management decisions that can count as active participation include approving new tenants, deciding rental terms, approving capital or repair expenditures, and other similar decisions.

An estate is treated as actively participating for tax years ending less than 2 years after the date of the decedent's death if the decedent would have satisfied the active participation requirements for the activity for the tax year the decedent died. Such an estate is a "qualifying estate."

The maximum special allowance that single individuals and married individuals filing a joint return for the tax year can qualify for is $25,000. The maximum is $12,500 in the case of married individuals who file separate returns for the tax year and who lived apart all times during the year. The maximum special allowance for which an estate can qualify is $25,000 reduced by the special allowance for which the surviving spouse qualifies.

If your modified adjusted gross income (defined below) is $100,000 or less ($50,000 or less in the case of married persons filing separately), your loss is deductible up to the amount of the maximum special allowance referred to in the preceding paragraph. If your modified adjusted gross income is more than $100,000 (more than $50,000 in the case of married persons filing separately), the special allowance is limited to 50% of the difference between $150,000 ($75,000 in the case of married persons filing separately) and your modified adjusted gross income. When modified adjusted gross income is $150,000 or more ($75,000 or more in the case of married persons filing separately), there is no special allowance.

Modified adjusted gross income is your adjusted gross income figured without taking into account any passive activity loss, any taxable social security or equivalent railroad retirement benefits, any deductible contributions to an IRA or certain other qualified retirement plans under section 219, the deduction allowed under section 164(f) for one-half of self-employment taxes, or the exclusion from income of interest from Series EE U.S. Savings Bonds used to pay higher education expenses.

Special rules for certain other activities.—Special rules apply to certain other activities. If you have net income (loss), deductions, or credits from any activity to which special rules apply, the partnership will identify the activity and all amounts relating to it on Schedule K-1 or on an attachment.

If you have net income subject to recharacterization under Temporary Regulations section 1.469-2T(f) and Regulations section 1.469-2(f), report such amounts according to the Instructions for Form 8582 (or Form 8810).

If you have net income (loss), deductions, or credits from any of the following activities, treat such amounts as nonpassive and report them as instructed in column (c) of Schedule K-1 or in these instructions:

1. Qualified low-income housing projects,

2. Working interests in oil and gas wells if you are a general partner, or

3. Trading personal property for the account of owners of interests in the activity.

Specific Instructions

General Information and Questions

Item F

Item F should show your share of the partnership's nonrecourse liabilities, partnership-level qualified nonrecourse financing, and other liabilities as of the end of the partnership's tax year. If you terminated your interest in the partnership during the tax year, Item F should show the share that existed immediately before the total disposition. A partner's "other liability" is any partnership liability for which a partner is personally liable.

Use the total of the three amounts for computing the adjusted basis of your partnership interest.

Generally, you may use only the amounts shown next to "Qualified nonrecourse financing" and "Other" to compute your amount at risk. Do not include any amounts that are not at risk if such amounts are included in either of these categories.

If your partnership is engaged in two or more different types of activities subject to the at-risk provisions, or a combination of at-risk activities and any other activity, the partnership should give you a statement showing your share of nonrecourse liabilities, partnership-level qualified nonrecourse financing, and other liabilities for each activity.

Qualified nonrecourse financing secured by real property used in an activity of holding real property that is subject to the at-risk rules is treated as an amount at risk. Qualified nonrecourse financing generally includes financing for which no one is personally liable for repayment that is borrowed for use in an activity of holding real property and that is loaned or guaranteed by a Federal, state, or local government or borrowed from a "qualified" person. Qualified persons include any persons actively and regularly engaged in the business of lending money, such as a bank or savings and loan association. Qualified persons generally do not include related parties (unless the nonrecourse financing is commercially reasonable and on substantially the same terms as loans involving unrelated persons), the seller of the property, or a person who receives a fee for the partnership's investment in the real property. See Pub. 925 for more information on qualified nonrecourse financing.

Both the partnership and you must meet the qualified nonrecourse rules on this debt before you can include the amount shown next to "Qualified nonrecourse financing" in your at-risk computation.

See **Limitations on Losses, Deductions, and Credits** on page 2 for more information on the at-risk limitations.

Item G

If the partnership is a registration-required tax shelter or has invested in a registration-required tax shelter, it should have completed Item G. If you claim or report any income, loss, deduction, or credit from a tax shelter, you must attach Form 8271 to your tax return. If the partnership has invested in a tax shelter, it must give you a copy of its Form 8271 with your Schedule K-1. Use the information on this Form 8271 to complete your Form 8271.

If the partnership itself is a registration-required tax shelter, use the information on Schedule K-1 (name of the partnership, partnership identifying number, and tax shelter registration number) to complete your Form 8271.

Item H

If the box in Item H is checked, you are a partner in a publicly traded partnership and must follow the rules discussed on page 3 under **Publicly traded partnerships.**

Lines 1 through 23

The amounts shown on lines 1 through 23 reflect your share of income, loss, credits, deductions, etc., from partnership business or rental activities without reference to limitations on losses or adjustments that may be required of you because of:

1. The adjusted basis of your partnership interest,

2. The amount for which you are at risk, or

3. The passive activity limitations. For information on these provisions, see **Limitations on Losses, Deductions, and Credits** on page 2.

If you are an individual and the passive activity rules do not apply to the amounts shown on your Schedule K-1, take the amounts shown in column (b) and enter them on the lines on your tax return as indicated in column (c). If the passive activity rules do apply, report the amounts shown in column (b) as indicated in the line instructions below.

If you are not an individual, report the amounts in column (b) as instructed on your tax return.

The line numbers in column (c) are references to forms in use for calendar year 1993. If you file your tax return on a calendar year basis, but your partnership files a return for a fiscal year, enter the amounts shown in column (b) on your tax return for the year in which the partnership's fiscal year ends. For example, if the partnership's tax year ends in February 1994, report the amounts in column (b) on your 1994 tax return.

If you have losses, deductions, or credits from a prior year that were not deductible or usable because of certain limitations, such as the basis rules or the at-risk limitations, take them into account in determining your net income, loss, or credits for this year. However, except for passive activity losses and credits, do not combine the prior-year amounts with any amounts shown on this Schedule K-1 to get a net figure to report on any supporting schedules, statements, or forms attached to your return. Instead, report the amounts on the attached schedule, statement, or form on a year-by-year basis.

If you have amounts other than those shown on Schedule K-1 to report on Schedule E (Form 1040), enter each item on a separate line of Part II of Schedule E.

Income

Line 1—Ordinary Income (Loss) From Trade or Business Activities

The amount reported for line 1 is your share of the ordinary income (loss) from the trade or business activities of the partnership. Generally, where you report this amount on Form 1040 depends on whether the amount is from an activity that is a passive activity to you. If you are an individual partner filing your 1993 Form 1040, find your situation below and report your line 1 income (loss) as instructed, after applying the basis and at-risk limitations on losses:

1. Report line 1 income (loss) from partnership trade or business activities in which you materially participated on Schedule E (Form 1040), Part II, column (i) or (k).

2. Report line 1 income (loss) from partnership trade or business activities in which you did not materially participate, as follows:

a. If income is reported on line 1, report the income on Schedule E, Part II, column (h). However, if the box in Item H is checked, report the income following the rules for **Publicly traded partnerships** on page 3.

b. If a loss is reported on line 1, report the loss following the Instructions for Form 8582, to determine how much of the loss can be reported on Schedule E, Part II, column (g). However, if the box in Item H is checked, report the loss following the rules for **Publicly traded partnerships** on page 3.

Line 2—Net Income (Loss) From Rental Real Estate Activities

Generally, the income (loss) reported on line 2 is a passive activity amount to all partners. There is an exception, however, for losses from a qualified low-income housing project. The passive activity loss limitations do not apply to losses incurred by qualified investors in qualified low-income housing projects. The partnership will have attached a schedule for line 2 to identify any such amounts.

If you are filing a 1993 Form 1040, use the following instructions to determine where to enter a line 2 amount:

1. If you have a loss (other than from a qualified low-income housing project) on line 2 and you meet **all** of the following conditions, enter the loss on Schedule E (Form 1040), Part II, column (g):

a. You actively participated in the partnership rental real estate activities. (See **Active participation in a rental real estate activity** on page 4.)

b. Rental real estate activities with active participation were your only passive activities.

c. You have no prior year unallowed losses from these activities.

d. Your total loss from the rental real estate activities was not more than $25,000 (not more than $12,500 if married filing separately and you lived apart from your spouse all year).

e. If you are a married person filing separately, you lived apart from your spouse all year.

f. You have no current or prior year unallowed credits from a passive activity.

g. Your modified adjusted gross income was not more than $100,000 (not more than $50,000 if married filing separately and you lived apart from your spouse all year).

h. Your interest in the rental real estate activity is **not** held as a limited partner.

2. If you have a loss on line 2 (other than from a qualified low-income housing project) and you **do not** meet all the conditions in **1** above, report the loss following the Instructions for Form 8582 to determine how much of the loss you can report on Schedule E (Form 1040), Part II, column (g). However, if the box in Item H is checked, report the loss following the rules for **Publicly traded partnerships** on page 3.

3. If you are a qualified investor reporting a qualified low-income housing project loss, report the loss on Schedule E, Part II, column (i).

4. If you have income on line 2, enter the income on Schedule E, Part II, column (h). However, if the box in Item H is checked, report the income following the rules for **Publicly traded partnerships** on page 3.

Line 3—Net Income (Loss) From Other Rental Activities

The amount on line 3 is a passive activity amount for all partners. Report the income or loss as follows:

1. If line 3 is a loss, report the loss following the Instructions for Form 8582. However, if the box in Item H is checked, report the loss following the rules for **Publicly traded partnerships** on page 3.

2. If income is reported on line 3, report the income on Schedule E (Form 1040), Part II, column (h). However, if the box in Item H is checked, report the income following the rules for **Publicly traded partnerships** on page 3.

Line 4—Portfolio Income (Loss)

Portfolio income or loss is not subject to the passive activity limitations. Portfolio income includes income not derived in the ordinary course of a trade or business from interest, dividends, annuities, or royalties and gain or loss on the sale of property that produces these types of income or is held for investment. Column (c) of Schedule K-1 tells individual partners where to report this income on Form 1040.

The partnership uses line 4f to report portfolio income other than interest, dividend, royalty, and capital gain (loss) income. It will attach a statement to tell you what kind of portfolio income is reported on line 4f. An example of portfolio income that could be reported on this line is income from a real estate mortgage investment conduit (REMIC) in which the partnership is a residual interest holder.

If the partnership has a residual interest in a REMIC, it will report on the statement your share of REMIC taxable income (net loss) that you report on Schedule E (Form 1040), Part IV, column (d). The statement will also report your share of any "excess inclusion" that you report on Schedule E, Part IV, column (c), and your share of section 212 expenses that you report on Schedule E, Part IV, column (e). If you itemize your deductions on Schedule A (Form 1040), you may also deduct these section 212 expenses as a miscellaneous deduction subject to the 2% adjusted gross income floor on Schedule A, line 20.

Line 5—Guaranteed Payments to Partners

Generally, amounts on this line are not part of a passive activity, and you should report them on Schedule E (Form 1040), Part II, column (k). For example, guaranteed payments for personal services paid to any partner are not passive activity income.

Line 6—Net Gain (Loss) Under Section 1231 (Other Than Due to Casualty or Theft)

If the amount on line 6 is from a rental activity, the section 1231 gain (loss) is a passive activity amount. Likewise, if the amount is from a trade or business activity and you did not materially participate in the activity, the section 1231 gain (loss) is a passive activity amount.

- If the amount is not a passive activity amount to you, report it on line 2, column (g) or (h), whichever is applicable, of **Form 4797,** Sales of Business Property. You do not have to complete the information called for in columns (b) through (f). Write "From Schedule K-1 (Form 1065)" across these columns.
- If gain is reported on line 6 and it is a passive activity amount to you, report the gain on line 2, column (h), of Form 4797.
- If a loss is reported on line 6 and it is a passive activity amount to you, see **Passive loss limitations** in the Instructions for Form 4797. You will need to report the loss following the Instructions for Form 8582 to determine how much of the loss is allowed on Form 4797. However, if the box in Item H is checked, report the loss following the rules for **Publicly traded partnerships** on page 3.

Line 7—Other Income (Loss)

Amounts on this line are other items of income, gain, or loss not included on lines 1 through 6. The partnership should give you a description and the amount of your share for each of these items.

Report loss items that are passive activity amounts to you following the Instructions for Form 8582. However, if the box in Item H is checked, report the loss following the rules for **Publicly traded partnerships** on page 3.

Report income or gain items that are passive activity amounts to you as instructed below.

The instructions given below tell you where to report line 7 items if such items are not passive activity amounts.

Line 7 items may include the following:

- Partnership gains from the disposition of farm recapture property (see Form 4797) and other items to which section 1252 applies.
- Income from recoveries of tax benefit items. A tax benefit item is an amount you deducted in a prior tax year that reduced your income tax. Report this amount on the "Other income" line of Form 1040 to the extent it reduced your tax.
- Gambling gains and losses.

1. If the partnership was **not** engaged in the trade or business of gambling, **(a)** report gambling winnings on Form 1040, line 22, and **(b)** deduct gambling losses to the extent of winnings on Schedule A, line 25.

2. If the partnership was engaged in the trade or business of gambling, **(a)** report gambling winnings in Part II of Schedule E, and **(b)** deduct gambling losses to the extent of winnings in Part II of Schedule E.

- Any income, gain, or loss to the partnership under section 751(b). Report this amount on Form 4797, line 11.
- Specially allocated ordinary gain (loss). Report this amount on Form 4797, line 11.
- Net gain (loss) from involuntary conversions due to casualty or theft. The partnership will give you a schedule that shows the amounts to be entered on **Form 4684,** Casualties and Thefts, line 34, columns (b)(i), (b)(ii), and (c).
- Net short-term capital gain or loss and net long-term capital gain or loss from Schedule D (Form 1065) that is **not** portfolio income (e.g., gain or loss from the disposition of nondepreciable personal property used in a trade or business activity of the partnership). Report a net short-term capital gain or loss on Schedule D (Form 1040), line 5, column (f) or (g), and a net long-term capital gain or loss on Schedule D (Form 1040), line 13, column (f) or (g).
- Any net gain or loss from section 1256 contracts. Report this amount on line 1 of **Form 6781,** Gains and Losses From Section 1256 Contracts and Straddles.

Deductions

Line 8—Charitable Contributions

The partnership will give you a schedule that shows the amount of contributions subject to the 50%, 30%, and 20% limitations. For more details, see the Form 1040 instructions.

If property other than cash is contributed and if the claimed deduction for one item or group of similar items of property exceeds $5,000, the partnership must give you a copy of **Form 8283,** Noncash Charitable Contributions, to attach to your tax return. Do not deduct the amount shown on this form. It is the partnership's contribution. Instead, deduct the amount shown on line 8 of your Schedule K-1 (Form 1065).

If the partnership provides you with information that the contribution was property other than cash and does not give you a Form 8283, see the Instructions for Form 8283 for filing requirements. Do not file Form 8283 unless the total claimed deduction for all contributed items of property exceeds $500.

Charitable contribution deductions are not taken into account in figuring your passive activity loss for the year. Do not enter them on Form 8582.

Line 9—Section 179 Expense Deduction

Use this amount, along with the total cost of section 179 property placed in service during the year from other sources, to complete Part I of **Form 4562,** Depreciation and Amortization. Use Part I of Form 4562 to figure your allowable section 179 expense deduction from all sources. Report the amount on line 12 of Form 4562 allocable to a passive activity from the partnership following the Instructions for Form 8582. However, if the box in Item H is checked, report this amount following the rules for **Publicly traded partnerships** on page 3. If the amount is not a passive activity deduction, report it on Schedule E (Form 1040), Part II, column (j).

Line 10—Deductions Related to Portfolio Income

Amounts entered on this line are deductions that are clearly and directly allocable to portfolio income (other than investment interest expense and section 212 expenses from a REMIC). Generally, you should enter line 10 amounts on Schedule A (Form 1040), line 20. See the Instructions for Schedule A, lines 20 and 25, for more information. These deductions are not taken into account in figuring your passive activity loss for the year. Do not enter them on Form 8582.

Line 11—Other Deductions

Amounts on this line are deductions not included on lines 8, 9, 10, 17e, and 18a, such as:

- Itemized deductions (Form 1040 filers enter on Schedule A (Form 1040)).

Note: *If there was a gain (loss) from a casualty or theft to property not used in a trade or business or for income-producing purposes, the partnership will notify you. You will have to complete your own Form 4684.*

- Any penalty on early withdrawal of savings.
- Soil and water conservation expenditures. See section 175 for limitations on the amount you are allowed to deduct.
- Expenditures for the removal of architectural and transportation barriers to the elderly and disabled that the partnership elected to treat as a current expense. The deductions are limited by section 190(c) to $15,000 per year from all sources.
- Any amounts paid during the tax year for insurance that constitutes medical care for you, your spouse, and your dependents. On line 26 of Form 1040, you may be allowed to deduct up to 25% of such amounts, even if you do not itemize deductions. If you do itemize deductions, enter on line 1 of Schedule A (Form 1040) any amounts not deducted on line 26 of Form 1040.
- Payments made on your behalf to an IRA, Keogh, or a simplified employee pension (SEP) plan. See Form 1040 instructions for lines 24a and 24b to figure your IRA deduction. Enter payments made to a Keogh or SEP plan on Form 1040, line 27. If the payments to a Keogh plan were to a defined benefit plan, the partnership should give you a statement showing the amount of the benefit accrued for the tax year.
- Interest expense allocated to debt-financed distributions. The manner in which you report such interest expense depends on your use of the distributed debt proceeds. See Notice 89-35, 1989-1 C.B. 675, for details.
- Interest paid or accrued on debt properly allocable to your share of a working interest in any oil or gas property (if your liability is not limited). If you did not materially participate in the oil or gas activity, this interest is investment interest reportable as described below; otherwise, it is trade or business interest.
- 1994 meals and entertainment expenses. If your tax year began in 1993, deduct 80% of this amount. Otherwise, you may deduct only 50% of this amount.

The partnership should give you a description and the amount of your share for each of these items.

Investment Interest

If the partnership paid or accrued interest on debts properly allocable to investment property, the amount of interest you are allowed to deduct may be limited.

For more information and the special provisions that apply to investment interest expense, get **Form 4952,** Investment Interest Expense Deduction, and **Pub. 550,** Investment Income and Expenses.

Line 12a—Interest Expense on Investment Debts

Enter this amount on Form 4952, line 1, along with your investment interest expense from Schedule K-1, line 11, if any, and from other sources to determine how much of your total investment interest is deductible.

Lines 12b(1) and (2)—Investment Income and Investment Expenses

Use the amounts on these lines to determine the amounts to enter in Part II of Form 4952.

Caution: *The amounts shown on lines 12b(1) and (2) include only investment income and expenses included on lines 4a, 4b, 4c, 4f, and 10 of this Schedule K-1. The partnership should attach a schedule that shows the amount of any investment income and expenses included on any other lines of this Schedule K-1. Be sure to take these amounts into account, along with the amounts on lines 12b(1) and 12b(2) and your investment income and expenses from other sources, when figuring the amounts to enter in Part II of Form 4952.*

Credits

Caution: *If you have credits that are passive activity credits to you, you must complete Form 8582-CR (or Form 8810 for corporations) in addition to the credit forms referenced below. See the Instructions for Form 8582-CR (or Form 8810) for more information.*

*Also, if you are entitled to claim more than one general business credit (e.g., investment credit, jobs credit, credit for alcohol used as fuel, research credit, low-income housing credit, enhanced oil recovery credit, disabled access credit, renewable electricity production credit, Indian employment credit, employer social security credit, and credit for contributions to certain community development corporations), you must complete **Form 3800,** General Business Credit, in addition to the credit forms referenced below. If you have more than one credit, see the instructions for Form 3800 for more information.*

Line 13a—Credit for Income Tax Withheld

Include the amount the partnership reports to you in the total that you enter on line 54, page 2, Form 1040. Be sure to check the box on line 54 and write "From Schedule K-1" in the margin.

Line 13b—Low-Income Housing Credit

Your share of the partnership's low-income housing credit is shown on line 13b. Any allowable credit is entered on **Form 8586,** Low-Income Housing Credit.

The partnership will report separately on line 13b(1) that portion of the low-income housing credit for property placed in service before 1990 with respect to which section 42(j)(5) applies. All other low-income housing credits for property placed in service before 1990 will be reported on line 13b(2). Line 13b(3) will report the low-income housing credit for property placed in service after 1989 with respect to which section 42(j)(5) applies. All other low-income housing credits for property placed in service after 1989 will be reported on line 13b(4).

Keep a separate record of the amount of low-income housing credit from each of these sources so that you will be able to correctly compute any recapture of low-income housing credit that may result from the disposition of all or part of your partnership interest. For more information, see the Instructions for Form 8586.

Caution: *You cannot claim the low-income housing credit on any qualified low-income housing project for which any person was allowed any benefit under section 502 of the Tax Reform Act of 1986.*

Line 13c—Qualified Rehabilitation Expenditures Related to Rental Real Estate Activities

The partnership should identify your share of the partnership's rehabilitation expenditures from each rental real estate activity. Enter the expenditures on the appropriate line of **Form 3468,** Investment Credit, to figure your allowable credit.

Line 13d—Credits (Other Than Credits Shown on Lines 13b and 13c) Related to Rental Real Estate Activities

The partnership will identify the type of credit and any other information you need to compute credits from rental real estate activities (other than the low-income housing credit and qualified rehabilitation expenditures).

Line 13e—Credits Related to Other Rental Activities

The partnership will identify the type of credit and any other information you need to compute credits from rental activities other than rental real estate activities.

Line 14—Other Credits

The partnership will identify the type of credit and any other information you need to compute credits related to a trade or business activity. Expenditures qualifying for the **(a)** rehabilitation credit from other than rental real estate activities, **(b)** energy credit, or **(c)** reforestation credit will be reported to you on line 23.

Credits that may be reported on line 13d, 13e, or 14 (depending on the type of activity they relate to) include the following:

- Nonconventional source fuel credit.
- Unused credits from cooperatives.
- The credit for increasing research activities and orphan drug credit. Enter this credit on **Form 6765,** Credit for Increasing Research Activities.
- Jobs credit. Enter this credit on **Form 5884,** Jobs Credit. See Form 5884 for definitions, special rules, and limitations.
- Credit for alcohol used as fuel. Enter this credit on **Form 6478,** Credit for Alcohol Used as Fuel.
- Disabled access credit. Enter this credit on **Form 8826,** Disabled Access Credit.
- Enhanced oil recovery credit. Enter this credit on **Form 8830,** Enhanced Oil Recovery Credit.
- Qualified electric vehicle credit. Enter this credit on **Form 8834,** Qualified Electric Vehicle Credit.
- Renewable electricity production credit. Enter this credit on **Form 8835,** Renewable Electricity Production Credit.
- Indian employment credit. Enter this credit on **Form 8845,** Indian Employment Credit.
- Employer social security credit. Enter this credit on **Form 8846,** Credit for Employer Social Security Taxes Paid on Certain Employee Cash Tips.
- Credit for contributions to certain community development corporations. Enter this credit on **Form 8847,** Credit for Contributions to Certain Community Development Corporations.

The passive activity limitations may limit the amount of credits on lines 13b, 13c, 13d, 13e, and 14 that you may take. Lines 13b, 13c, 13d, and 13e credits are related to the rental activities of the partnership and are passive activity credits to all partners. Line 14 credits are related to the trade or business activities of the partnership and are passive activity credits to all partners who did not materially participate in the trade or business activity. In general, credits from passive activities are limited to the tax attributable to passive activities.

But if you actively participated in a rental real estate activity, you may be able to use the line 13d credits against tax on other income. The amount of these credits you can use is limited to their deduction equivalent up to $25,000 (net of losses from rental real estate activities deductible against up to $25,000 of other income).

You may also claim the credits on lines 13b and 13c against tax on other income, subject to the same $25,000 limitation, even if you did not actively participate in a rental real estate activity. Line 13e credits are limited to tax attributable to passive activities. The $25,000 deduction equivalent does not apply to line 13e and line 14 credits.

Self-Employment

If you and your spouse are both partners, each of you must complete and file your own **Schedule SE (Form 1040),** Self-Employment Tax, to report your partnership net earnings (loss) from self-employment.

Line 15a—Net Earnings (Loss) From Self-Employment

If you are a general partner, reduce this amount before entering it on Schedule SE (Form 1040) by any section 179 expense deduction claimed, unreimbursed partnership expenses claimed, and depletion claimed on oil and gas properties. Do not reduce net earnings from self-employment by any separately stated deduction for health insurance expenses.

If the amount on this line is a loss, enter only the deductible amount on Schedule SE (Form 1040). See **Limitations on Losses, Deductions, and Credits** on page 2.

If your partnership is an options dealer or a commodities dealer, see section 1402(i).

If your partnership is an investment club, see Rev. Rul. 75-525, 1975-2 C.B. 350.

Line 15b—Gross Farming or Fishing Income

If you are an individual partner, enter the amount from this line, as an item of information, on Schedule E (Form 1040), Part V, line 41. Also use this amount to figure net earnings from self-employment under the farm optional method on Schedule SE (Form 1040), Section B, Part II.

Line 15c—Gross Nonfarm Income

If you are an individual partner, use this amount to figure net earnings from self-employment under the nonfarm optional method on Schedule SE (Form 1040), Section B, Part II.

Adjustments and Tax Preference Items

Use the information reported on lines 16a through 16e (as well as your adjustments and tax preference items from other sources) to prepare your **Form 6251,** Alternative Minimum Tax—Individuals; **Form 4626,** Alternative Minimum Tax—Corporations; or Schedule H of **Form 1041,** U.S. Fiduciary Income Tax Return.

Lines 16d(1) and 16d(2)—Gross Income From, and Deductions Allocable to, Oil, Gas, and Geothermal Properties

The amounts reported on these lines include only the gross income from, and deductions allocable to, oil, gas, and geothermal properties that are included on line 1 of Schedule K-1. The partnership should have attached a schedule that shows any income from or deductions allocable to such properties that are included on lines 2 through 11 and line 23 of Schedule K-1. Use the amounts reported on lines 16d(1) and 16d(2) and the amounts on the attached schedule to help you determine the net amount to enter on line 14f of Form 6251.

Line 16e—Other Adjustments and Tax Preference Items

Enter the information on the schedule attached by the partnership for line 16e on the applicable lines of Form 6251.

Foreign Taxes

Use the information on lines 17a through 17g and attached schedules to figure your foreign tax credit. For more information, get **Form 1116,** Foreign Tax Credit—Individual, Fiduciary, or Nonresident Alien Individual, and the related instructions; **Form 1118,** Foreign Tax Credit—Corporations, and the related instructions; and **Pub. 514,** Foreign Tax Credit for Individuals.

Other

Lines 18a and 18b

The partnership will show on line 18a the total qualified expenditures to which an election under section 59(e) may apply. It will identify the type of expenditure on line 18b. If there is more than one type of expenditure, the amount of each type will be listed on an attachment. Generally, section 59(e) allows each partner to elect to deduct certain expenses ratably over the number of years in the applicable period rather than deduct the full amount in the current year. Under the election, you may deduct circulation expenditures ratably over a 3-year period. Research and experimental expenditures and mining exploration and development costs qualify for a writeoff period of 10 years. Intangible drilling and development costs may be deducted over a 60-month period, beginning with the month in which such costs were paid or incurred. If you make this election, these items are not treated as adjustments or tax preference items for purposes of the alternative minimum tax. Make the election on Form 4562.

Because each partner decides whether to make the election under section 59(e), the partnership cannot provide you with the amount of the adjustment or tax preference item related to the expenses listed on line 18a. You must decide both how to claim the expenses on your return and compute the resulting adjustment or tax preference item.

Line 19—Tax-Exempt Interest Income

You must report on your return, as an item of information, your share of the tax-exempt interest received or accrued by the partnership during the year. Individual partners should report this amount on Form 1040, line 8b. Increase the adjusted basis of your interest in the partnership by this amount.

Line 20—Other Tax-Exempt Income

Increase the adjusted basis of your interest in the partnership by the amount shown on line 20, but do not include it in income on your tax return.

Line 21—Nondeductible Expenses

The nondeductible expenses paid or incurred by the partnership are not deductible on your tax return. Decrease the adjusted basis of your interest in the partnership by this amount.

Lines 22a and 22b—Recapture of Low-Income Housing Credit

A section 42(j)(5) partnership will report recapture of a low-income housing credit on line 22a. All other partnerships will report recapture of a low-income housing credit on line 22b. Keep a separate record of recapture from each of these sources so that you will be able to correctly compute any recapture of low-income housing credit that may result from the disposition of all or part of your partnership interest. For more information, get **Form 8611,** Recapture of Low-Income Housing Credit.

Supplemental Information

Line 23

Amounts shown on line 23 include:

1. Taxes paid on undistributed capital gains by a regulated investment company. (Form 1040 filers enter your share of these taxes on line 59, check the box for Form 2439, and add the words "Form 1065.")

2. Number of gallons of each fuel used during the tax year in a use qualifying for the credit for taxes paid on fuels and the applicable credit per gallon. Also your share of the credit allowed for the purchase of qualified diesel-powered highway vehicles. Use this information to complete **Form 4136,** Credit for Federal Tax Paid on Fuels.

3. Your share of gross income from the property, share of production for the tax year, etc., needed to figure your depletion deduction for oil and gas wells. The partnership should also allocate to you a share of the adjusted basis of each partnership oil or gas property. See Pub. 535 for how to figure your depletion deduction.

4. Recapture of the section 179 expense deduction. If the recapture was caused by a disposition of the property, include the amount on Form 4797, line 18. The recapture amount will be limited to the amount you deducted in earlier years.

5. Recapture of certain mining exploration expenditures (section 617).

6. Any information or statements you need to comply with requirements under section 6111 (regarding tax shelters) or section 6662(d)(2)(B)(ii) (regarding adequate disclosure of items that may cause an understatement of income tax on your return).

7. Farm production expenses. You may be eligible to elect to deduct these expenses currently or capitalize them under section 263A. Get **Pub. 225,** Farmer's Tax Guide, and Temporary Regulations section 1.263A-1T(c).

8. Any information you need to compute the interest due under section 453(l)(3) with respect to the disposition of certain timeshares and residential lots on the installment method. If you are an individual, report the interest on Form 1040, line 53. Write "453(l)(3)" and the amount of the interest on the dotted line to the left of line 53.

9. Any information you need to compute the interest due under section 453A(c) with respect to certain installment sales. If you are an individual, report the interest on Form 1040, line 53. Write "453A(c)" and the amount of the interest on the dotted line to the left of line 53.

10. Any information you need to compute the interest due or to be refunded under the look-back method of section 460(b)(2) on certain long-term contracts. Use **Form 8697,** Interest Computation Under the Look-Back Method for Completed Long-Term Contracts, to report any such interest.

11. Any information you need relating to interest expense that you are required to capitalize under section 263A for production expenditures. See Notice 88-99, 1988-2 C.B. 422, for more information.

12. Any information you need to compute unrelated business taxable income under section 512(a)(1) (but excluding any modifications required by paragraphs (8) through (15) of section 512(b)) for a partner that is a tax-exempt organization.

Note: *A partner is required to notify the partnership of its tax-exempt status.*

13. Your share of expenditures qualifying for the **(a)** rehabilitation credit from other than rental real estate activities, **(b)** energy credit, or **(c)** reforestation credit. Enter the expenditures on the appropriate line of Form 3468 to figure your allowable credit.

14. Investment credit properties subject to recapture. Any information you need to figure your recapture tax on **Form 4255,** Recapture of Investment Credit. See the Form 3468 on which you took the original credit for other information you need to complete Form 4255.

You may also need Form 4255 if you disposed of more than one-third of your interest in a partnership.

15. Any information you need to figure your recapture of the qualified electric vehicle credit. See Pub. 535 for details, including how to figure the recapture.

16. Any other information you may need to file your return not shown elsewhere on Schedule K-1.

The partnership should give you a description and the amount of your share for each of these items.

*U.S. Government Printing Office: 1993 — 345-268

Form **SS-4**
(Rev. December 1993)
Department of the Treasury
Internal Revenue Service

Application for Employer Identification Number

(For use by employers, corporations, partnerships, trusts, estates, churches, government agencies, certain individuals, and others. See instructions.)

EIN

OMB No. 1545-0003
Expires 12-31-96

Please type or print clearly.

1 Name of applicant (Legal name) (See instructions.)

2 Trade name of business, if different from name in line 1

3 Executor, trustee, "care of" name

4a Mailing address (street address) (room, apt., or suite no.)

5a Business address, if different from address in lines 4a and 4b

4b City, state, and ZIP code

5b City, state, and ZIP code

6 County and state where principal business is located

7 Name of principal officer, general partner, grantor, owner, or trustor—SSN required (See instructions.) ▶

8a Type of entity (Check only one box.) (See instructions.)

☐ Sole Proprietor (SSN) ______
☐ REMIC
☐ Personal service corp.
☐ State/local government
☐ National guard
☐ Other nonprofit organization (specify) ______ (enter GEN if applicable) ______
☐ Other (specify) ▶ ______
☐ Estate (SSN of decedent) ______
☐ Plan administrator-SSN ______
☐ Other corporation (specify) ______
☐ Federal government/military
☐ Church or church controlled organization
☐ Trust
☐ Partnership
☐ Farmers' cooperative

8b If a corporation, name the state or foreign country (if applicable) where incorporated ▶ | State | Foreign country

9 Reason for applying (Check only one box.)

☐ Started new business (specify) ▶ ______
☐ Hired employees
☐ Created a pension plan (specify type) ▶ ______
☐ Banking purpose (specify) ▶
☐ Changed type of organization (specify) ▶ ______
☐ Purchased going business
☐ Created a trust (specify) ▶ ______
☐ Other (specify) ▶

10 Date business started or acquired (Mo., day, year) (See instructions.)

11 Enter closing month of accounting year. (See instructions.)

12 First date wages or annuities were paid or will be paid (Mo., day, year). **Note:** *If applicant is a withholding agent, enter date income will first be paid to nonresident alien. (Mo., day, year)* . . . . ▶

13 Enter highest number of employees expected in the next 12 months. **Note:** *If the applicant does not expect to have any employees during the period, enter "0."* . . . . ▶

Nonagricultural	Agricultural	Household

14 Principal activity (See instructions.) ▶

15 Is the principal business activity manufacturing? . . . . ☐ **Yes** ☐ **No**
If "Yes," principal product and raw material used ▶

16 To whom are most of the products or services sold? Please check the appropriate box. ☐ Business (wholesale)
☐ Public (retail) ☐ Other (specify) ▶ ☐ N/A

17a Has the applicant ever applied for an identification number for this or any other business? . . . . ☐ **Yes** ☐ **No**
Note: *If "Yes," please complete lines 17b and 17c.*

17b If you checked the "Yes" box in line 17a, give applicant's legal name and trade name, if different than name shown on prior application.

Legal name ▶ Trade name ▶

17c Enter approximate date, city, and state where the application was filed and the previous employer identification number if known.

Approximate date when filed (Mo., day, year)	City and state where filed	Previous EIN

Under penalties of perjury, I declare that I have examined this application, and to the best of my knowledge and belief, it is true, correct, and complete.

Business telephone number (include area code)

Name and title (Please type or print clearly.) ▶

Signature ▶ Date ▶

Note: *Do not write below this line. For official use only.*

Please leave blank ▶	Geo.	Ind.	Class	Size	Reason for applying

For Paperwork Reduction Act Notice, see attached instructions. Cat. No. 16055N Form **SS-4**

General Instructions

(Section references are to the Internal Revenue Code unless otherwise noted.)

Purpose

Use Form SS-4 to apply for an employer identification number (EIN). An EIN is a nine-digit number (for example, 12-3456789) assigned to sole proprietors, corporations, partnerships, estates, trusts, and other entities for filing and reporting purposes. The information you provide on this form will establish your filing and reporting requirements.

Who Must File

You must file this form if you have not obtained an EIN before and

- You pay wages to one or more employees.
- You are required to have an EIN to use on any return, statement, or other document, even if you are not an employer.
- You are a withholding agent required to withhold taxes on income, other than wages, paid to a nonresident alien (individual, corporation, partnership, etc.). A withholding agent may be an agent, broker, fiduciary, manager, tenant, or spouse, and is required to file **Form 1042,** Annual Withholding Tax Return for U.S. Source Income of Foreign Persons.
- You file **Schedule C,** Profit or Loss From Business, or **Schedule F,** Profit or Loss From Farming, of **Form 1040,** U.S. Individual Income Tax Return, and have a Keogh plan or are required to file excise, employment, or alcohol, tobacco, or firearms returns.

The following must use EINs even if they do not have any employees:

- Trusts, except the following:

1. Certain grantor-owned revocable trusts (see the Instructions for Form 1040).

2. Individual Retirement Arrangement (IRA) trusts, unless the trust has to file **Form 990-T,** Exempt Organization Business Income Tax Return (See the Instructions for Form 990-T.)

- Estates
- Partnerships
- REMICS (real estate mortgage investment conduits) (See the instructions for **Form 1066,** U.S. Real Estate Mortgage Investment Conduit Income Tax Return.)
- Corporations
- Nonprofit organizations (churches, clubs, etc.)
- Farmers' cooperatives
- Plan administrators (A plan administrator is the person or group of persons specified as the administrator by the instrument under which the plan is operated.)

Note: *Household employers are not required to file Form SS-4 to get an EIN. An EIN may be assigned to you without filing Form SS-4 if your only employees are household employees (domestic workers) in your private home. To have an EIN assigned to you, write "NONE" in the space for the EIN on **Form 942,** Employer's Quarterly Tax Return for Household Employees, when you file it.*

When To Apply for A New EIN

New Business.—If you become the new owner of an existing business, **DO NOT** use the EIN of the former owner. If you already have an EIN, use that number. If you do not have an EIN, apply for one on this form. If you become the "owner" of a corporation by acquiring its stock, use the corporation's EIN.

Changes in Organization or Ownership.—If you already have an EIN, you may need to get a new one if either the organization or ownership of your business changes. If you incorporate a sole proprietorship or form a partnership, you must get a new EIN. However, **DO NOT** apply for a new EIN if you change only the name of your business.

File Only One Form SS-4.—File only one Form SS-4, regardless of the number of businesses operated or trade names under which a business operates. However, each corporation in an affiliated group must file a separate application.

EIN Applied For, But Not Received.—If you do not have an EIN by the time a return is due, write "Applied for" and the date you applied in the space shown for the number. **DO NOT** show your social security number as an EIN on returns.

If you do not have an EIN by the time a tax deposit is due, send your payment to the Internal Revenue service center for your filing area. (See **Where To Apply** below.) Make your check or money order payable to Internal Revenue Service and show your name (as shown on Form SS-4), address, kind of tax, period covered, and date you applied for an EIN.

For more information about EINs, see **Pub. 583,** Taxpayers Starting a Business and **Pub. 1635,** EINs Made Easy.

How To Apply

You can apply for an EIN either by mail or by telephone. You can get an EIN immediately by calling the Tele-TIN phone number for the service center for your state, or you can send the completed Form SS-4 directly to the service center to receive your EIN in the mail.

Application by Tele-TIN.—Under the Tele-TIN program, you can receive your EIN over the telephone and use it immediately to file a return or make a payment. To receive an EIN by phone, complete Form SS-4, then call the Tele-TIN phone number listed for your state under **Where To Apply.** The person making the call must be authorized to sign the form (see **Signature block** on page 3).

An IRS representative will use the information from the Form SS-4 to establish your account and assign you an EIN. Write the number you are given on the upper right-hand corner of the form, sign and date it.

You should mail or FAX the signed SS-4 ***within 24 hours*** *to the Tele-TIN Unit at the service center address for your state.* The IRS representative will give you the FAX number. The FAX numbers are also listed in Pub. 1635.

Taxpayer representatives can receive their client's EIN by phone if they first send a facsimile (FAX) of a completed **Form 2848,** Power of Attorney and Declaration of Representative, or **Form 8821,** Tax Information Authorization, to the Tele-TIN unit. The Form 2848 or Form 8821 will be used solely to release the EIN to the representative authorized on the form.

Application by Mail.—Complete Form SS-4 at least 4 to 5 weeks before you will need an EIN. Sign and date the application and mail it to the service center address for your state. You will receive your EIN in the mail in approximately 4 weeks.

Where To Apply

The Tele-TIN phone numbers listed below will involve a long-distance charge to callers outside of the local calling area, and should be used only to apply for an EIN. THE NUMBERS MAY CHANGE WITHOUT NOTICE. Use 1-800-829-1040 to verify a number or to ask about an application by mail or other Federal tax matters.

If your principal business, office or agency, or legal residence in the case of an individual, is located in:	Call the Tele-TIN phone number shown or file with the Internal Revenue Service center at:
Florida, Georgia, South Carolina	Attn: Entity Control Atlanta, GA 39901 (404) 455-2360
New Jersey, New York City and counties of Nassau, Rockland, Suffolk, and Westchester	Attn: Entity Control Holtsville, NY 00501 (516) 447-4955
New York (all other counties), Connecticut, Maine, Massachusetts, New Hampshire, Rhode Island, Vermont	Attn: Entity Control Andover, MA 05501 (508) 474-9717
Illinois, Iowa, Minnesota, Missouri, Wisconsin	Attn: Entity Control Stop 57A 2306 E. Bannister Rd. Kansas City, MO 64131 (816) 926-5999
Delaware, District of Columbia, Maryland, Pennsylvania, Virginia	Attn: Entity Control Philadelphia, PA 19255 (215) 574-2400

Indiana, Kentucky, Michigan, Ohio, West Virginia	Attn: Entity Control Cincinnati, OH 45999 (606) 292-5467
Kansas, New Mexico, Oklahoma, Texas	Attn: Entity Control Austin, TX 73301 (512) 462-7843
Alaska, Arizona, California (counties of Alpine, Amador, Butte, Calaveras, Colusa, Contra Costa, Del Norte, El Dorado, Glenn, Humboldt, Lake, Lassen, Marin, Mendocino, Modoc, Napa, Nevada, Placer, Plumas, Sacramento, San Joaquin, Shasta, Sierra, Siskiyou, Solano, Sonoma, Sutter, Tehama, Trinity, Yolo, and Yuba), Colorado, Idaho, Montana, Nebraska, Nevada, North Dakota, Oregon, South Dakota, Utah, Washington, Wyoming	Attn: Entity Control Mail Stop 6271-T P.O. Box 9950 Ogden, UT 84409 (801) 620-7645
California (all other counties), Hawaii	Attn: Entity Control Fresno, CA 93888 (209) 452-4010
Alabama, Arkansas, Louisiana, Mississippi, North Carolina, Tennessee	Attn: Entity Control Memphis, TN 37501 (901) 365-5970

If you have no legal residence, principal place of business, or principal office or agency in any state, file your form with the Internal Revenue Service Center, Philadelphia, PA 19255 or call (215) 574-2400.

Specific Instructions

The instructions that follow are for those items that are not self-explanatory. Enter N/A (nonapplicable) on the lines that do not apply.

Line 1.—Enter the legal name of the entity applying for the EIN exactly as it appears on the social security card, charter, or other applicable legal document.

Individuals.—Enter the first name, middle initial, and last name.

Trusts.—Enter the name of the trust.

Estate of a decedent.—Enter the name of the estate.

Partnerships.—Enter the legal name of the partnership as it appears in the partnership agreement.

Corporations.—Enter the corporate name as set forth in the corporation charter or other legal document creating it.

Plan administrators.—Enter the name of the plan administrator. A plan administrator who already has an EIN should use that number.

Line 2.—Enter the trade name of the business if different from the legal name. The trade name is the "doing business as" name.

Note: *Use the full legal name on line 1 on all tax returns filed for the entity. However, if you enter a trade name on line 2 and choose to use the trade name instead of the legal name, enter the trade name on all returns you file. To prevent processing delays and errors,* ***always*** *use either the legal name only or the trade name only on all tax returns.*

Line 3.—Trusts enter the name of the trustee. Estates enter the name of the executor, administrator, or other fiduciary. If the entity applying has a designated person to receive tax information, enter that person's name as the "care of" person. Print or type the first name, middle initial, and last name.

Line 7.—Enter the first name, middle initial, last name, and social security number (SSN) of a principal officer if the business is a corporation; of a general partner if a partnership; and of a grantor owner, or trustor if a trust.

Line 8a.—Check the box that best describes the type of entity applying for the EIN. If not specifically mentioned, check the "other" box and enter the type of entity. Do not enter N/A.

Sole proprietor.—Check this box if you file Schedule C or F (Form 1040) and have a Keogh plan, or are required to file excise, employment, or alcohol, tobacco, or firearms returns. Enter your SSN (social security number) in the space provided.

Plan administrator.—If the plan administrator is an individual, enter the plan administrator's SSN in the space provided.

Withholding agent.—If you are a withholding agent required to file Form 1042, check the "other" box and enter "withholding agent."

REMICs.—Check this box if the entity has elected to be treated as a real estate mortgage investment conduit (REMIC). See the Instructions for Form 1066 for more information.

Personal service corporations.—Check this box if the entity is a personal service corporation. An entity is a personal service corporation for a tax year only if:

- The principal activity of the entity during the testing period (prior tax year) for the tax year is the performance of personal services substantially by employee-owners.
- The employee-owners own 10 percent of the fair market value of the outstanding stock in the entity on the last day of the testing period.

Personal services include performance of services in such fields as health, law, accounting, consulting, etc. For more information about personal service corporations, see the instructions to **Form 1120,** U.S. Corporation Income Tax Return, and **Pub. 542,** Tax Information on Corporations.

Other corporations.—This box is for any corporation other than a personal service corporation. If you check this box, enter the type of corporation (such as insurance company) in the space provided.

Other nonprofit organizations.—Check this box if the nonprofit organization is other than a church or church-controlled organization and specify the type of nonprofit organization (for example, an educational organization.)

If the organization also seeks tax-exempt status, you must file either **Package 1023** or **Package 1024,** Application for Recognition of Exemption. Get **Pub. 557,** Tax-Exempt Status for Your Organization, for more information.

Group exemption number (GEN).—If the organization is covered by a group exemption letter, enter the four-digit GEN. (Do not confuse the GEN with the nine-digit EIN.) If you do not know the GEN, contact the parent organization. Get Pub. 557 for more information about group exemption numbers.

Line 9.—Check only **one** box. Do not enter N/A.

Started new business.—Check this box if you are starting a new business that requires an EIN. If you check this box, enter the type of business being started. **DO NOT** apply if you already have an EIN and are only adding another place of business.

Changed type of organization.—Check this box if the business is changing its type of organization, for example, if the business was a sole proprietorship and has been incorporated or has become a partnership. If you check this box, specify in the space provided the type of change made, for example, "from sole proprietorship to partnership."

Purchased going business.—Check this box if you purchased an existing business. DO NOT use the former owner's EIN. Use your own EIN if you already have one.

Hired employees.—Check this box if the existing business is requesting an EIN because it has hired or is hiring employees and is therefore required to file employment tax returns. **DO NOT** apply if you already have an EIN and are only hiring employees. If you are hiring household employees, see **Note** under **Who Must File** on page 2.

Created a trust.—Check this box if you created a trust, and enter the type of trust created.

Note: *DO NOT file this form if you are the individual-grantor/owner of a revocable trust. You must use your SSN for the trust. See the instructions for Form 1040.*

Created a pension plan.—Check this box if you have created a pension plan and need this number for reporting purposes. Also, enter the type of plan created.

Banking purpose.—Check this box if you are requesting an EIN for banking purposes only and enter the banking purpose (for example, a bowling league for depositing dues, an investment club for dividend and interest reporting, etc.).

Other (specify).—Check this box if you are requesting an EIN for any reason other than those for which there are checkboxes, and enter the reason.

Line 10.—If you are starting a new business, enter the starting date of the business. If the business you acquired is already operating, enter the date you acquired the business. Trusts should enter the date the trust was legally created. Estates should enter the date of death of the decedent whose name appears on line 1 or the date when the estate was legally funded.

Line 11.—Enter the last month of your accounting year or tax year. An accounting or tax year is usually 12 consecutive months, either a calendar year or a fiscal year (including a period of 52 or 53 weeks). A calendar year is 12 consecutive months ending on December 31. A fiscal year is either 12 consecutive months ending on the last day of any month other than December or a 52-53 week year. For more information on accounting periods, see **Pub. 538,** Accounting Periods and Methods.

Individuals.—Your tax year generally will be a calendar year.

Partnerships.—Partnerships generally must adopt the tax year of either (1) the majority partners; (2) the principal partners; (3) the tax year that results in the least aggregate (total) deferral of income; or (4) some other tax year. (See the Instructions for **Form 1065,** U.S. Partnership Return of Income, for more information.)

REMICs.—Remics must have a calendar year as their tax year.

Personal service corporations.—A personal service corporation generally must adopt a calendar year unless:

- It can establish a business purpose for having a different tax year, or
- It elects under section 444 to have a tax year other than a calendar year.

Trusts.—Generally, a trust must adopt a calendar year except for the following:

- Tax-exempt trusts,
- Charitable trusts, and
- Grantor-owned trusts.

Line 12.—If the business has or will have employees, enter the date on which the business began or will begin to pay wages. If the business does not plan to have employees, enter N/A.

Withholding agent.—Enter the date you began or will begin to pay income to a nonresident alien. This also applies to individuals who are required to file Form 1042 to report alimony paid to a nonresident alien.

Line 14.—Generally, enter the exact type of business being operated (for example, advertising agency, farm, food or beverage establishment, labor union, real estate agency, steam laundry, rental of coin-operated vending machine, investment club, etc.). Also state if the business will involve the sale or distribution of alcoholic beverages.

Governmental.—Enter the type of organization (state, county, school district, or municipality, etc.).

Nonprofit organization (other than governmental).—Enter whether organized for religious, educational, or humane purposes, and the principal activity (for example, religious organization—hospital, charitable).

Mining and quarrying.—Specify the process and the principal product (for example, mining bituminous coal, contract drilling for oil, quarrying dimension stone, etc.).

Contract construction.—Specify whether general contracting or special trade contracting. Also, show the type of work normally performed (for example, general contractor for residential buildings, electrical subcontractor, etc.).

Food or beverage establishments.—Specify the type of establishment and state whether you employ workers who receive tips (for example, lounge—yes).

Trade.—Specify the type of sales and the principal line of goods sold (for example, wholesale dairy products, manufacturer's representative for mining machinery, retail hardware, etc.).

Manufacturing.—Specify the type of establishment operated (for example, sawmill, vegetable cannery, etc.).

Signature block.—The application must be signed by: (1) the individual, if the applicant is an individual, (2) the president, vice president, or other principal officer, if the applicant is a corporation, (3) a responsible and duly authorized member or officer having knowledge of its affairs, if the applicant is a partnership or other unincorporated organization, or (4) the fiduciary, if the applicant is a trust or estate.

Some Useful Publications

You may get the following publications for additional information on the subjects covered on this form. To get these and other free forms and publications, call 1-800-TAX-FORM (1-800-829-3676).

Pub. 1635, EINs Made Easy

Pub. 538, Accounting Periods and Methods

Pub. 541, Tax Information on Partnerships

Pub. 542, Tax Information on Corporations

Pub. 557, Tax-Exempt Status for Your Organization

Pub. 583, Taxpayers Starting A Business

Pub. 937, Employment Taxes and Information Returns

Package 1023, Application for Recognition of Exemption

Package 1024, Application for Recognition of Exemption Under Section 501(a) or for Determination Under Section 120

Paperwork Reduction Act Notice

We ask for the information on this form to carry out the Internal Revenue laws of the United States. You are required to give us the information. We need it to ensure that you are complying with these laws and to allow us to figure and collect the right amount of tax.

The time needed to complete and file this form will vary depending on individual circumstances. The estimated average time is:

Recordkeeping	7 min.
Learning about the law or the form	18 min.
Preparing the form	44 min.
Copying, assembling, and sending the form to the IRS	20 min.

If you have comments concerning the accuracy of these time estimates or suggestions for making this form more simple, we would be happy to hear from you. You can write to both the **Internal Revenue Service,** Attention: Reports Clearance Officer, PC:FP, Washington, DC 20224; and the **Office of Management and Budget,** Paperwork Reduction Project (1545-0003), Washington, DC 20503. **DO NOT** send this form to either of these offices. Instead, see **Where To Apply** on page 2.

*U.S. Government Printing Office: 1993 — 363-331/99125

SCHEDULE D (Form 1040)

Department of the Treasury Internal Revenue Service

Capital Gains and Losses

▶ Attach to Form 1040. ▶ See Instructions for Schedule D (Form 1040).

▶ Use lines 20 and 22 for more space to list transactions for lines 1 and 9.

OMB No. 1545-0074

1993

Attachment Sequence No. **12**

Name(s) shown on Form 1040 | Your social security number

Part I Short-Term Capital Gains and Losses—Assets Held One Year or Less

	(a) Description of property (Example: 100 sh. XYZ Co.)	(b) Date acquired (Mo., day, yr.)	(c) Date sold (Mo., day, yr.)	(d) Sales price (see page D-3)	(e) Cost or other basis (see page D-3)	(f) LOSS If (e) is more than (d), subtract (d) from (e)	(g) GAIN If (d) is more than (e), subtract (e) from (d)
1							
2	Enter your short-term totals, if any, from line 21 2						
3	**Total short-term sales price amounts.** Add column (d) of lines 1 and 2 . . . 3						
4	Short-term gain from Forms 2119 and 6252, and short-term gain or (loss) from Forms 4684, 6781, and 8824 4						
5	Net short-term gain or (loss) from partnerships, S corporations, and fiduciaries from Schedule(s) K-1 5						
6	Short-term capital loss carryover from 1992 Schedule D, line 38 6						
7	Add lines 1, 2, and 4 through 6, in columns (f) and (g) 7					( )	
8	**Net short-term capital gain or (loss).** Combine columns (f) and (g) of line 7 8						

Part II Long-Term Capital Gains and Losses—Assets Held More Than One Year

	(a) Description of property	(b) Date acquired	(c) Date sold	(d) Sales price	(e) Cost or other basis	(f) LOSS	(g) GAIN
9							
10	Enter your long-term totals, if any, from line 23 10						
11	**Total long-term sales price amounts.** Add column (d) of lines 9 and 10 . . . 11						
12	Gain from Form 4797; long-term gain from Forms 2119, 2439, and 6252; and long-term gain or (loss) from Forms 4684, 6781, and 8824 12						
13	Net long-term gain or (loss) from partnerships, S corporations, and fiduciaries from Schedule(s) K-1 13						
14	Capital gain distributions 14						
15	Long-term capital loss carryover from 1992 Schedule D, line 45 15						
16	Add lines 9, 10, and 12 through 15, in columns (f) and (g) 16					( )	
17	**Net long-term capital gain or (loss).** Combine columns (f) and (g) of line 16 17						

Part III Summary of Parts I and II

18 Combine lines 8 and 17. If a loss, go to line 19. If a gain, enter the gain on Form 1040, line 13. **Note:** *If both lines 17 and 18 are gains, see the* ***Schedule D Tax Worksheet*** *on page D-4* . . **18**

19 If line 18 is a (loss), enter here and as a (loss) on Form 1040, line 13, the **smaller** of these losses:

a The (loss) on line 18; **or**

b ($3,000) or, if married filing separately, ($1,500) . . . . **19** ( )

Note: *See the* ***Capital Loss Carryover Worksheet*** *on page D-4 if the loss on line 18 exceeds the loss on line 19* ***or*** *if Form 1040, line 35, is a loss.*

Name(s) shown on Form 1040. Do not enter name and social security number if shown on other side. | Your social security number

Part IV Short-Term Capital Gains and Losses—Assets Held One Year or Less *(Continuation of Part I)*

(a) Description of property (Example: 100 sh. XYZ Co.)	(b) Date acquired (Mo., day, yr.)	(c) Date sold (Mo., day, yr.)	(d) Sales price (see page D-3)	(e) Cost or other basis (see page D-3)	(f) LOSS If (e) is more than (d), subtract (d) from (e)	(g) GAIN If (d) is more than (e), subtract (e) from (d)
20						
21 Short-term totals. Add columns (d), (f), and (g) of line 20. Enter here and on line 2 .	21					

Part V Long-Term Capital Gains and Losses—Assets Held More Than One Year *(Continuation of Part II)*

(a) Description of property	(b) Date acquired	(c) Date sold	(d) Sales price	(e) Cost or other basis	(f) LOSS	(g) GAIN
22						
23 Long-term totals. Add columns (d), (f), and (g) of line 22. Enter here and on line 10 .	23					

*U.S. Government Printing Office: 1994 — 301-628/00112

How To Save On Attorney Fees

Millions of Americans know they need legal protection, whether it's to get agreements in writing, protect themselves from lawsuits, or document business transactions. But too often these basic but important legal matters are neglected because of something else millions of Americans know: legal services are expensive.

They don't have to be. In response to the demand for affordable legal protection and services, there are now specialized clinics that process simple documents. Paralegals help people prepare legal claims on a freelance basis. People find they can handle their own legal affairs with do-it-yourself legal guides and kits. Indeed, this book is a part of this growing trend.

Highlight

When are these alternatives to a lawyer appropriate? If you hire an attorney, how can you make sure you're getting good advice for a reasonable fee? Most importantly, do you know how to lower your legal expenses?

When are these alternatives to a lawyer appropriate? If you hire an attorney, how can you make sure you're getting good advice for a reasonable fee? Most importantly, do you know how to lower your legal expenses?

When there is no alternative

Make no mistake: serious legal matters require a lawyer. The tips in this book can help you reduce your legal fees, but there is no alternative to good professional legal services in certain circumstances:

- When you are charged with a felony, you are a repeat offender, or jail is possible.
- When a substantial amount of money or property is at stake in a lawsuit.
- When you are a party in an adversarial divorce or custody case.
- When you are an alien facing deportation.

- When you are the plaintiff in a personal injury suit that involves large sums of money.
- When you're involved in very important transactions.

Are you sure you want to take it to court?

Consider the following questions before you pursue legal action:

 ***What are your financial resources?***

Money buys experienced attorneys, and experience wins over first-year lawyers and public defenders. Even with a strong case, you may save money by not going to court. Yes, people win millions in court. But for every big winner there are ten plaintiffs who either lose or win so little that litigation wasn't worth their effort.

Highlight

Even with a strong case, you may save money by not going to court.

 ***Do you have the time and energy for a trial?***

Courts are overbooked, and by the time your case is heard your initial zeal may have grown cold. If you can, make a reasonable settlement out of court. On personal matters, like a divorce or custody case, consider the emotional toll on all parties. Any legal case will affect you in some way. You will need time away from work. A newsworthy case may bring press coverage. Your loved ones, too, may face publicity. There is usually good reason to settle most cases quickly, quietly, and economically.

 ***How can you settle your disputes without litigation?***

Consider *mediation.* In mediation, each party pays half the mediator's fee and, together, they attempt to work out a compromise informally. *Binding arbitration* is another alternative. For a small fee, a trained specialist serves as judge, hears both sides, and hands down a ruling that both parties have agreed to accept.

So you need an attorney

Having done your best to avoid litigation, if you still find yourself headed for court, you will need an attorney. To get the right attorney at a reasonable cost, be guided by these four questions:

 ***What type of case is it?***

You don't seek a foot doctor for a toothache. Find an attorney experienced in your type of legal problem. If you can get recommendations from clients who have recently won similar cases, do so.

Where will the trial be held?

You want a lawyer familiar with that court system and one who knows the court personnel and the local protocol—which can vary from one locality to another.

Should you hire a large or small firm?

Hiring a senior partner at a large and prestigious law firm sounds reassuring, but chances are the actual work will be handled by associates—at high rates. Small firms may give your case more attention but, with fewer resources, take longer to get the work done.

Highlight

High fees may reflect a firm's luxurious offices, high-paid staff and unmonitored expenses, while low estimates may mean "unexpected" costs later.

What can you afford?

Hire an attorney you can afford, of course, but know what a fee quote includes. High fees may reflect a firm's luxurious offices, high-paid staff and unmonitored expenses, while low estimates may mean "unexpected" costs later. Ask for a written estimate of all costs and anticipated expenses.

How to find a good lawyer

Whether you need an attorney quickly or you're simply open to future possibilities, here are seven nontraditional methods for finding your lawyer:

1. ***Word of mouth:*** Successful lawyers develop reputations. Your friends, business associates and other professionals are potential referral sources. But beware of hiring a friend. Keep the client-attorney relationship strictly business.
2. ***Directories:*** The Yellow Pages and the Martin-Hubbell Lawyer Directory (in your local library) can help you locate a lawyer with the right education, background and expertise for your case.
3. ***Databases:*** A paralegal should be able to run a quick computer search of local attorneys for you using the Westlaw or Lexis database.
4. ***State bar association:*** Bar associations are listed in phone books. Along with lawyer referrals, your bar association can direct you to low-cost legal clinics or specialists in your area.
5. ***Law schools:*** Did you know that a legal clinic run by a law school gives law students hands-on experience? This may fit your legal needs. A third-year law student loaded with enthusiasm and a little experience might fill the bill quite inexpensively—or even for free.
6. ***Advertisements:*** Ads are a lawyer's business card. If a "TV attorney" seems to have a good track record with your kind of case, why not call? Just don't be swayed by the glamour of a high-

profile attorney.

7. ***Your own ad:*** A small ad describing the qualifications and legal expertise you're seeking, placed in a local bar association journal, may get you just the lead you need.

How to hire and work with your attorney

No matter how you hear about an attorney, you must interview him or her in person. Call the office during business hours and ask to speak to the attorney directly. Then explain your case briefly and mention how you obtained the attorney's name. If the attorney sounds interested and knowledgeable, arrange for a visit.

Highlight

Explain your case briefly and mention how you obtained the attorney's name. If the attorney sounds interested and knowledgeable, arrange for a visit.

The ten-point visit:

1. Note the address. This is a good indication of the rates to expect.
2. Note the condition of the offices. File-laden desks and poorly maintained work space may indicate a poorly run firm.
3. Look for up-to-date computer equipment and an adequate complement of support personnel.
4. Note the appearance of the attorney. How will he or she impress a judge or jury?
5. Is the attorney attentive? Does the attorney take notes, ask questions, follow up on points you've mentioned?
6. Ask what schools he or she has graduated from, and feel free to check credentials with the state bar association.
7. Does the attorney have a good track record with your type of case?
8. Does he or she explain legal terms to you in plain English?
9. Are the firm's costs reasonable?
10. Will the attorney provide references?

Hiring the attorney

Having chosen your attorney, make sure all the terms are agreeable. Send letters to any other attorneys you have interviewed, thanking them for their time and interest in your case and explaining that you have retained another attorney's services.

Request a letter from your new attorney outlining your retainer agreement. The letter should list all fees you will be responsible for as well as the billing arrangement. Did you arrange to pay in installments? This should be noted in your retainer agreement.

Controlling legal costs

Highlight

Don't be afraid to question legal bills. It's your case and your money!

Legal fees and expenses can get out of control easily, but the client who is willing to put in the effort can keep legal costs manageable. Work out a budget with your attorney. Create a timeline for your case. Estimate the costs involved in each step.

Legal fees can be straightforward. Some lawyers charge a fixed rate for a specific project. Others charge contingency fees (they collect a percentage of your recovery, usually 35-50 percent, if you win and nothing if you lose). But most attorneys prefer to bill by the hour. Expenses can run the gamut, with one hourly charge for taking depositions and another for making copies.

Have your attorney give you a list of charges for services rendered and an itemized monthly bill. The bill should explain the service performed, who performed the work, when the service was provided, how long it took, and how the service benefits your case.

Ample opportunity abounds in legal billing for dishonesty and greed. There is also plenty of opportunity for knowledgeable clients to cut their bills significantly if they know what to look for. Asking the right questions and setting limits on fees is smart and can save you a bundle. Don't be afraid to question legal bills. It's your case and your money!

When the bill arrives

- ***Retainer fees:*** You should already have a written retainer agreement. Ideally, the retainer fee applies toward case costs, and your agreement puts that in writing. Protect yourself by escrowing the retainer fee until the case has been handled to your satisfaction.
- ***Office visit charges:*** Track your case and all documents, correspondence, and bills. Diary all dates, deadlines and questions you want to ask your attorney during your next office visit. This keeps expensive office visits focused and productive, with more accomplished in less time. If your attorney charges less for phone consultations than office visits, reserve visits for those tasks that must be done in person.

- ***Phone bills:*** This is where itemized bills are essential. Who made the call, who was spoken to, what was discussed, when was the call made, and how long did it last? Question any charges that seem unnecessary or excessive (over 60 minutes).
- ***Administrative costs:*** Your case may involve hundreds, if not thousands, of documents: motions, affidavits, depositions, interrogatories, bills, memoranda, and letters. Are they all necessary? Understand your attorney's case strategy before paying for an endless stream of costly documents.
- ***Associate and paralegal fees:*** Note in your retainer agreement which staff people will have access to your file. Then you'll have an informed and efficient staff working on your case, and you'll recognize their names on your bill. Of course, your attorney should handle the important part of your case, but less costly paralegals or associates may handle routine matters more economically. Note: Some firms expect their associates to meet a quota of billable hours, although the time spent is not always warranted. Review your bill. Does the time spent make sense for the document in question? Are several staff involved in matters that should be handled by one person? Don't be afraid to ask questions. And withhold payment until you have satisfactory answers.

Highlight

Note in your retainer agreement which staff people will have access to your file. Then you'll have an informed and efficient staff working on your case, and you'll recognize their names on your bill.

- ***Court stenographer fees:*** Depositions and court hearings require costly transcripts and stenographers. This means added expenses. Keep an eye on these costs.
- ***Copying charges:*** Your retainer fee should limit the number of copies made of your complete file. This is in your legal interest, because multiple files mean multiple chances others may access your confidential information. It is also in your financial interest, because copying costs can be astronomical.
- ***Fax costs:*** As with the phone and copier, the fax can easily run up costs. Set a limit.
- ***Postage charges:*** Be aware of how much it costs to send a legal document overnight, or a registered letter. Offer to pick up or deliver expensive items when it makes sense.
- ***Filing fees:*** Make it clear to your attorney that you want to minimize the number of court filings in your case. Watch your bill and question any filing that seems unnecessary.
- ***Document production fee:*** Turning over documents to your

opponent is mandatory and expensive. If you're faced with reproducing boxes of documents, consider having the job done by a commercial firm rather than your attorney's office.

- ***Research and investigations:*** Pay only for photographs that can be used in court. Can you hire a photographer at a lower rate than what your attorney charges? Reserve that right in your retainer agreement. Database research can also be extensive and expensive; if your attorney uses Westlaw or Nexis, set limits on the research you will pay for.

Highlight

Surprise costs are so routine they're predictable. Budget a few thousand dollars over what you estimate your case will cost. It usually is needed.

- ***Expert witnesses:*** Question your attorney if you are expected to pay for more than a reasonable number of expert witnesses. Limit the number to what is essential to your case.
- ***Technology costs:*** Avoid videos, tape recordings, and graphics if you can use old-fashioned diagrams to illustrate your case.
- ***Travel expenses:*** Travel expenses for those connected to your case can be quite costly unless you set a maximum budget. Check all travel-related items on your bill, and make sure they are appropriate. Always question why the travel is necessary before you agree to pay for it.
- ***Appeals costs:*** Losing a case often means an appeal, but weigh the costs involved before you make that decision. If money is at stake, do a cost-benefit analysis to see if an appeal is financially justified.
- ***Monetary damages:*** Your attorney should be able to help you estimate the total damages you will have to pay if you lose a civil case. Always consider settling out of court rather than proceeding to trial when the trial costs will be high.
- ***Surprise costs:*** Surprise costs are so routine they're predictable. The judge may impose unexpected court orders on one or both sides, or the opposition will file an unexpected motion that increases your legal costs. Budget a few thousand dollars over what you estimate your case will cost. It usually is needed.
- ***Padded expenses:*** Assume your costs and expenses are legitimate. But some firms do inflate expenses—office supplies, database searches, copying, postage, phone bills—to bolster their bottom line. Request copies of bills your law firm receives from support services. If you are not the only client represented on a bill, determine those charges related to your case.

Keeping it legal without a lawyer

The best way to save legal costs is to avoid legal problems. There are hundreds of ways to decrease your chances of lawsuits and other nasty legal encounters. Most simply involve a little common sense. You can also use your own initiative to find and use the variety of self-help legal aid available to consumers.

11 situations in which you may not need a lawyer

Highlight

The best way to save legal costs is to avoid legal problems.

1. ***No-fault divorce:*** Married couples with no children, minimal property, and no demands for alimony can take advantage of divorce mediation services. A lawyer should review your divorce agreement before you sign it, but you will have saved a fortune in attorney fees. A marital or family counselor may save a seemingly doomed marriage, or help both parties move beyond anger to a calm settlement. Either way, counseling can save you money.
2. ***Wills:*** Do-it-yourself wills and living trusts are ideal for people with estates of less than $600,000. Even if an attorney reviews your final documents, a will kit allows you to read the documents, ponder your bequests, fill out sample forms, and discuss your wishes with your family at your leisure, without a lawyer's meter running.
3. ***Incorporating:*** Incorporating a small business can be done by any business owner. Your state government office provides the forms and instructions necessary. A visit to your state offices will probably be necessary to perform a business name check. A fee of $100-$200 is usually charged for processing your Articles of Incorporation. The rest is paperwork: filling out forms correctly; holding regular, official meetings; and maintaining accurate records.
4. ***Routine business transactions:*** Copyrights, for example, can be applied for by asking the US Copyright Office for the appropriate forms and brochures. The same is true of the US Patent and Trademark Office. If your business does a great deal of document preparation and research, hire a certified paralegal rather than paying an attorney's rates. Consider mediation or binding arbitration rather than going to court for a business dispute. Hire a human resources/benefits administrator to head off disputes

concerning discrimination or other employee charges.

5. ***Repairing bad credit:*** When money matters get out of hand, attorneys and bankruptcy should not be your first solution. Contact a credit counseling organization that will help you work out manageable payment plans so that everyone wins. It can also help you learn to manage your money better. A good company to start with is the Consumer Credit Counseling Service, 1-800-388-2227.
6. ***Small Claims Court:*** For legal grievances amounting to a few thousand dollars in damages, represent yourself in Small Claims Court. There is a small filing fee, forms to fill out, and several court visits necessary. If you can collect evidence, state your case in a clear and logical presentation, and come across as neat, respectful and sincere, you can succeed in Small Claims Court.

Highlight

If your business does a great deal of document preparation and research, hire a certified paralegal rather than paying an attorney's rates.

7. ***Traffic Court:*** Like Small Claims Court, Traffic Court may show more compassion to a defendant appearing without an attorney. If you are ticketed for a minor offense and want to take it to court, you will be asked to plead guilty or not guilty. If you plead guilty, you can ask for leniency in sentencing by presenting mitigating circumstances. Bring any witnesses who can support your story, and remember that presentation (some would call it acting ability) is as important as fact.
8. ***Residential zoning petition:*** If a homeowner wants to open a home business, build an addition, or make other changes that may affect his or her neighborhood, town approval is required. But you don't need a lawyer to fill out a zoning variance application, turn it in, and present your story at a public hearing. Getting local support before the hearing is the best way to assure a positive vote; contact as many neighbors as possible to reassure them that your plans won't adversely affect them or the neighborhood.
9. ***Government benefit applications:*** Applying for veterans' or unemployment benefits may be daunting, but the process doesn't require legal help. Apply for either immediately upon becoming eligible. Note: If your former employer contests your application for unemployment benefits and you have to defend yourself at a hearing, you may want to consider hiring an attorney.
10. ***Receiving government files:*** The Freedom of Information Act gives every American the right to receive copies of government information

about him or her. Write a letter to the appropriate state or federal agency, noting the precise information you want. List each document in a separate paragraph. Mention the Freedom of Information Act, and state that you will pay any expenses. Close with your signature and the address the documents should be sent to. An approved request may take six months to arrive. If it is refused on the grounds that the information is classified or violates another's privacy, send a letter of appeal explaining why the released information would not endanger anyone. Enlist the support of your local state or federal representative, if possible, to smooth the approval process.

11. ***Citizenship:*** Arriving in the United States to work and become a citizen is a process tangled in bureaucratic red tape, but it requires more perseverance than legal assistance. Immigrants can learn how to obtain a "Green Card," under what circumstances they can work, and what the requirements of citizenship are by contacting the Immigration Services or reading a good self-help book.

Highlight

Arriving in the United States to work and become a citizen is a process tangled in bureaucratic red tape, but it requires more perseverance than legal assistance.

Save more; it's E-Z

When it comes to saving attorneys' fees, E-Z Legal Forms is the consumer's best friend. America's largest publisher of self-help legal products offers legally valid forms for virtually every situation. E-Z Legal Kits and E-Z Legal Guides include all necessary forms with a simple-to-follow manual of instructions or a layman's book. E-Z Legal Books are a legal library of forms and documents for everyday business and personal needs. E-Z Legal Software provides those same forms on disk for customized documents at the touch of the keyboard.

You can add to your legal savvy and your ability to protect yourself, your loved ones, your business and your property with a range of self-help legal titles available through E-Z Legal Forms. See the product descriptions and order form at the back of this guide.

(*How To Save On Attorney Fees* was compiled and written by Valerie Hope Goldstein.)

E•Z Legal Guides

- ***Complete information***
- ***Full instructions***
- ***Do-it-yourself forms***
- ***Only $14.95 each***

Living Will & Powers of Attorney

Dying with dignity is on the minds of every baby boomer and every boomer's parents. They are looking for information, for answers, for the forms they need to fill out now, while they are healthy. They'll find it all in one simple book, the *Guide to Living Will & Powers of Attorney*.

Stock No.: G106
$14.95 8.5" x 11"
128 pages Soft cover
ISBN 1-56382-406-X

Immigration

This simple guide explains the various ways America allows aliens to qualify for "green cards," offers step-by-step directions in the petition and application processes, and prepares immigrants to become naturalized citizens. An excellent reference book complete with federally required forms.

Stock No.: G113
$14.95 8.5" x 11"
176 pages Soft cover
ISBN 1-56382-413-2

Divorce

Spouses facing an amicable divorce shouldn't have to face off with contentious lawyers. This guide explains when a do-it-yourself divorce is appropriate, provides the forms necessary, takes the reader through the legal steps, and provides state-by-state information for filing for divorce.

Stock No.: G102
$14.95 8.5" x 11"
160 pages Soft cover
ISBN 1-56382-402-7

Credit Repair

Anyone can improve bad credit with the help of this guide. From discovering exactly what a credit report contains to challenging false information and turning unfavorable reports into glowing reports, it's all in this guide. Sample letters help the reader contact the right authorities and assert his or her consumer rights.

Stock No.: G103
$14.95 8.5" x 11"
176 pages Soft cover
ISBN 1-56382-403-5

Bankruptcy

How does someone file bankruptcy without adding to their debts? With the *E-Z Legal Guide to Bankruptcy.* Takes the confusion out of bankruptcy by taking the reader through the forms, the law, even the state and federal exemptions.

Stock No.: G100
$14.95 8.5" x 11"
128 pages Soft cover
ISBN 1-56382-400-0

Small Claims Court

The reader prepares for his day in court with this guide, which explains the process for the plaintiff and the defendant, offers options to an actual court case, and more. For anyone who has ever thought about taking someone to court.

Stock No.: G109
$14.95 8.5" x 11"
128 pages Soft cover
ISBN 1-56382-409-4

Employment Law

This is a handy reference for anyone with questions about hiring, wages and benefits, privacy, discrimination, injuries, sexual harassment, unions, and unemployment. Written in simple language from the perspectives of both the employer and the employee.

Stock No.: G112
$14.95 8.5",x 11"
112 pages Soft cover
ISBN 1-56382-412-4

Traffic Court

For most American drivers, traffic tickets are an annoying fact of life. But sometimes the motorist doesn't deserve the ticket. This guide tells how and why to fight a ticket, and how to handle a police stop, read a traffic ticket, and take it to court and win.

Stock No.: G110
$14.95 8.5" x 11"
112 pages Soft cover
ISBN 1-56382-410-8

Trademarks and Copyrights

When someone has a great idea and wants to protect it, this book provides the basics of copyright and trademark law: when to get a lawyer, when simply to fill out the right paperwork. Cuts through the volumes of technical information found elsewhere to provide what the layman must know.

Stock No.: G114
$14.95 8.5" x 11"
192 pages Soft cover
ISBN 1-56382-404-3

Personnel Director

America's #1 Employee Management System!

Personnel Director manages employees more efficiently, effectively and legally – without expensive legal fees. A collection of over 240 personnel agreements, forms, letters and documents for virtually every size and type of business. Forms document employee turnover, set policy, put agreements in writing and keep all necessary records. Perfect for time-starved small or midsize businesses that want to protect themselves and their employees.

Stock No.: BK302
$24.95 8.5" x 11"
290 pages Soft cover
ISBN 1-56382-302-0

E·Z LEGAL BOOKS®

Corporate Secretary

When business owners are ready to incorporate, they don't need a lawyer, they need *Corporate Secretary*. It provides over 170 minutes, resolutions, notices and other essential documents for companies, whether they are small or midsize, private or public, non-profit or for profit, "S" or "C." Helps any corporation hold regular, official meetings and document the votes and transactions of its directors and shareholders.

Stock No.: BK304
$24.95 8.5" x 11"
270 pages Soft cover
ISBN 1-56382-304-7

Credit Manager

Business owners stop credit losses and get paid with *Credit Manager*, a complete credit and collection system of over 200 letters, agreements, notices, memos and other documents. *Credit Manager* is for any organization that wants to avoid troublesome disputes and legal liability while enforcing its legal rights and fulfilling legal obligations in credit and collections.

Stock No.: BK303
$24.95 8.5" x 11"
260 pages Soft cover
ISBN 1-56382-303-9

Family Record Organizer

Family Record Organizer contains every form the well-organized household needs to keep life running smoothly, from travel planning to family event scheduling to monthly goal setting. Special sections on business records, investment and financial records, and purchase and maintenance records make it perfect for the home business. E-Z Legal's recordkeeping forms organize every aspect of your life.

Stock No.: BK300
$24.95 8.5" x 11"
226 pages Soft cover
ISBN 1-56382-300-4

Index